A Theory of Indexical Shift

Linguistic Inquiry Monographs
Samuel Jay Keyser, general editor

A complete list of books published in the Linguistic Inquiry Monographs series appears at the back of this book.

A Theory of Indexical Shift
Meaning, Grammar, and Crosslinguistic Variation

Amy Rose Deal

The MIT Press
Cambridge, Massachusetts
London, England

© 2020 Massachusetts Institute of Technology

All rights reserved. No part of this book may be reproduced in any form by any electronic or mechanical means (including photocopying, recording, or information storage and retrieval) without permission in writing from the publisher.

This book was set in Syntax and Times Roman by Westchester Publishing Services.

Printed and bound in the United States of America.

Library of Congress Cataloging-in-Publication Data

Names: Deal, Amy Rose, author.
Title: A theory of indexical shift : meaning, grammar, and crosslinguistic variation / Amy Rose Deal.
Description: Cambridge : The MIT Press, 2020. | Series: Linguistic inquiry monographs ; 82 | Includes bibliographical references and index.
Identifiers: LCCN 2019049201 | ISBN 9780262044189 (hardcover) | ISBN 9780262539210 (paperback)
Subjects: LCSH: Indexicals (Semantics) | Nez Percé language—Semantics.
Classification: LCC P325.5.I54 D43 2020 | DDC 497/.4124—dc23
LC record available at https://lccn.loc.gov/2019049201

10 9 8 7 6 5 4 3 2 1

To Barak

The unseen is proved by the seen,
Till that becomes unseen and receives proof in its turn.
—Walt Whitman

Contents

Series Foreword   xi
Preface   xiii

1 **Introduction**   1

2 **Indexicals and Operators: A Nez Perce Case Study**   7
   2.1 Analysis Types   9
        2.1.1 The Quotation Analysis   9
        2.1.2 The Nonindexical Analysis   14
        2.1.3 The Partial Quotation Analysis   16
        2.1.4 The Binding Analysis   19
        2.1.5 The Context Pronoun Analysis   21
        2.1.6 The Pragmatic Analysis   23
   2.2 The Shifty Operator Theory of Indexical Shift   27
        2.2.1 Meanings for Indexicals and Operators   28
        2.2.2 Operators in Syntactic Structures   33
        2.2.3 The Overwriting Nature of Context Shift   36
        2.2.4 Conclusion to the Case Study   44
   2.3 Epilogue: Operators beyond Nez Perce   45

3 **Shifty Asymmetries**   49
   3.1 Dimensions of Variation   49
        3.1.1 Which Verbs Are Involved in Shifting   49
        3.1.2 Which Indexicals Shift (with Which Verbs)   52
        3.1.3 How Much Optionality is Permitted in Indexical Shift   54
        3.1.4 Which Indexicals Must Be Read *De Se* When Shifted   59
   3.2 Deriving the Asymmetries   64
        3.2.1 Regulating Which Indexicals Shift   64
        3.2.2 The Effect of Verbs   68
        3.2.3 Back to the *De Se*   70

4 **Extending the Theory**   77
   4.1 Temporal Indexicals   78

4.2 Lexical Bundling   83
    4.2.1 Verbs of Cognition and the Second Person   83
    4.2.2 Temporal/Locative Bundling in Korean   87
4.3 Remarks on Single-Operator Analyses   89
4.4 Summary of Predictions   93

5 Beyond Indexical Shift   97
5.1 From Mixed Quotation to Free Indirect Discourse   98
5.2 Sign Language Role Shift   103
5.3 Fake Indexicals   104
5.4 Indexiphors   107
5.5 Closing Remarks   120

6 Conclusions   123

A Remarks on Shift Together   125

B Nez Perce Grammatical Background   133

Notes   141
References   159
Index   173

Series Foreword

We are pleased to present the eighty-second volume in the series *Linguistic Inquiry Monographs*. These monographs present new and original research beyond the scope of the article. We hope they will benefit our field by bringing to it perspectives that will stimulate further research and insight.

Originally published in limited edition, the *Linguistic Inquiry Monographs* are now more widely available. This change is due to the great interest engendered by the series and by the needs of a growing readership. The editors thank the readers for their support and welcome suggestions about future directions for the series.

Samuel Jay Keyser
for the Editorial Board

Preface

This book owes its existence in no small part to an invitation I wasn't sure whether to accept. It came from Craige Roberts, Jefferson Barlew, and Eric Synder, who were organizing a special session of the Linguistic Society of America annual meeting on Perspectival Expressions and the *De Se* Crosslinguistically. While I had long maintained an interest in the topic, owing both to my individual work on Nez Perce indexical shift and to my joint work with Cathy O'Connor on perspectival aspects of Northern Pomo grammar, I hesitated, feeling I had already said my bit and wondering whether I could come up with anything additional to say. For reasons I don't quite remember, I said yes, and from there I was lucky in two different ways. One was the kind of luck (sometimes called inspiration) that happens most often when a project has been set aside for a while and then returned to. In my first round of work on indexical shift, I had discovered that person and locative indexicals were different in shifty environments in two different ways, one to do with optionality of shift and the other to do with *de se* interpretation, but I hadn't been able to show how these two properties could be connected. Upon returning to the topic, four years later, I had the experience of the elusive connection suddenly jumping out. The second type of luck was the kind that happens when, to speak metaphorically, the little thread one is pulling turns out to lead to a main seam. Every language is a mix of pieces shaped by the deep factors of human cognition and evolution and the more shallow happenstance of history and arbitrary choice. In learning, likewise, some aspects of an individual language are idiosyncratic and must be learned by rote; others, owing to deeper parts of the system, could not be otherwise. The analyst who embarks on an empirical project rarely gets to know in advance which pieces are which. For me, I could not have known in my initial summers of fieldwork on the subject that the Nez Perce indexical shift system would turn out to provide the first inklings of a larger theory, one that can both organize what we know about indexical shift thus far and predict what we may hope to know in the future. That, at least, is what I will contend.

I have many individuals and groups to thank for feedback, discussion, and helpful data points along the way, including Pranav Anand, Carolyn Anderson, Amir Anvari, Mark Baker, Seth Cable, Kathryn Davidson, Kai von Fintel, Irene Heim, Peter Jenks, Sunwoo Jeong, Min-Joo Kim, Sarah Murray, Sumiyo Nishiguchi, Yangsook Park, Tom Roeper, Philippe Schlenker, Roger Schwarzschild, Yasu Sudo, and Sandhya Sundaresan; audience members at Berkeley, the University of Massachusetts, MIT, the University of Michigan, the University of Connecticut, Frankfurt, the SIAS attitudes group in summer 2016, the 22nd Workshop on Structure and Constituency of the Languages of the Americas (at the University of British Columbia in spring 2017), the Rutgers Semantics/Pragmatics workshop in spring 2017, Sinn und Bedeutung 22 (at the University of Potsdam in fall 2017), and the Alphabet of Universal Grammar workshop (at the British Academy in summer 2019); and of course audience members and organizers at the LSA annual meeting 2016. I'm especially grateful to Sarah Murray and two anonymous reviewers for extensive comments on versions of this manuscript, as well as to colleagues at MIT and Harvard for their hospitality while I worked on this project during a fall 2016 sabbatical leave (especially Jay Jasanoff, who lent me his Widener Library office space), and to the American Council of Learned Societies and the College of Letters and Science at the University of California, Berkeley, for sabbatical support.

All Nez Perce judgments in this book were provided by Nez Perce elders Bessie Scott and Florene Davis, whom I cannot thank enough for their patient teaching and years of friendship. *Qe'ciyew'yew'!*

Amy Rose Deal
January 8, 2020

1 Introduction

Indexicals are a class of linguistic items identifiable by the particular way in which their meaning depends on an utterance event. Among this class, in English, are *I* and *you*, *here* and *now*, *tomorrow* and *today*. So inherent to this lexical class is its particular type of dependence on utterance that non-indexical paraphrases invariably fail to capture it, even when those paraphrases are themselves in some way context-dependent. So it is that when Anna and Berta watch a televised speech together, they may use definite expressions such as *the speaker* or *the person talking* to form a coherent disagreement about the subject on screen:

(1) *A coherent disagreement*
    Anna: The speaker / the person talking is in Washington.
    Berta: No, the speaker / the person talking is not in Washington.

A version with the indexical *I*, on the other hand, fails not only in its attempt to refer to a third party; it does not even achieve the status of a coherent disagreement.[1]

(2) *Not a coherent disagreement*
    Anna: I'm in Washington.
    Berta: No, I'm not in Washington.

The well-formed disagreement in (1) demonstrates that descriptions such as *the speaker* and *the person talking* can, in principle, be used to refer to the same individual regardless of who it is that utters them. *I*, on the other hand, has no such option. In (2), it simply cannot refer to the same person when used by Anna as when used by Berta. Whatever *I* means, then, it cannot be the same as the meaning of *the speaker* or *the person talking*. This basic fact undergirds the celebrated direct reference theory of indexicals, where, as Kaplan (1989, 491) put it: "The speaker refers to himself when he uses *I*, and no pointing to another or believing that he is another or intending to refer to another can defeat this reference."

Examples (1) and (2) are presented in English, but it is probably fair to say that this contrast could be replicated in every language. Typologists have after all found no language lacking a first person (Cysouw 2003, 83). In Nez Perce (Sahaptian; USA), for instance, the pattern in (3) reproduces the English pattern exactly. (I parenthesize the English translations here to highlight that the disagreement is judged incoherent without any English provided.)[2]

(3) *Not a coherent disagreement (in Nez Perce)*
  Anna: 'Iin kiy-u' Kemiex-px.
    1SG.NOM go-PROSP Kamiah-to
    (I'm going to Kamiah.)
  Berta: Weet'u 'iin kiy-u' Kemiex-px.
    NEG 1SG.NOM go-PROSP Kamiah-to
    (I'm not going to Kamiah.)

Yet this finding should not lure us into thinking that semantic variation is excluded in matters related to indexicality. In fact, it only takes a small modification to the pattern to see a rather different crosslinguistic picture emerge, bringing with it an apparent challenge to the core Kaplanian theory. The modification involves embedding indexical expressions under speech or attitude verbs. This manipulation, of course, has no effect on the facts in standard English. Discourse (4) is no more coherent than (2): modulo quotation, English *I* is just as utterance-dependent in speech and attitude reports as in matrix clauses.

(4) *Still not a coherent disagreement*
  Anna: Casey said that I'm in Washington.
  Berta: No, Casey didn't say that I'm in Washington.

In contrast to the behavior of unembedded indexicals in (2) and (3), this behavior of embedded indexicals is not universal. Suppose that the first-person pronoun, embedded in a speech or attitude report, could refer to the author of the report—the thinker, that is, with a verb of thought, or the speaker, with a verb of speech. This is clearly not possible in English, for if it were, then (4) would achieve coherence as a disagreement about Casey's statements about his own location. But this reading *is* possible in Nez Perce sentences such as (5) and (6), where the embedded first-person pronouns may refer to the attitude author:

(5) Mipx　　Beth　　　hi-neek-Ø-e　　　　　　　[*pro*
　　where.to Beth.NOM 3SUBJ-think-P-REM.PAST [1SG
　　kuu-se-Ø　　　　]?
　　go-IMPERF-PRES]
　　Where did Beth$_i$ think she$_i$ was going?³

(6) Kii　　　hii-wes　　　　'iniit　　　　yox̂　　ke Jack
　　this.NOM 3SUBJ-be.PRES house.NOM RP.NOM C Jack.NOM
　　hi-hi-ce-Ø　　　　　　　['iin　　　hani-Ø-ya　　　　　].
　　3SUBJ-say-IMPERF-PRES [1SG.NOM make-P-REM.PAST]
　　This is the house that Jack$_i$ says he$_i$ built.

No surprise, then, that in Nez Perce, disagreements of the form in (4) are indeed coherent:

(7) *A coherent disagreement (in Nez Perce)*
　　　　Anna: Naaqc k'ay'kin Caan　　　hi-i-cee-ne,
　　　　　　　one　　week　　John.NOM 3SUBJ-say-IMPERF-REM.PAST
　　　　　　　[watiisx　　　*pro* kiy-u'　　'itamyaanwas-x].
　　　　　　　[1.day.away 1SG go-PROSP town-to　　　　　]
　　　　　　　Last week John said he would go to town tomorrow.
　　　　Berta: Weet'u Caan　　　　hi-i-cee-ne,　　　　　　　　　[watiisx
　　　　　　　NEG　　John.NOM 3SUBJ-say-IMPERF-REM.PAST [1.day.away
　　　　　　　pro kiy-u'　　'itamyaanwas-x].
　　　　　　　1SG go-PROSP town-to　　　　　]
　　　　　　　John didn't say he would go to town tomorrow.

Notably, these behaviors of the first person in Nez Perce do not require quotation of the embedded clause: the clause hosting the indexical remains transparent for questioning and relativization in (5) and (6) and hosts a clearly nonquoted temporal adverb in (7). Rather, independent of clausal quotation, the embedded indexical draws its reference from an attitude event instead of from the overall utterance. This demonstrates the phenomenon of *indexical shift*.

Over the past two decades, the study of indexical shift has come into its own as a major front in the investigation of natural language semantics. The empirical progress has been significant: the phenomenon has been reported for languages spanning five continents and at least ten language families.⁴ Theoretical progress has been substantial as well, as new empirical discoveries have been mined for insights into the nature of indexicality, quantification, quotation, and context-dependence. As this progress has unfolded, the field has seen a steady accumulation of small discoveries about ways in which indexical-shifting languages are different not just from standard English, but also from each other. Such discoveries reveal that the true theory of indexicality is responsible not just for a binary choice between languages like English and languages like Nez Perce, but ultimately for a range of ways in which languages may allow or disallow indexical shift. This suggests that we may best appreciate how indexical shift works by better understanding the ways it does and does not vary across languages.

This is the project I take up in this book. My central goal is to advance and justify a constrained typology of indexical shift—a picture of variation that is at once rich enough to capture the known facts and also restrictive enough to make predictions about currently unknown data points. This is in line with similar projects at the intersection of formal semantics and language typology in the domains of bare nominals (Chierchia 1998), generalized quantifiers (Matthewson 2013), and degree constructions (Beck et al. 2009), among other areas. To achieve this goal for shifty indexicals it will be necessary to answer three questions:

1. What are the major dimensions of variation in indexical shift?
2. What theory of indexical shift can best account for both commonalities and variation within and across the set of languages instantiating the phenomenon?
3. What are the natural seams that separate indexical shift from surface-similar phenomena?

I will say at once that these questions must be approached in the knowledge that large gaps remain in our understanding of embedded indexicals across a wide variety of languages. The goal is that the predictions from this study will be testable in additional languages in future work, where perhaps they will be disconfirmed in favor of some improved alternative. In the meantime, the (eternal) absence of fully exhaustive data cannot excuse us from theorizing. By outlining a constrained typology now, we prepare to more quickly grasp the import of new language types that may (or may not) ultimately be discovered in the future.

The plan of the book is as follows. The next chapter serves as an in-depth introduction to indexical shift via a case study of one language, Nez Perce, and the evidence it provides in favor of the basic approach to indexical shift I adopt here: the *shifty operator theory* (Anand and Nevins 2004, Anand 2006, Sudo 2012, Deal 2014, Shklovsky and Sudo 2014, Park 2016). On this theory, indexical shift results from the presence of syntactic elements—operators—that change the context relative to which their complement is interpreted. Indexicals, then, retain their standard Kaplanian analysis as directly referential expressions. The difference between a language such as Nez Perce and a language such as standard English is that the latter lacks elements that modify the context of interpretation.

The recognition of such operators sets the stage for the rest of the book, which addresses the three questions listed above. The heart of the proposal is presented in chapter 3, which begins by outlining four dimensions of variation in indexical shift along with corresponding initial generalizations about the crosslinguistic patterns. This chapter draws most extensively on studies of six languages (Matses, Navajo, Nez Perce, Slave, Uyghur, and Zazaki) that instantiate patterns also found in numerous others. To account for the generalizations laid out in this chapter, I propose, first, that languages allowing shift of multiple types of indexicals (e.g., first person, second person, locative) may allow multiple shifty operators to stack in the left periphery of finite clauses; stacking is regulated by standard syntactic constraints on functional structure in a way that explains several of the crosslinguistic generalizations. Second, the semantic contributions of these operators may vary, in a way that explains a core generalization about indexical shift and interpretation *de se*.

With the basic proposal on the table, chapter 4 elaborates the theory along two further dimensions. In section 4.1, I extend the account to temporal indexicals, drawing on evidence from Korean and a nonstandard variety of English. In section 4.2, I discuss lexical "bundling" of shifty operators (to borrow a term from Pylkkänen 2008), that is, cases where a shifty operator forms a single lexical unit along with another operator or other material. This discussion draws on case studies of second-person indexicals in Uyghur (Sudo 2012) and adverbial indexicals in Korean (Park 2016). I then present an overview of the predictions of the final account as developed here.

This leaves the question of how indexical shift may be distinguished from surface-similar phenomena, which is the subject of chapter 5. Here I contrast indexical shift with four distinct though partially related phenomena—Free Indirect Discourse, sign language Role Shift (particularly in American Sign Language and French Sign Language), fake indexicality in focus constructions, and *indexiphoricity* (i.e., "[first] personal logophoricity")—with the goal of clarifying the controls that are needed to test the constrained typology on new data sets.

2 Indexicals and Operators: A Nez Perce Case Study

The right theory of embedded indexicals is one that allows us to correctly predict crosslinguistic patterns while at the same time getting the details of particular languages right. In this chapter, we take first steps toward the general picture by beginning with the very specific. We lead off with a case study of indexical shift in one language, Nez Perce, and its consequences for the choice among a variety of competing views on shifty indexicality. As we will see, an adequate theory of indexical shift in Nez Perce must respond to four desiderata:

1. It is specific to speech and attitude reports.
2. It operates on a whole-clause basis.
3. It allows for the behavior of shifty indexicals to be distinguished from the behavior of bindable, anaphoric elements.
4. It is sensitive to the structure of the embedded clause.

Taken jointly, I will argue, these desiderata suggest an approach where shifty indexicals are indeed indexical: they obtain their value directly as a function of the context of interpretation, in keeping with the classic approach from Kaplan (1989). Furthermore, shift need not result from quotation (whether at the clausal or subclausal level). Rather, indexical shift is attributable to a class of operators which, syntactically, occupy the periphery of certain complement clauses, and which, semantically, determine coordinates of the context against which their complement is interpreted. This is the *shifty operator theory* (Anand and Nevins 2004, Anand 2006, Sudo 2012, Deal 2014, Shklovsky and Sudo 2014, Park 2016). The first of the properties listed just above distinguishes this approach from the binding-based theory developed by von Stechow (2003) (see section 2.1.4); the second distinguishes it from the partial quotation approach developed by Maier (2007, 2012, 2014a, 2016) (see section 2.1.3); the third distinguishes it both from Schlenker's pronoun-based proposal (Schlenker 1999,

2003, 2011; also Sharvit 2008, Koev 2013; see section 2.1.5) and from the anaphora- or presupposition-based approaches developed by Hunter and Asher (2005), Bittner (2014), and Roberts (2015) (see section 2.1.6).

This chapter has two parts. The first introduces the phenomenon of indexical shift in Nez Perce by way of consideration of a series of potential analysis types. This begins in section 2.1 with discussion of an initial analysis in terms of clausal quotation. In this language, embedded clauses may host indexical elements that draw their reference from an attitude event, rather than from the overall context of utterance, whether or not the clause that hosts them shows the distinctive opacity of a clausal quote. How should such data be analyzed? I consider and reject five possibilities: that the putative indexicals are instead definite descriptions (section 2.1.2); that the indexicals are individually quoted, and thus the clause that hosts them is partially quoted (section 2.1.3); that the putative indexicals are instead bound pronouns subject to feature transmission under binding (section 2.1.4); that the indexicals have a complex internal representation involving bindable context pronouns (section 2.1.5); and that the speech and attitude verbs that permit indexical shift in their complements do so directly by making a particular perspective pragmatically salient (section 2.1.6). Each hypothesis will fail in some way—but the point of the exercise is not merely to observe failure but to notice *why* these hypotheses fail. In each case, a systematic shortcoming of the proposed hypothesis brings out one or more of the four generalizations listed above—a set of generalizations that the correct analysis, whatever it is, will have to explain. The second part of the chapter takes up this challenge. I lay out a basic analysis in terms of shifty operators, showing how it explains this set of generalizations. (This analysis will be built on and slightly modified in the chapters that follow.) Finally, as an epilogue to the case study proper, I indicate additional types of support for this general view that can be found in languages other than Nez Perce.

Two words of caution are in order. First, the reader is advised that I will not devote significant attention in this chapter to morphosyntactic questions raised by glossing the Nez Perce examples, even though this task is nontrivial in various ways. (How do we know there are null pronouns in certain cases? How do we recover their features?) For that discussion, the curious reader is referred to appendix B. Second, while I will consider a range of approaches for Nez Perce that are clearly inspired by previous work, I will not aim to fully review the space of previous analyses in any major depth. For that the reader is referred to Anand (2006), Schlenker (2011), and to the original works cited throughout the chapter.

2.1 Analysis Types

2.1.1 The Quotation Analysis

Nez Perce shows a distinction between what in traditional terms would be called direct versus indirect reporting. In (8a), for instance, the embedded clause contains a third-person pronoun co-referring with the matrix subject, *Sue*. In (8b), the same reference is accomplished with a first-person pronoun.

(8) Context: Sue and Claire are students in a class. Sue is feeling sick. She asks Claire to tell this to the teacher. Claire approaches the teacher and says:
    a. Sue   hi-i-caa-qa   [*pro*
       Sue.NOM 3SUBJ-say-IMPERF-REC.PAST [3SG
       hi-k'oomay-ca-Ø   ].
       3SUBJ-be.sick-IMPERF-PRES]
       Sue$_i$ said that she$_i$ is sick.
    b. Sue   hi-i-caa-qa   ['iin
       Sue.NOM 3SUBJ-say-IMPERF-REC.PAST [1SG.NOM
       k'oomay-ca-Ø   ].
       be.sick-IMPERF-PRES]
       Sue$_i$ said that she$_i$ is sick. / Sue said, "I am sick."

What is the nature of this distinction? To a first pass, it looks to be something quite familiar—the difference between the presence and absence of clausal quotation. A zealous punctuator might thus wish to add quotation marks in the places where I have indicated clause boundaries with square brackets—but only in (8b).

Preliminary diagnoses call for follow-up exams. In English, we might hope to confirm a diagnosis of clausal quotation by investigating relatively simple matters such as the possibility of a complementizer or sequence of tense.[1] We see for instance that *that* is possible in (9), and a simultaneous reading of embedded past tense obtains in (9b), but no such options are open for the clausal quotation variants in (10).

(9) a. Sue said **that** she is sick.
    b. Sue said that she was sick.
       Appropriate scenario: Sue used the words "I am sick."
(10) a. * Sue said **that** "I am sick."
     b. Sue said, "I was sick."
       Inappropriate scenario: Sue used the words "I am sick."

Tests like these turn out to be quite varied in their applicability across languages. Some languages have complementizers that may be used equally well in the introduction of quoted and nonquoted clauses; relevant morphemes include Hindi *ki* (Anand 2006, 81), Mishar Tatar *diep* (Podobryaev 2014, section 3.1.2.1), and Tsez =λ*in* (Polinsky 2015). Still others show no overt complementizers in either case, whether for the introduction of quotes or nonquoted complements—and Nez Perce is a language of this type. (So too are Kiowa [Andrew McKenzie, pers. comm.] and many languages of China, including Mandarin.) Similarly, many languages lack a sequence of tense rule (or sequence of tense mechanism of whatever sort) and therefore broadly disallow simultaneous readings of embedded past tense in past tense attitude reports; this is the situation for instance in Hebrew, Japanese, and Russian (Ogihara and Sharvit 2012). Nez Perce is a language of this type, too (Deal 2019c).²

If we hope to reliably diagnose quotation crosslinguistically, we must then ask: why should these diagnostics be so fragile? The answer is perhaps because they have little to do with the nature of quotation itself. In the case of complementizers, the issue concerns not the quote, but the way the quote is integrated into a larger sentence. Languages may or may not vary in the syntactic nature of this integration, but they certainly vary in the phonological signatures thereof (i.e., whether a complementizer is overt or null). In the case of sequence of tense, the relevant diagnostic turns on properties not of the quoted clause, but of its nonquoted alternative—in other words, what varies crosslinguistically is the interpretation of sentences like (9b), not (10b). Outside of quotation, a language may or may not have a sequence of tense rule allowing for past tense in an embedded clause to receive a simultaneous reading. Sequence of tense therefore does not directly diagnose quotation itself. When available, it diagnoses only the absence of quotation. The distinction is a relevant one in view of the fact that the precise conditions on the application of sequence of tense rules are nontrivial (see, e.g., von Stechow 1995, Ogihara 1996). In a language with sequence of tense, an attitude report failing to show the sequence of tense pattern could be a quote, but it could also be a case where these conditions are not met for some other reason.

Why is quotation incompatible with sequence of tense? To pick a concrete example: why may we not report Sue's words "I am sick" with the sentence *Sue said, "I was sick"* (as in (10b))? This judgment has the distinction of broad crosslinguistic applicability (I am not aware of any language for which the facts are otherwise) as well as clear connections to other ways in which quotations, both in English and crosslinguistically, are syntactically and semantically opaque. This opacity can be seen, for instance, for *wh*-movement, (11); for negative polarity licensing, (12); and for descriptions *de re*, (13).

(11) * Who did Mary say, "I handed the bag to"?
cf. Who did Mary say she handed the bag to?
(12) # Mary never said "I handed the bag to anyone." (unacceptable unless Mary has said something ungrammatical)
cf. Mary never said she handed the bag to anyone.
(13) Context: Mary said that Sue is walking around in the woods near her house. Unbeknownst to her, Sue is a secret agent.
\# Mary said, "A secret agent is walking around in the woods near my house."
cf. Mary said that a secret agent is walking around in the woods near her house.

The distinctive opacity of quoted clauses plausibly arises in connection with a central aspect of what it is to be a quote: quotations showcase not only what is said but also *how* it is said, along both linguistic and extralinguistic dimensions (Banfield 1973, Clark and Gerrig 1990, Clark 1996, Recanati 2001, inter alia). Quotations may thus feature a language or dialect distinct from that of the containing clause; slips, disfluencies, errors, or simply idiosyncratic lexical or phonological properties; and (particularly outside of written language) distinctive tone or affective phonology conveying a range of emotional or physical states. In all these respects, quotations involve mention or demonstration of language, rather than simply use. The quoted material resembles the original utterance in certain relevant respects, in the maximal case repeating the original verbatim.[3]

What can these diagnostics tell us about our initial impression concerning Nez Perce sentences like those in (8)? In (8b), an embedded first-person pronoun refers not to the overall speaker (Claire) but to the matrix subject (Sue). Do embedded clauses like this one behave opaquely, as we might expect if they are quotes? They do not. In (14), the subject of the embedded clause is a first-person pronoun, and the object has been *wh*-moved into the matrix clause. Note that the embedded first-person pronoun refers to person A (the matrix subject) and not to the overall speaker.

(14) Isii-ne$_2$ A.   hi-i-caa-qa   [cewcewin'es-ki
who-ACC   A.NOM 3SUBJ-say-IMPERF-REC.PAST [phone-with
pro   'e-muu-ce-Ø t_2]?
1SG   3OBJ-call-IMPERF-PRES   ]
Colloquial: Who did A.$_i$ say she$_i$ was calling?
Literal: Who did A.$_i$ say I$_i$ am calling?
Compare quotation: *Who did A. say, "I am calling"?

We can be sure that there is indeed cross-clausal movement here due to the case-marking of the *wh*-word *'isiine* 'who'. This bears an accusative case marker that could only have been licensed in the lower clause.[4] The same combination of movement and a first-person subject is seen in relativization in (15), which was previewed in chapter 1; here the first-person pronoun happens to be overt. (For this example and those that follow, readers are invited to construct their own English quotation paraphrases and confirm that they are, indeed, ungrammatical.)

(15) Kii   hii-wes   'iniit   yox̂$_1$ ke Jack
     this.NOM   3SUBJ-be.PRES   house.NOM RP.NOM   C   Jack
     hi-hi-ce-Ø   ['iin   hani-Ø-ya t_1].
     3SUBJ-say-IMPERF-PRES [1SG.NOM make-P-REM.PAST   ]
     Colloquial: This is the house that Jack$_i$ says he$_i$ built.
     Literal: This is the house that Jack$_i$ says I$_i$ built.

The pattern can also be demonstrated with indexicals other than the first person. In (16), the most embedded clause contains a second-person pronoun referring to the object of the embedding verb, rather than the overall addressee.[5] This clause is again transparent for Ā movement, in this case relativization.

(16) Manaa we'nikt   'u-us   haama-nm,   ke ko-nya$_1$ T.-nm
     how   name.NOM   3GEN-be.PRES man-GEN   C   RP-ACC   T-ERG
     pee-Ø-n-e   R.-ne, ['ee   'o-opayata-yo'qa t_1]?
     3/3-say-P-REM.PAST R-ACC [2SG.CL 3OBJ-help-MODAL   ]
     Colloquial: What is the name of the man that T told R$_i$ that he$_i$ should help?
     Literal: What is the name of the man that T told R$_i$ that you$_i$ should help?

And in (17), the Ā-transparent embedded clause contains the locative indexical *kinix* 'from here' referring to the location of the event described by the main clause (Lewiston), rather than the location of the overall utterance (Lapwai).

(17) Context: Elicited in Lapwai, ID. Lewiston is the closest major city.
     Miniku cewcewin'es$_2$ *pro* hi-i-caa-qa   Simiinikem-pe
     which phone.NOM   3SG 3SUBJ-say-IMPERF-REC.PAST Lewiston-LOC
     [t_2 hi-muu-no'qa   kinix   met'u weet'u t_2 hi-muu-no'qa
     [3SUBJ-call-MODAL from.here but   NEG   3SUBJ-call-MODAL
     konix   ]?
     from.there]
     Colloquial: Which phone did they say in Lewiston can call from Lewiston but not from Lapwai?
     Literal: Which phone did they say in Lewiston$_i$ can call from here$_i$ but not from there$_j$?

One general conclusion from this type of data is that the presence of an indexical element that does not draw its reference from the context of utterance is not necessarily diagnostic of the presence of a clausal quote. This of course immediately calls into question our initial diagnosis of the complement of (8b) as a quote. Sentential quotation is a possible analysis for that material, but (14)–(17) show that it is not the *only* analysis consistent with the facts.

A further demonstration of this point comes from *de re* reporting. In the scenario given for sentence (18), the speaker, but not Beth, is aware that Harold is a teacher:

(18) Context: Beth told me she met Harold. She doesn't know he is a teacher. When we are in class, I say to someone else:
Beth-nim   hi-hi-n-e   *pro*
Beth-ERG   3SUBJ-say-P-REM.PAST   1SG.ACC
[*pro* 'e-wewkuny-Ø-e   sepehitemenew'etuu-ne].
[1SG 3OBJ-meet-P-REM.PAST teacher-ACC   ]
Colloquial: Beth told me she met the teacher.
Literal: Beth$_i$ told me$_j$ I$_i$ met the teacher.

Given this context, the description *sepehitemenew'etuune* 'the teacher' must be read *de re*. (There is no appropriate reading *de dicto*: Beth would not assent to this description of Harold.) The clause containing this description is thus not opaque in the way we expect were it to be quoted—yet it contains, again, a first-person indexical referring to the matrix subject.

The same applies in examples like (19), which differs from (18) in several ways—the *de re* term is a name (*Calvin*), the embedded indexical is an object rather than a subject, and the verb is 'think' rather than 'say'.[6]

(19) Context: My neighbor Mary complains to me that a cat has been digging up her flowers. She tells me about the cat and it sounds like it was my cat Calvin, even though Mary doesn't know what cat it was. I say to my husband: *Mary thinks Calvin is digging up her flowers.*
pro   hi-neki-se-Ø   [Calvin-nim
3SG   3SUBJ-think-IMPERF-PRES   [Calvin-ERG
hi-p'la-yay'-sa-Ø   *pro*   laatis   ].
3SUBJ-dig-μ-IMPERF-PRES   1SG.ACC   flower.NOM]
Colloquial: She thinks Calvin is digging up her flowers.
Literal: She$_i$ thinks Calvin is digging up my$_i$ flowers.

This type of fact reinforces the conclusion from Ā-movement. Reported speech or thought containing shifty indexicals in Nez Perce simply need not showcase *how* something has been said in the way that quotations characteristically do. No surprise, then, that word order variation and other types of simple paraphrase are accepted in clauses with indexical shift:

(20) Context: On day 1, Mary says:
      Fido-nm   hi-ken'ip-Ø-e   *pro*.
      Fido-ERG 3SUBJ-bite-P-REM.PAST 1SG.ACC
      (Fido bit me.)
   On day 2, I say to you:
   a. ✓ Meeli   hi-i-caa-qa
      Mary.NOM 3SUBJ-say-IMPERF-REC.PAST
      [hi-ken'ip-Ø-e   *pro*   Fido-nm].
      [3SUBJ-bite-P-REM.PAST 1SG.ACC Fido-ERG]
      Literal: Mary said, bit me Fido.
   b. ✓ Meeli   hi-i-caa-qa   [ciq'aamqal-nim
      Mary.NOM 3SUBJ-say-IMPERF-REC.PAST [dog-ERG
      hi-ken'ip-Ø-e   *pro*   ].
      3SUBJ-bite-P-REM.PAST 1SG.ACC]
      Literal: Mary said, the/a dog bit me.

Whatever is responsible for the behavior of indexicals in embedded clauses in Nez Perce, it is not something that comes with the characteristic properties of clausal quotation.

2.1.2 The Nonindexical Analysis

A first alternative approach to these facts begins with the hypothesis that first- and second-person pronouns, in some languages, are not in fact indexical at all—rather, they are definite descriptions. From this point of view, the Nez Perce first-person pronoun is semantically parallel not to English *I*, but to *the speaker*; the second-person pronoun is parallel not to *you*, but to *the addressee*; and—extending this view beyond personal pronouns—the locative is parallel not to *here* but to *the utterance location* (or perhaps *the vicinity of the speaker*, as per Harbour 2016). The most accurate English paraphrase of (14) will be *Who did A say the speaker was calling?*, where indeed it is possible for *the speaker* to refer either to A or to the person asking the overall question.

In seminal work on the meanings of indexicals, Kaplan (1989) argues against a variant of this analysis as applied to English, and a generalized version of his argument can be applied to the Nez Perce case as well. What Kaplan notices is that intuitive synonymies such as that between *I* and *the person uttering this sentence* or simply *the speaker* markedly fail to hold in certain environments of quantification.[7] This can be clearly seen in English with adverbial quantifiers such as *if* clauses or *whenever* clauses, making for a sharp difference in the meaning of the two examples in (21).

(21) a.   Whenever Obama is speaking, the speaker is a former president.
      b.   # Whenever Obama is speaking, I am a former president.

What we see in these examples is that an ordinary description like *the speaker* may covary with the adverbial quantifier, while the reference of the indexical remains rigidly determined.

When we run this test in Nez Perce, we find exactly the same distinction between a description like *c'iix̂new'eet* 'the speaker' and the first person. The former covaries with a 'whenever'-quantifier, but the latter cannot.

(22) a.   Ke   mawa   T.   hi-c'iiq-tetu-Ø,   **c'iix̂-new'eet**
            C   when   T.NOM 3SUBJ-speak-HAB.SG-PRES speak-AGT.NOM
            hii-wes   haama.
            3SUBJ-be.PRES man.NOM
            Whenever T speaks, the speaker is a man.
      b.   # Ke mawa T.   hi-c'iiq-ce-Ø,   **'iin**   wees
            C   when   T.NOM 3SUBJ-speak-IMPERF-PRES 1SG.NOM be.PRES
            haama.
            man.NOM
            Consultant (female): "Whenever [T] is speaking, I am a man … ?!"

The same fact is in evidence for the second-person pronoun *'iim*, (23), which thus should not be taken to mean 'the listener'. The same goes as well as for the locative adverb *kine* 'here', as in (24), which thus does not mean 'the speech location'. Note that these expressions are different from the locative expression *kona* 'there', which may covary with a quantifier just as its English translation may, (25). We thus diagnose *kona* as nonindexical.

(23) # Ke kaa   A.-nim pee-c'iiq-ce-Ø   P.-a,   **'iim**   wees
        C   then   A-ERG 3/3-speak-IMPERF-PRES P-ACC, 2SG.NOM be.PRES
        haacwal.
        boy.NOM
        When A talks to P, you are a boy.
        Consultant: "You are a boy?"

(24) # Ke mine Obama hi-c'iiq-tetu-Ø, 'ilx̂nii-we
C where Obama.NOM 3SUBJ-speak-HAB.SG-PRES many-HUMAN
kine hi-wsiix titooqan.
here 3SUBJ-be.PRES.PL person.NOM
Wherever Obama speaks, many people are here.
Consultant: "I don't think you say *kine* [here] ... you're saying *ke mine*, 'wherever,' so I think you have to say *kona* [there]."

(25) Ke mine Obama hi-c'iiq-tetu-Ø, 'ilx̂nii-we
C where Obama.NOM 3SUBJ-speak-HAB.SG-PRES, many-HUMAN
kona hi-wsiix titooqan.
there 3SUBJ-be.PRES.PL person.NOM
Wherever Obama speaks, many people are there.

We conclude that Nez Perce, just like English, has a set of indexical elements that can be distinguished from nonindexicals in terms of binding by adverbial quantifiers. Nez Perce unembedded first person, second person, and *kine* 'here' behave like English unembedded indexicals. It is not merely the presence of quantification that facilitates indexical shift: where Nez Perce and English come apart is only in *embedding under speech and attitude predicates*. It is here that the effect of indexical shift must be localized.

2.1.3 The Partial Quotation Analysis

In this connection it may be helpful to return to the idea that clauses embedded under speech and attitude verbs are special in their ability to host quotations. We have seen that shifty indexical subjects are possible in environments where the object is *wh*-moved or interpreted *de re*; the object could not, thus, be in the scope of quotation.[8] Such reasoning applies, for instance, to examples like (26).

(26) Context: Beth told me she met Harold. She doesn't know he is a teacher.
When we are in class, I say to someone else:
Beth-nim hi-hi-n-e *pro*
Beth-ERG 3SUBJ-say-P-REM.PAST 1SG.ACC
[*pro* 'e-wewkuny-Ø-e sepehitemenew'etuu-ne].
[1SG 3OBJ-meet-P-REM.PAST teacher-ACC]
Beth told me she met the teacher.
cf. quotation: #Beth told me, "I met the teacher." (Inappropriate for this *de re* report.)

Rather than abandoning a quotation analysis entirely, let us now consider that we might revise it, in particular by assigning a rather more narrow scope to the quotation operation. Instead of applying at the sentence level, let us suppose that quotation applies only to the individual indexical (and perhaps its associated agreement): cf. *Beth told me that "I" met the teacher.* On this strategy, explored by Maier (2007, 2012, 2014a), shifty indexicality falls under the purview of theories of partial or mixed quotation.[9]

The essential advantage of the partial quotation view is that it lets quotation of one phrase (e.g., the subject) be independent of complications that might arise for its clausemate (e.g., the object). Putting one indexical under a quotation operator has no bearing on anything else in the clause. Yet it is precisely for this reason that the partial quotation view runs into trouble. When one person indexical in a given embedded clause is shifty, other person indexicals must be shifty too; conversely, when one person indexical fails to be shifty, other clausemate person indexicals cannot be shifty either.

To see this, first consider baseline sentence (27). Here the embedded subject is an unshifted indexical, *'ee* 'you'. Also inside the embedded clause is a third-person pronoun co-referring with the matrix subject *Lori*.

(27) Lori   hi-neki-se-Ø   ['ee   wees   qetu   kuhet
     Lori.NOM 3SUBJ-think-IMPERF-PRES [2SG.CL be.PRES more tall
     'ip-nim-x   ].
     3SG-OBL-to]
     Lori$_i$ thinks that you$_j$ are taller than her$_i$.

If indexical shift arises through quotation of the individual indexicals, we expect to be able to swap the third-person pronoun of this sentence for a (quoted) first person shifty indexical referring to Lori while preserving the truth value of the sentence. (We know that first-person shifty indexicals are possible in 'think' reports: see, e.g., example (19).) But this is completely impossible. The sentence that results from this swap, (28), does not allow its first-person indexical to have a shifty reading. In the presence of an unshifty second person, first person must be unshifty as well.

(28) Lori   hi-neki-se-Ø   ['ee   wees   qetu   kuhet
     Lori.NOM 3SUBJ-think-IMPERF-PRES [2SG.CL be.PRES more tall
     'iin-im-x   ].
     1SG-OBL-to]
     Lori$_i$ thinks that you$_j$ are taller than me$_k$/ ✗"me"$_i$.

This type of fact holds regardless of the particular position of the two indexicals in the embedded clause. In (29a), the embedded third-person subject co-refers with the matrix subject and is clausemate with an unshifted second-person object. Given the presence of the unshifted pronoun, the third-person subject cannot be replaced with a shifty first-person pronoun *salva veritate*:

(29) a. 'Iin-im   lawtiwaa-nm hi-i-caa-qa   *pro*
      1SG-GEN friend-ERG   3SUBJ-say-IMPERF-REC.PAST 1SG
      [*pro* 'ee   hi-sok-saa-qa   ].
      [3SG 2SG.CL 3SUBJ-recognize-IMPERF-REC.PAST]
      My friend$_i$ told me he$_i$ recognized you.
   b. 'Iin-im   lawtiwaa-nm hi-i-caa-qa   *pro*
      1SG-GEN friend-ERG   3SUBJ-say-IMPERF-REC.PAST 1SG
      [*pro* 'ee   sok-saa-qa   ].
      [1SG 2SG.CL recognize-IMPERF-REC.PAST]
      My friend$_i$ told me I$_j$ / ✗"I"$_i$ recognized you.

The broader pattern is seen in (30), presented here with four potential readings. On the most natural reading of this sentence, both embedded pronouns are shifty (and thus refer to the speaker's husband and sister, respectively).[10] Also possible is a reading where neither pronoun is shifty, and thus they refer to the addressee and the speaker, respectively. But it is entirely impossible for one pronoun to be shifty while the other remains unshifty.

(30) Ne-'níc-em   pee-Ø-n-e   'in-haama-na,
     1SG-older.sister-ERG 3/3-say-P-REM.PAST 1SG-husband-ACC
     ['im-im   ciq'aamqal hi-twehkey'k-Ø-e   'iin-e   ].
     [2SG-GEN dog(ERG) 3SUBJ-chase-P-REM.PAST 1SG-ACC]
     a.   My sister$_s$ told my husband$_h$ that his$_h$ dog chased her$_s$.
     b. ? My sister$_s$ told my husband$_h$ that your dog chased me.
     c. ✗ My sister$_s$ told my husband$_h$ that your dog chased her$_s$.
     d. ✗ My sister$_s$ told my husband$_h$ that his$_h$ dog chased me.

The same pattern obtains in cases where both pronouns are first person:

(31) Ne-'níc-em   pee-Ø-n-e   'in-haama-na,
     1SG-older.sister-ERG 3/3-say-P-REM.PAST 1SG-husband-ACC
     ['iin-im   ciq'aamqal hi-twehkey'k-Ø-e   'iin-e   ].
     [1SG-GEN dog(ERG) 3SUBJ-chase-P-REM.PAST 1SG-ACC]
     a.   My sister$_s$ told my husband$_h$ that her$_s$ dog chased her$_s$.
     b. ? My sister$_s$ told my husband$_h$ that my dog chased me.
     c. ✗ My sister$_s$ told my husband$_h$ that my dog chased her$_s$.
     d. ✗ My sister$_s$ told my husband$_h$ that her$_s$ dog chased me.

The pattern here is one established by Rice (1986) and especially Anand and Nevins (2004) and Anand (2006) (and one which we return to later in this chapter):

(32) *Shift Together: Person*
     In a given embedded clause, either all or no person indexicals are shifty.

The Shift Together pattern holds as well for locative indexicals:[11]

(33) *Shift Together: Locative*
In a given embedded clause, either all or no locative indexicals are shifty.

Because both locative indexicals in (34) must refer to the same location, the desired interpretation 'from Idaho to California' is unavailable. The only reading of (34) is thus the anomalous one where both indexicals refer to the same location.[12]

(34) Context: Elicited in Lapwai, Idaho.
  # Ke-x kaa *pro* ciklii-toq-o' California-px, *pro*
  C-1 then 1SG return-back-PROSP California-to 1SG
  'e-nees-Ø-nu' *pro* [*pro* we-ke'eyk-Ø-e
  3OBJ-O.PL-say-PROSP 3PL.ACC [1SG fly-go-P-REM.PAST
  kinix kine-px].
  from.here here-to]
  When I return home to California ...
  a. ✗ I will tell them that I flew from here$_{Idaho}$ to here$_{California}$.
  b. ✗ I will tell them that I flew from here$_{California}$ to here$_{Idaho}$.

Similarly, because both locative indexicals in (35) must refer to the same location, the only reading of the sentence is one where it reports the utterance of a contradiction (namely, that a single place is hotter than itself):[13]

(35) # 'In-lawtiwaa-nm paasx̂a-pa hi-hi-n-e *pro*, [kine
  my-friend-ERG Boise-LOC 3SUBJ-say-P-REM.PAST 1SG [here
  hii-wes qetu 'iyeeqis kin-ix].
  3SUBJ-be.PRES more hot here-from]
  a. ✗ My friend in Boise told me it was hotter here than there.
  b. ✗ My friend in Boise told me it was hotter there than here.

Given (32) and (33), the essential trouble for the partial quotation view is that it posits too fine-grained a tool. Indexical shift is a clause-level phenomenon. Patterns of Shift Together call for a treatment of embedded indexicals above the level of the indexicals themselves.[14]

2.1.4 The Binding Analysis

We are now at the point of requiring some kind of mechanism that ensures that elements with a particular referent take a particular shape—for example, in (27)–(28), first-person shifty indexical versus third-person pronoun—in the environment of certain other semantically similar elements. Such mechanisms are familiar, of course, in the domain of binding theory, and this suggests that perhaps binding effects could be responsible for the restrictions on Nez Perce shifty indexicals. This type of hypothesis is naturally coupled with a treatment of shifty indexicals as ordinary (semantically third-person) bound pronouns in disguise, which has been explored in work by von Stechow (2003).[15]

To assess this view, let us first rephrase the Shift Together generalizations in (32) and (33) as a constraint on binding: in a given embedded clause, either all or no person elements / locative elements are *bound*. Then we ask: does a parallel generalization hold for bindable elements that are *not* disguised as indexicals, as we might expect if binding plays the crucial role?

A ready test is afforded by Nez Perce temporal adverbials. Applying the adverbial binding test from section 2.1.2 to the translation equivalents of *today* and *tomorrow*—*kii taaqc* and *watiisx*, respectively—we find that these adverbials are in fact not indexical, in spite of their colloquial translations (brought out by the (a) examples):

(36) *kii taaqc* ≠ English *today*
    a. Weet'u *pro* hipt   ha-ani-siix-Ø   **kii taaqc**.
       not   3PL food.NOM 3SUBJ-make-IMPERF.PL-PRES same.day
       They're not making food today.
    b. Ke-m kaa   *pro*   'ew-'nii-se-Ø   laqaas-na
       C-2   then 2SG 3OBJ-give-IMPERF-PRES mouse-ACC
       cicyuk'iisin' k'aɫk'aɫ, kaa   *pro*   hi-wewluq-o'qa
           cookie.NOM   then 3SG 3SUBJ-want-MODAL
       qahasnim wee'ikt **kii taaqc**.
           milk.NOM   same.day
       When you give a mouse a cookie, he wants some milk that same day (#today).[16]

(37) *watiisx* ≠ English *tomorrow*[17]
    a. **Watiisx**   *pro*   ciq'aamqal-niin 'itamyaanwas-x pe-ky-u'.
       1.day.away 1SG dog-with   town-to   S.PL-go-PROSP
       Tomorrow I'm going into town with my dog.
    b. Ke-x mawa   *pro*   capaakayx-tato-Ø   'aatamoc, kaa   **watiisx**
       C-1   when 1SG wash-HAB.SG-PRES car.NOM   then 1.day.away
       hi-weeqi-yo'qa.
       3SUBJ-rain-MODAL
       Whenever I wash my car, the next day (#tomorrow) it rains.

This gives us the fodder we need to test whether the Shift Together effect reflects a general principle of binding. Is it the case, in a given embedded clause, that either all or none of the temporal adverbials must be bound by the attitudinal quantification? It is not, as the interpretation of (38) shows. In this sentence embedded *kii taaqc* is interpreted as bound ('the same day as the reported speech event'), whereas embedded *watiisx* is interpreted as free ('one day after the overall utterance / tomorrow').

(38) Naaqc k'ay'x-pa, weet 'aayat hi-i-cee-ne [*pro*
one week-LOC, Y.N lady.NOM 3SUBJ-say-IMPERF-REM.PAST [1SG
kiy-u' kii taaqc 'itq'o watiisx]?
go-PROSP same.day or 1.day.away]
One week ago$_{t_1}$, did the lady say$_{t_1}$ she would go that same day$_{t_1}$ or tomorrow$_{t^*+1}$?

Also possible is the reverse pattern, bound *watiisx* ('one day after the attitude event') and free *kii taaqc* ('the same day as the overall utterance / today'):

(39) Halx̂pawit'aasx, Harold hi-cuukwe-ce-ne [*pro*
Saturday Harold.NOM 3SUBJ-know-IMPERF-REM.PAST [1SG
wek-u' łepwey-pe watiisx halx̂paawit-pa kaa kii taaqc lepiti-pe
be-PROSP Lapwai-LOC 1.day.away Sunday-LOC and same.day two-LOC
ka'aw-pa].
day-LOC]
On Saturday$_{t_1}$, Harold knew that I would be in Lapwai the next day$_{t_1+1}$, Sunday, and today$_{t^*}$, Tuesday.

Such findings point to an important difference between indexical elements and nonindexical temporal adverbs. This is unexpected if both types of elements are to be handled by the same general set of binding constraints. The data set points to an analysis of the Shift Together constraint on shifty indexicals that is particular to truly *indexical* elements. Bindable anaphoric elements are subject to no such requirement.[18]

2.1.5 The Context Pronoun Analysis

An alternative version of a binding-based approach offers a potentially more successful response to the Shift Together data. We have seen that Shift Together effects are not paralleled by "Bind Together" effects for other anaphoric elements. Might indexicals then be somehow special in the way that they are bound, such that they should be subject to different constraints? Perhaps, for instance, indexicals are not bound as type *e* elements, on par with classic treatments of bound third-person pronouns; rather, they are complex expressions that merely contain potentially bindable context pronouns. A binding theory for context pronouns might in principle be rather different than the binding theory for individual pronouns (cp. Percus 2000). This type of view has been explored by Schlenker (1999, 2003, 2011).

If indexicals compose with context pronouns, we might imagine that these pronouns come in two varieties. Ordinary context pronouns $c_1 \ldots c_n$ are bindable by attitude predicates, resulting in shifty readings; a distinguished context pronoun, c^*, picks out the context of utterance, resulting in unshifty readings.[19] Certainly, if indexicals in a language with optional indexical shift may compose with either c_i or c^*, Shift Together effects will not be derived: those that compose with c_i will shift, whereas those that compose with c^* will not. (Like the partial quotation view reviewed in section 2.1.3, this view is too fine-grained.) Yet this view allows a repair (Schlenker 2011): a language might require its indexicals to depend on c^*, and then allow attitude contexts to feature binding of this distinguished variable. The result is that all indexicals depend on the same bound context variable. This produces a reading where all indexicals shift.

The prediction is that indexical shift should be a purely all-or-nothing affair, for all types of indexicals. If a language shows Shift Together effects, we do not expect that language to allow clauses where some classes of indexicals are shifted (e.g., person) but others are not (e.g., locative). Once c^* has been bound, all indexicals that depend on this value will show shifty readings. But this undergenerates the readings possible in Nez Perce sentences containing both person and locative indexicals. We have seen that person indexicals and locative indexicals each show Shift Together effects with others of their class. Across classes, however, there is more freedom. In (40) and (41), we see that first person may shift while locative *kine* 'here' does not. (We return to this type of data in section 3.1.3.)

(40) Context: my friend is calling me on his cellphone and describing his location. He is trying to make it to Lapwai, but he is lost.
Pro hi-hi-ce-Ø   [*pro* kine paay-ca-Ø   ],
3SG 3SUBJ-say-IMPERF-PRES [1SG here arrive-IMPERF-PRES]
met'u weet'u *pro* hi-paay-ca-Ø   kine.
but   not   3SG 3SUBJ-arrive-IMPERF-PRES here
He$_i$ says he$_i$ is arriving here, but he is not arriving here.

(41) Context: I travel to the town where my dad grew up and I go to the address he said he grew up at. Someone sees me looking at the house and I explain:
Na'-toot-am   hi-i-cee-ne   *pro* [*pro* kine
my-father-ERG 3SUBJ-say-IMPERF-REM.PAST 1SG [1SG here
tew'yenik-Ø-e   ].
live-P-REM.PAST]
My father told me he used to live here.

To derive the unshifty reading of *kine* 'here' in these examples, we must allow this indexical to compose with a context pronoun that is not bound. If Nez Perce requires its indexicals to compose with c^*, shifty readings result when

c^* is bound and unshifty readings result when c^* remains unbound. The mixed readings in (40) and (41) cannot be derived: c^* must be bound for the person indexical to be shifty, but must be free for the locative indexical to be unshifty. If, conversely, Nez Perce allows its indexicals to compose either with c^* or with a regular c_i variable, we fail to predict any Shift Together effects whatsoever. As on the partial quotation view, indexical shift becomes an every-item-for-itself type of matter.

2.1.6 The Pragmatic Analysis

This last type of analysis points us to a further potential avenue—one that ties together indexicals and embedding verbs not in terms of binding but rather in terms of their special pragmatics. Indexicals are special in the way that they relate to a discourse: unembedded indexicals draw their reference from the utterance event. What if indexicals could be "anchored" in some way to an alternative speech or attitude event, made salient by the use of a speech or attitude verb? On such a view, the Shift Together generalizations discussed in section 2.1.3 could perhaps be taken to reflect the particular mechanisms by which a speech or attitude event becomes salient. The salient speech or attitude event and the original utterance event are not treated on a par. Rather, in order for indexicals to shift, the reported speech or attitude event must be ranked more highly in terms of salience than the original utterance event is. Indexicals, in turn, draw their reference from the most highly ranked speech or attitude event. Thus if one indexical shifts, other indexicals must shift as well. (Different levels of salience might be accorded to different participants in an attitude, producing some freedom in mixing person and locative indexicals.) This general analytical strategy is explored by Bittner (2014) and Roberts (2015).

The advantage of this view is that it treats indexical shift as a natural concomitant of verb meaning. Use of an attitude verb introduces an attitude state simply by virtue of what the verb means; an attitude state, in turn, can be used to calculate the reference of indexicals. Given the core role of pragmatic mechanisms in regulating the connection between the verb and indexical elements, we expect that the possibility of indexical shift should be potentially affected by pragmatic manipulations, but, conversely, unaffected by syntactic manipulations of the speech or attitude complement. After all, it is the meaning of the verb, rather than the syntactic details of the complementation structure, that determines which potential anchors for indexicals are sufficiently salient.

Testing this prediction requires consideration of a broader range of complementation structures than we have seen thus far. In addition to the simple clausal complementation structure that has been exemplified thus far in this chapter, the Nez Perce verb *neki* 'think' also occurs in a prolepsis structure: the matrix attitude verb takes an object, originating in the matrix clause, which is construed (to a first pass) as coreferential with a pronoun inside the clausal complement.[20] The matrix object must be interpreted *de re*, with scope over the verb (Deal 2018a). In Deal (2017) (largely following Salzmann 2017a,b), I defend the structure in (42) for this type of complementation in Nez Perce. Here an operator on the edge of the embedded CP binds an embedded pronoun. This produces an intensional property that serves as the first argument to a *de re* attitude verb (cp. Heim 1994).

(42) Structure of proleptic complementation

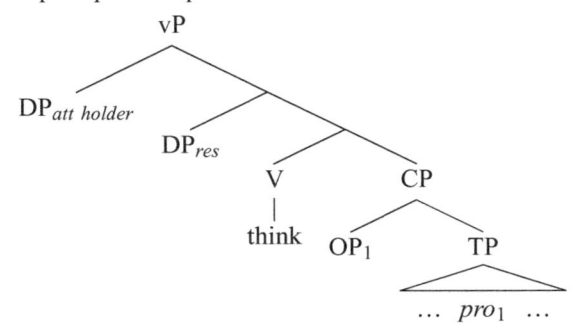

```
              vP
             /  \
       DP_att holder
               \
               DP_res
                   \
                  V    CP
                  |   /  \
                think OP_1  TP
                            /\
                           ... pro_1 ...
```

In Nez Perce, structures of this type can be recognized morphosyntactically in several ways. Most notably, given the presence of an object in the matrix clause, this clause shows transitive case and agreement (discussed in more detail in appendix B): the attitude holder DP (if overt) appears in the ergative case, the *res* DP (if overt) appears in the accusative case, and the attitude verb agrees with both the attitude holder DP (as subject) and the *res* DP (as object). These morphosyntactic effects can be seen by comparing minimal pairs of simple clausal complementation structures, as in the (a) examples that follow, with prolepsis, as in the (b) examples.[21] (*Res* arguments are bolded for ease of identification.)

(43) Context: My neighbor Mary sees a cat catching a magpie. It turns out it was my cat, Calvin, but Mary doesn't know that. She just tells me about the fight and what the cat looked like. When I get home, Calvin is there and he's all dirty and messed up. To explain what happened I say:
    a. Mary   hi-neki-se-Ø
       Mary.NOM 3SUBJ-think-IMPERF-PRES
       [**Calvin-nim** pee-cepeqick-Ø-e   'ek'eex-ne   ].
       [Calvin-ERG 3/3-catch-P-REM.PAST magpie-ACC]
       Mary thinks Calvin caught a magpie.

b. Mary-nim **Calvin-ne** pee-nek-se-Ø [*pro*
Mary-ERG Calvin-ACC 3/3-think-IMPERF-PRES [3SG.ERG
pee-cepeqick-Ø-e 'ek'eex-ne].
3/3-catch-P-REM.PAST magpie-ACC]
Mary thinks Calvin caught a magpie.

(44) Context: There is a friendly dog, but it scares people because they think it's a wolf, just based on how it looks. When I point to it I say:
 a. *Pro* hi-nek-siix-Ø [**kii** **ciq'aamqal**
 3PL.NOM 3SUBJ-think-IMPERF.PL-PRES [this.NOM dog.NOM
 hii-wes himiin' weet'u ciq'aamqal].
 3SUBJ-be.PRES wolf.NOM NEG dog.NOM]
 They think that this dog is a wolf, not a dog.
 b. *Pro* pee-nek-six-Ø **ki-nye ciq'aamqal-a**, [*pro*
 3PL.ERG 3/3-think-IMPERF.PL-PRES this-ACC dog-ACC [3SG
 hii-wes himiin' weet'u ciq'aamqal].
 3SUBJ-be.PRES wolf.NOM NEG dog.NOM]
 They think that this dog is a wolf, not a dog.

Note that all four of these sentences express *de re* reports. In (43), Mary does not identify the cat in question as Calvin. In (44), we have a case of mistaken identity—the proposition believed *de dicto* would be contradictory. Differences between these sentences are thus unlikely to be in their meanings—each pair reports the same attitude *de re*—but rather in the compositional path by which the meaning is obtained. Indeed, given the morphosyntactic profile of prolepsis, differences in compositional structure between the two variants are quite likely. In prolepsis sentences (43b) and (44b), the *res* is an argument of the matrix verb, whose lexical semantics forces a *de re* reading (see Deal 2018a). In nonprolepsis counterparts (43a) and (44a), the *res* shows no special morphosyntactic behavior; there is no sign of covert *res*-movement, for instance.[22] This suggests that the *de re* reading in (43a) and (44a) is achieved with the help of concept generators (Percus and Sauerland 2003a, Anand 2006, Charlow and Sharvit 2014, Pearson 2015, Sharvit 2018) or alternative in situ *de re* mechanisms (e.g., Ninan 2012).

Now, in arguing against a clausal quotation account in section 2.1.1, I showed that shift is possible for indexicals whose clausemate is interpreted *de re*. One such case is (45). Note that this sentence does not feature prolepsis. Rather, it features *de re* in situ, plausibly via concept generators, as in (43a) and (44a). (Observe in particular that the attitude verb shows no object agreement and that the *res* argument is not marked accusative.)

(45) Context: My neighbor Mary complains to me that a cat has been digging up her flowers. She tells me about the cat and it sounds like it was my cat Calvin, even though Mary doesn't know what cat it was. I say to my husband: *Mary thinks Calvin is digging up her flowers.*
Pro hi-neki-se-Ø
3SG.NOM 3SUBJ-think-IMPERF-PRES
[Calvin-nim hi-p'la-yay'-sa-Ø   *pro*   laatis   ].
[Calvin-ERG 3SUBJ-dig-µ-IMPERF-PRES 1SG.ACC flower.NOM]
She$_i$ thinks Calvin is digging up her$_i$ flowers.

Crucially, the possibility of indexical shift in a *de re* context is sensitive to the way the *de re* reading is compositionally derived. In contrast to nonproleptic (45), the proleptic version disfavors indexical shift:[23]

(46) Context: same.
  a. ?? *Pro*   pee-nek-se-Ø   Calvin-ne   [*pro*
     3SG.ERG 3/3-think-IMPERF-PRES Calvin-ACC [3SG.ERG
     hi-p'la-yay'-sa-Ø   *pro*   laatis   ].
     3SUBJ-dig-µ-IMPERF-PRES 1SG.ACC flower.NOM]
     Intended: She$_i$ thinks Calvin is digging up her$_i$ flowers.
  b. *Pro*   pee-nek-se-Ø   Calvin-ne   [*pro*
     3SG.ERG 3/3-think-IMPERF-PRES Calvin-ACC [3SG.ERG
     paa-p'la-yay'-sa-Ø   *pro*   laatis   ].
     3/3-dig-µ-IMPERF-PRES 3SG.ACC flower.NOM]
     She$_i$ thinks Calvin is digging up her$_i$ flowers.

The same interaction between complementation type and indexical shift is seen in (47), where consultants' judgments were more categorical:

(47) Context: There is a BBQ with a lot of food on different tables. People are there with their families and their dogs. Mary leaves her food on one table and then she sees a dog come up to it. Next thing she knows, the food is missing.
  a. Indexical shift is possible with ordinary complementation:
     Meeli   hi-neki-se-Ø   [ciq'aamqal-nim
     Mary.NOM 3SUBJ-think-IMPERF-PRES [dog-ERG
     hi-ip-eny-Ø-e   *pro*   hipt   ].
     3SUBJ-eat-µ-P-REM.PAST 1SG.ACC food.NOM]
     Mary thinks a dog ate her food.

b. Prolepsis is possible without indexical shift:
   Meeli-nim **ciq'aamqal-na** pee-nek-se-Ø   [*pro*
   Mary-ERG   dog-ACC   3/3-think-IMPERF-PRES [3SG.ERG
   pee-p-eny-Ø-e   *pro*   hipt   ].
   3/3-eat-µ-P-REM.PAST 3SG.ACC food.NOM]
   Mary thinks a dog ate her food.
c. Prolepsis and indexical shift cannot be combined:
   # Meeli-nim **ciq'aamqal-na** pee-nek-se-Ø   [*pro*
   Mary-ERG   dog-ACC   3/3-think-IMPERF-PRES [3SG.ERG
   hi-ip-eny-Ø-e   *pro*   hipt   ].
   3SUBJ-eat-µ-P-REM.PAST 1SG.ACC food.NOM]
   Intended: Mary thinks a dog ate her food.

The disfavoring of indexical shift in proleptic structures is particularly notable in view of the fact that Nez Perce speakers typically prefer indexical shift whenever it is possible (see note 10). These facts strongly suggest that the possibility of indexical shift is influenced not only by sentence meaning or pragmatics, by also by syntactic factors. And this means that the role of verbs in making particular perspectives salient, independent of the syntax of complementation, cannot be the full story. The structure of the embedded clause matters for indexical shift. These data point to a theory of indexical shift that is specific to cases of straightforward CP complementation—not the type found in prolepsis.[24]

2.2 The Shifty Operator Theory of Indexical Shift

Indexical shift in Nez Perce is specific to speech and attitude reports; it operates on a whole-clause basis; it allows for the behavior of shifty indexicals to be distinguished from the behavior of bindable, anaphoric elements; it is sensitive to the structure of the embedded clause. Having established these generalizations, it is time to lay out a theoretical framework that can explain them. The framework I present in this section is the shifty operator theory of indexical shift, as originally proposed by Anand and Nevins (2004) and subsequently developed by a range of authors (Anand 2006, Sudo 2012, Deal 2014, Shklovsky and Sudo 2014, Park 2016). While I will deviate in a few presentational respects from the *loci classici* of the shifty operator view (Anand and Nevins 2004, Anand 2006), I will adhere closely to their spirit. My focus will be on the core mechanics of operator-based indexical shift, as applied to Nez Perce, and the central generalizations this approach delivers (including those laid out in the previous section).

2.2.1 Meanings for Indexicals and Operators

We begin with a familiar proposal for what indexicals mean—indeed the standard idea in the linguistics literature, owing to Kaplan (1989). The proposal is simple: the meaning of an indexical is directly determined by context. Different indexicals are distinguished from one another by the particular function they apply to context, for instance:

(48) a. $[\![I]\!]^{c,i,g} = author(c)$
 b. $[\![here]\!]^{c,i,g} = loc(c)$

Note that these denotations are provided relative to a context c, index i, and assignment g. The denotations in (48) themselves make few demands of these elements. They place no demands whatsoever on index or assignment, and so far as contexts are concerned, they require merely that these be sufficient to uniquely identify an author (who we might think of as a speaker, in the case of a context of speech) and a location. Clearly, many types of formal objects are sufficient to play this narrow role. For instance, a context could be thought of, as per Lewis, as "a location—time, place, and possible world—where a sentence is said" (1980, 79). On this conception, a context might be thought of as a part of a possible world, a Kratzerian situation (Kratzer 1989). But it would work equally well so far as the meanings in (48) are concerned to model context in a rather different way, one more closely associated with Kaplan's views. As this view would have it, a context is a tuple of author, addressee, location, time, and world. It is a mathematical object, an ordered list, not a part of a possible world at all.[25]

This second conception of contexts makes the context parameter of interpretation at least partially formally parallel to the index, or what Kaplan calls the *circumstance of evaluation*. The traditional role of the index is to manage information about world and time dependence. So, an index must consist at least of a tuple $\langle w, t \rangle$—a world and a time—where w is shifted by intensional operators and t by temporal ones (each presented below in a more or less grossly oversimplified caricature):

(49) $[\![PAST\ I\ swim]\!]^{c,\langle w,t \rangle,g} = 1$ iff $\exists t' : t' < t.[\![I\ swim]\!]^{c,\langle w,t' \rangle,g} = 1$
 $= 1$ iff $\exists t' : t' < t.[\![swim]\!]^{c,\langle w,t' \rangle,g}([\![I]\!]^{c,\langle w,t' \rangle,g}) = 1$
 $= 1$ iff $\exists t' : t' < t.author(c)$ swims at t' in w

(50) $[\![Mona\ says\ I\ surf]\!]^{c,\langle w,t \rangle,g} = 1$ iff $\forall w' : w'$ is compatible with what Mona says in w . $[\![I\ surf]\!]^{c,\langle w',t \rangle,g} = 1$
 $= 1$ iff $\forall w' : w'$ is compatible with what Mona says in $w.author(c)$ surfs at t in w'

It would not disturb a theory of intensional or temporal operators to imagine that the index contained other sorts of information as well, for instance, the additional information that would be required in order to make it fully parallel to the tuple-conception of a context. Both as far as indexicals are concerned (regarding context) and so far as intensional and temporal operators are concerned (regarding index), context and index *both* might be modeled as tuples of an author, addressee, location, time, and world (von Stechow 2003, von Stechow and Zimmermann 2005, Anand 2006).[26]

Modeling index structure in this fashion opens up the possibility of a view of attitude verb meaning that goes quite a bit beyond the caricature in (50), in a way that turns out to be useful for handling indexical shift. Rather than simply quantifying over (accessible) worlds (as in (50)), or world-time pairs, an attitude verb may quantify over richly centered indices whose coordinates are drawn in part from the circumstances of the attitude.[27] The predicate *say*, for instance, can be given the following syncategorematic denotation (cp. Anand and Nevins 2004, section 5.1.1; Anand 2006, 109; and especially Sudo 2012, 233):

(51) $[\![SAY\ \alpha]\!]^{c,i,g} = \lambda x. \forall i' \in R_{say}(x,i) [\![\alpha]\!]^{c,i',g}$
where $i' \in R_{say}(x,i)$ iff
a. $w(i')$ is compatible with what x says at i
b. $author(i')$ is an individual in $w(i')$ that x identifies at i as herself
c. $addr(i')$ is an individual in $w(i')$ that x identifies at i as her addressee
d. $loc(i')$ is a location in $w(i')$ that x identifies at i as her spatial location
e. $time(i')$ is a time in $w(i')$ that x identifies at i as her temporal location

Such a predicate composes with a complement that provides a function from indices to truth values.[28] This may be accomplished via a rule of Intensional Function Application (Heim and Kratzer 1998):

(52) *Intensional Function Application*
If α is a branching node and $\{\beta, \gamma\}$ the set of its daughters, then for any context c, index i, and assignment g: if $[\![\beta]\!]^{c,i,g}$ is a function whose domain contains $\lambda i'.[\![\gamma]\!]^{c,i',g}$, then $[\![\alpha]\!]^{c,i,g} = [\![\beta]\!]^{c,i,g}(\lambda i'.[\![\gamma]\!]^{c,i',g})$

The accessibility relation introduced by the predicate ensures that the only indices relevant for the interpretation of its complement will be those that match both what is said (in terms of the world coordinate of the index) and the self-locating perspective of the attitude holder (in terms of other coordinates of the index).[29] For a simple sentence such as *Mona says I surf*, this more rich representation of the attitudinal quantifier yields, in the end, the same result. Information about various coordinates of the index (e.g., author) is not invoked by anything in the embedded clause. It is this that will be different in cases of indexical shift. In these cases, information about a range of coordinates of the index proves potentially relevant for the semantics of the last, most distinctive element of our basic story—the shifty operator.

The function of a shifty operator may be appreciated with the help of an ambiguous sentence like Nez Perce (53). This sentence has both a nonshifty reading, (a), and a shifty reading, (b).

(53) Isii-ne$_i$ A.   hi-i-caa-qa
     who-ACC A.NOM 3SUBJ-say-IMPERF-REC.PAST
     [(OP) cewcewin'es-ki   pro   'e-muu-ce-Ø   t$_i$]?
     [phone-with   1SG   3OBJ-call-IMPERF-PRES   ]

   a. Who did A say I was calling?
   b. Who did A$_i$ say she$_i$ was calling?

As the glossing now indicates, the two readings reflect a structural ambiguity: on reading (b), but not on reading (a), a context-shifting operator OP is present in the left periphery of the embedded clause. When the operator is absent, the embedded first-person indexical is interpreted in the standard way as drawing its reference from the author coordinate of the utterance context. This delivers the unshifted reading.

(54) $[\![pro.1\text{SG}]\!]^{c,i,g} = author(c)$

When the operator is present, the meaning of the indexical (what Kaplan calls its "character") does not change, but the context against which it is evaluated does. The operator requires that its complement, including the indexical, be interpreted with respect to a set of contexts c' such that the author function applied to c' yields the author of the reported attitude, in this case person A. This delivers the shifted reading.

(55) $[\![pro.1\text{SG}]\!]^{c',i,g} = author(c') = A$

How does the operator effect this change? How are values for c' determined? The answer takes advantage of the fact that shifty operators occupy attitude complements, where attitude verbs quantify over indices in the general way indicated in (51) (Anand and Nevins 2004). The operator's function is to overwrite the context parameter of interpretation for its complement with the (bound) index parameter.[30] Anand and Nevins propose that this overwriting may be total (cp. Stalnaker's 1978 diagonal operator). This operator is defined syncategorematically in (56a) (following Anand and Nevins), but may equally well be defined categorematically as in (56b). As the categorematic version indicates, a shifty operator composes with a complement that provides a function from indices to a function from contexts to truth values. This composition requires a rule beyond Intensional Function Application; I follow Anand (2006) in calling the additional rule *Monstrous Function Application*.[31] (In what follows, I will largely stick to categorematic presentation, and assume that composition of a shifty operator and its complement proceeds via rule (57). I represent both context and index as being of type κ.)

(56) a. $[\![\text{OP}_\forall \, \alpha]\!]^{c,i,g} = [\![\alpha]\!]^{i,i,g}$
 b. $[\![\text{OP}_\forall]\!]^{c,i,g} = \lambda p \in D_{<\kappa, \kappa t>} . p(i)(i) = 1$

(57) *Monstrous Function Application*
If α is a branching node and $\{\beta, \gamma\}$ is the set of its daughters, then for any context c, index i, and assignment g: if $[\![\beta]\!]^{c,i,g}$ is a function whose domain contains $\lambda i' . \lambda c' . [\![\gamma]\!]^{c',i',g}$, then $[\![\alpha]\!]^{c,i,g} = [\![\beta]\!]^{c,i,g}(\lambda i' . \lambda c' . [\![\gamma]\!]^{c',i',g})$

Note that the adoption of operators that change contexts, and the corresponding rule of Monstrous Function Application, is a departure from the otherwise orthodox Kaplanian view we have adopted thus far. (Indeed, Kaplan famously dubbed context-changing operators "monsters begat by elegance" and sought to ban them by fiat. See Kaplan 1989, section VIII.) This departure is a limited one: it does not affect the semantics of attitude verbs (or other temporal or modal operators), as in (51), nor does Monstrous Function Application replace the more limited rule of Intensional Function Application from (52). In other words: the theory does not require that *all* intensional manipulation change the context—it merely allows that *some* does. This limited change, as we will see shortly, should not puzzle us. It is this that fundamentally makes indexical shift possible.

In addition to total overwriting of context, as in (56), Anand and Nevins also propose that overwriting may be partial, affecting some coordinates of context but not others. The operator in (58) overwrites only the author and addressee coordinates of context. Because all indices quantified over by a verb like (51) have an author coordinate that is a (*de se*) counterpart of the attitude holder and an addressee coordinate that is a (*de te*) counterpart of the reported addressee, a 'say' complement containing this operator will require that first- and second-person indexicals refer to the reported speaker and reported addressee, respectively, rather than the utterance speaker and utterance addressee. (Following standard notation for variable assignments, I represent modified contexts, e.g., c modified only so as to substitute x for the original value of coordinate α, as $c^{x/\alpha}$.)

(58) $[\![\text{OP}_{\text{PERS}}]\!]^{c,i,g} = \lambda p \in D_{<\kappa, \kappa t>} . p(i)(c^{\text{author}(i)/\text{author}, \text{addr}(i)/\text{addr}}) = 1$

Note that the operator defined in (58) may cause its complement to be evaluated with respect to an "improper context"—one that does not correspond to any actual circumstance of utterance or attitude-holding (cp. Kaplan 1989, 509; Schlenker 2018): the author and addressee coordinates have shifted but the rest of the context has not. It was precisely this type of behavior that Lewis (1980) sought to prevent with his conception of contexts as locations (parts of worlds), rather than formal tuples. If partial shiftability of this type turns out to be necessary for the analysis of indexical shift, as I will argue, then it turns out we do have linguistic reason to prefer the tuple-conception of contexts over the location-conception. Indexicals in isolation can be handled equally well on either conception, but shifty operators cannot.

To appreciate this proposal in action, let us consider the shifty and unshifty readings for the embedded clause in (53), repeated here:

(59) Isii-ne$_2$ A.   hi-i-caa-qa
   who-ACC A.NOM 3SUBJ-say-IMPERF-REC.PAST
   [(OP) cewcewin'es-ki   *pro*   'e-muu-ce-Ø t_2]?
   [phone-with   1SG 3OBJ-call-IMPERF-PRES   ]

   a. Who did A say I was calling?
   b. Who did A$_i$ say she$_i$ was calling?

The derivation of reading (a) proceeds straightforwardly, as shown in (60). The attitude verb quantifies over SAY indices, as defined in (51). Coordinates of the index matter for the contribution of the embedded clause because the verb *call* is world- and time-sensitive. The semantics of the embedded first-person subject and the embedded trace object are determined by the context and assignment, respectively; neither of these is manipulated within this portion of the structure.[32]

(60) a. $[\![A\ SAY\ [_{CP}\ I\ CALL\ t_2]\ ]\!]^{c,i,g} = 1$ iff $\forall i' \in R_{say}(A, i)[\![I\ CALL\ t_2\ ]\!]^{c,i',g} = 1$
   b. $[\![\ A\ SAY\ [_{CP}\ I\ CALL\ t_2]\ ]\!]^{c,i,g} = 1$ iff $\forall i' \in R_{say}(A, i)[$ author(c) calls $g(2)$ at $t(i')$ in $w(i')\ ]$

The derivation of reading (b) is different only in that a shifty operator is present, just below the attitude verb. In (61) I assume this operator is OP$_{PERS}$ (though the reader can verify that the choice of OP$_\forall$ would yield the same result here).

(61) a. $[\![A\ SAY\ [_{CP}\ OP_{PERS}\ I\ CALL\ t_2]]\!]^{c,i,g} = 1$ iff
      $\forall i' \in R_{say}(A, i)[\![\ OP_{PERS}\ I\ CALL\ t_2\ ]\!]^{c,i',g} = 1$
   b. Monstrous Function Application:
      $[\![\ OP_{PERS}\ I\ CALL\ t_2\ ]\!]^{c,i',g} = 1$ iff
      $[\lambda p \in D_{<\kappa,\kappa t>}.p(i')(c^{author(i')/author, addr(i')/addr}) = 1]\ (\lambda i''.\lambda c''.$
      $[\![\ I\ CALL\ t_2]\!]^{c'',i'',g}) = 1$

c. β-Reduction (twice):
$[\![\text{OP}_{\text{PERS}}\ I\ CALL\ t_2]\!]^{c,i',g} = 1$ iff
$[\![I\ CALL\ t_2]\!]^{c^{author(i')/author,addr(i')/addr},i',g} = 1$

d. Lexical Entries for Embedded Material:
$[\![I\ CALL\ t_2]\!]^{c^{author(i')/author,addr(i')/addr},i',g} = 1$
iff $author(c^{author(i')/author,addr(i')/addr})$ calls $g(2)$ at $t(i')$ in $w(i')$
$[\![I\ CALL\ t_2]\!]^{c^{author(i')/author,addr(i')/addr},i',g} = 1$ iff $author(i')$ calls $g(2)$ at $t(i')$ in $w(i')$

e. Result for Overall Structure from Line (a):
$[\![A\ SAY\ [_{CP}\ \text{OP}_{\text{PERS}}\ I\ CALL\ t_2]]\!]^{c,i,g} = 1$ iff $\forall i' \in R_{say}(A, i)[\ author(i')$ calls $g(2)$ at $t(i')$ in $w(i')]$

Here, as before, the attitude verb quantifies over SAY indices—author-addressee-location-time-world tuples that meet the requirements imposed by the verb 'say'—but this time the quantification over author coordinates of the index has a downstream effect. The shifty operator, sitting in the scope of the quantification over indices, overwrites the author and addressee coordinates of context for the interpretation of its complement with information drawn from this quantification. For the indexical pronoun, which itself sits in the scope of the shifty operator, the result is that the author value is calculated with respect to shifted contexts. These contexts in particular are those that contain the original location-time-world information, but contain as author coordinates those who A identifies as herself in the various worlds compatible with what she says. (The same goes, mutatis mutandis, for addressee coordinates.) The upshot is that the embedded indexical picks out *de se* counterparts of A, the reported speaker. Information about the utterance speaker, as represented by the original context, is not available for the interpretation of the embedded first person.

This demonstration reveals that the shifty operator view provides a way to interpret embedded first-person pronouns with shifted reference in the absence of clausal quotation. The fact that the coargument of the shifty indexical in (59) is the trace of *wh*-movement provides no special obstacle. While quotation may involve mention or demonstration of language, no such factors play a role in indexical shift. It is rather the manipulation of the context (treated formally as a parameter of interpretation) that determines the shifted reading.

2.2.2 Operators in Syntactic Structures

To see how this approach compares to the various alternative analyses discussed in section 2.1, we begin by consideration of the consequences of positing shifty operators *qua* covert syntactic items.[33] Shifty operators are not open-class lexical items. They are functional elements, and so we expect their position in the clause to be relatively invariable and crosslinguistically consistent—an expectation that plays a significant role in the theory developed in chapter 3. Just what is this position? The answer turns out to connect closely with two of the desiderata for a theory of indexical shift with which we began this chapter: the restriction to speech and attitude reports and sensitivity to the structure of the embedded clause.

The evidence we have seen thus far in this chapter provides several reasons to think that the position of shifty operators is quite high. First, subject indexicals undergo shift; the position of the operator therefore must be above the subject position. If subjects are interpreted in Spec,TP, this suggests a position in the C domain. Second, as we saw in section 2.1.6, indexical shift is possible only in cases of straightforward CP complementation (rather than prolepsis):

(62) Indexical shift is possible without prolepsis:
Meeli hi-neki-se-Ø [ciq'aamqal-nim
Mary.NOM 3SUBJ-think-IMPERF-PRES [dog-ERG
hi-ip-eny-Ø-e pro hipt].
3SUBJ-eat-μ-P-REM.PAST 1SG.ACC food.NOM]
Mary thinks a dog ate her food.

(63) Indexical shift is impossible with prolepsis:
Meeli-nim ciq'aamqal-na pee-nek-se-Ø [*pro*
Mary-ERG dog-ACC 3/3-think-IMPERF-PRES [3SG.ERG
hi-ip-eny-Ø-e pro hipt].
3SUBJ-eat-μ-P-REM.PAST 1SG.ACC food.NOM]
Intended: Mary thinks a dog ate her food.

Proleptic embeddings feature a different C domain than simple CP embeddings do, given the structure in (42); there must be an operator in CP that binds an embedded pronoun. A reasonable conclusion is that shifty operators belong to the finite C system—either they instantiate a particular type of finite C^0 (as Anand 2006, 109 and Sudo 2012, 216 discuss) or they participate in a selectional relationship with such a head. (I will flesh out a version of this second option in chapters 3 and 4.) Either type of syntactic fact about the location of the operator allows us to tie the possibility of indexical shift to the precise syntactic details of the complementation structure.[34] The structure of the embedded clause matters for indexical shift because the shifty operator is an element in this structural representation.

This raises a question about matrix clauses. Matrix clauses have much in common structurally with the type of embedded clause that supports shifty operators. Could shifty operators be present at the matrix level? Indeed they could—but note that this would have no impact whatsoever on the interpretation of indexicals, so long as the shifty operator does not itself fall in the scope of a quantifier over indices. To see this, we start with a definition of truth at a context (and assignment) that builds from Kaplan (1989, 547):

(64) A sentence α is true at a context c and assignment g iff $[\![\alpha]\!]^{c,c,g} = 1$

Truth at a context-assignment pair is defined in terms of truth at a context, *index*, and assignment: a sentence is true at c, g just in case it is true at context c, an index identical to c, and assignment g. If we can count on extragrammatical mechanisms to indicate to us which context and assignment the speaker takes to be operative, we can provide "starting values" for context, assignment, *and index*—the last of these copied directly from the value for context. In an environment in which the index has not been shifted (e.g., by an attitude predicate), the contribution of a shifty operator—copying coordinates from the index onto the corresponding coordinates of the context—will therefore have no effect. After all, each pair of coordinates already has the same value to begin with. Thus:

(65) A sentence [OP α] is true at a context c and assignment g iff α is true at c and g, where OP is any operator that copies index values onto context values.

These considerations cast light on the origin of the restriction of indexical shift to complements of speech and attitude verbs. Of special interest in that connection are indexicals in matrix sentences such as (66):

(66) # Ke mawa T. hi-c'iiq-ce-Ø, 'iin wees
     C when T.NOM 3SUBJ-speak-IMPERF-PRES 1SG.NOM be.PRES
     haama.
     man.NOM
     Consultant (female): "Whenever [T] is speaking, I am a man ... ?!"

Here we have a matrix clause that contains a plausible adverbial quantifier over indices, a "whenever" clause. If a shifty operator were possible *between* this quantifier and the matrix subject indexical, we would expect that indexical to allow a shifty reading. The impossibility of such a reading suggests that shifty operators must occupy an extremely high position in the C domain—one higher than the highest possible attachment site of adverbial quantifiers. Thus (67) may be a possible structure, but (68) cannot be:

(67) Possible structure:

ke mawa T. hic'iiqce 'whenever T speaks'   *'iin wees haama* 'I am a man'

(68) Impossible structure:

ke mawa T. hic'iiqce 'whenever T speaks'

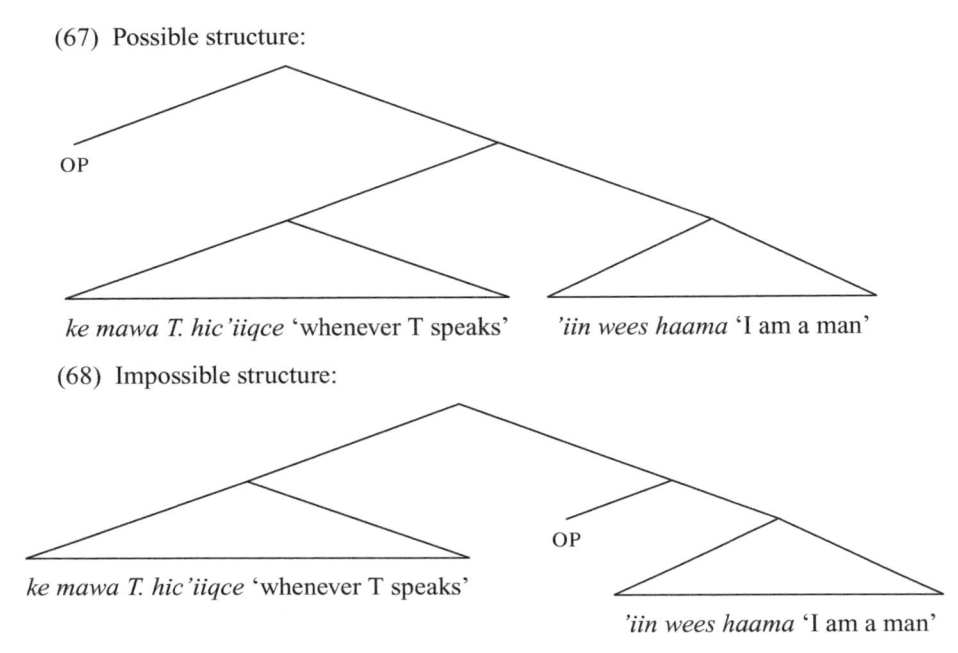

'iin wees haama 'I am a man'

What is special about speech and attitude complements, then, is not just that these CPs are large enough to host shifty operators, but that shifty operators within these CPs are able to fall within the scope of a quantifier over indices. For a quantifier over indices to outscope a shifty operator, the quantifier must belong to the next clause up. This suggests that shifty operators in fact occupy an extremely high position in syntactic structure.

2.2.3 The Overwriting Nature of Context Shift

A second set of differences from alternative analyses lies in the overwriting nature of context shift. In the scope of an operator that overwrites context with respect to coordinate r, information about the utterance value for coordinate r is unavailable. There is a technical sense in which this makes indexical shift similar to binding: in the scope of an abstractor over binding index n, information about the utterance assignment for binding index n is unavailable. Thus the utterance assignment g may be such that $g(2)$ = Lindy, but in the scope of an abstraction over index 2, this utterance-determined value will be unavailable:[35]

(69) $[\![\text{the person who 2 } t_2 \text{ greeted her}_2 \text{ friend}]\!]^{c,i,g}$ = the unique person x such that x greeted x's friend
$\neq$ the unique person x such that x greeted Lindy's friend

Much the same logic underlies the approach to Shift Together effects. In the scope of a shifty operator OP$_{PERS}$ (for instance), information about the utterance-determined values for author and addressee are unavailable. Thus, when the operator is present in (70), all first-person indexicals shift, yielding reading (70a). To avoid this effect on one indexical, the shifty operator must be taken out of the structure. This yields reading (70b), where no first person indexicals shift. No other readings can be derived.

(70) Ne-'níc-em pee-Ø-n-e 'in-haama-na,
1SG-older.sister-ERG 3/3-say-P-REM.PAST 1SG-husband-ACC
['iin-im ciq'aamqal hi-twehkey'k-Ø-e 'iin-e].
[1SG-GEN dog(ERG) 3SUBJ-chase-P-REM.PAST 1SG-ACC]
 a. My sister$_s$ told my husband$_h$ that her$_s$ dog chased her$_s$.
 b. ? My sister$_s$ told my husband$_h$ that my dog chased me.
 c. ✗ My sister$_s$ told my husband$_h$ that my dog chased her$_s$.
 d. ✗ My sister$_s$ told my husband$_h$ that her$_s$ dog chased me.

Of course, in the case of binding, there is always the option of switching the binder and bound element to a different indexation, allowing for other indexed material to receive its interpretation in keeping with values determined by the utterance assignment:

(71) Where $g(2)$ = Lindy:
⟦*the person who 3 t$_3$ greeted her$_2$ friend*⟧^{c,i,g} = the unique person x such that x greeted Lindy's friend

But there is no similar option for indexical elements. Unlike a variable assignment, which may map an unlimited number of binding indices to an unlimited number of different individuals, contexts of interpretation store a limited amount of information—only one author value and one addressee value at a time. All first-person indexicals depend on the very same feature of interpretation—the author coordinate of context—and the shifty operator overwrites this coordinate for the interpretation of its entire complement. An embedded first-person indexical can pick up reference from a shifted context c' only if an author-shifting operator is present at the edge of a clause containing it. The presence of this operator in turn forces all other first-person indexicals within the local complement clause to have shifty readings.

 Overall, what a theory of context overwriting leads us to expect for Shift Together effects is, at minimum, the following (where classes of indexicals are first person, second person, locative, and temporal):[36]

(72) *Shift Together*
If one indexical of class Ψ picks up reference from context c, then all indexicals of class Ψ within the same minimal attitude complement must also pick up reference from context c.

While the name of this constraint follows Anand and Nevins (2004) and Anand (2006), the formulation departs from their precise formulations; for example, "all shiftable indexicals within an attitude-context domain must pick up reference from the same context" (Anand 2006, 100). (It also differs in the same way from a similar generalization formulated by Oshima 2006, 192.) The version of the generalization given in (72) records only that clausemate indexicals *that depend on the same coordinate of context* must shift together: that one first person indexical, for instance, should be required to shift together with a clausemate first person indexical, as in (70), follows from the overwriting nature of context shift. I take the reformulation to be a friendly amendment, as the shifty operator theory developed by Anand and Nevins (2004) and Anand (2006) predicts only the narrower version used here.[37] This is because it contains indexical shifters other than $OP_Ψ$, for instance, the OP_{PERS} shifter introduced in (58). I elaborate further on the formulation and consequences of the Shift Together constraint in appendix A.

Beyond this, two types of remarks about Shift Together effects are in order. First, note that the precise predictions in terms of which types of indexicals should shift together in part depends on the degree to which attitude complements may contain shifters that affect only some contextual coordinates but not others. The fact that first- and second-person indexicals must shift together in Nez Perce, as we see in (73), indicates that the language does not allow attitude complements to contain shifters affecting only the author coordinate of context or only the addressee coordinate:

(73) Ne-'níc-em pee-Ø-n-e 'in-haama-na,
1SG-older.sister-ERG 3/3-say-P-REM.PAST 1SG-husband-ACC
['im-im ciq'aamqal hi-twehkey'k-Ø-e 'iin-e].
[2SG-GEN dog(ERG) 3SUBJ-chase-P-REM.PAST 1SG-ACC]
  a.   My sister$_s$ told my husband$_h$ that his$_h$ dog chased her$_s$.
  b.   ? My sister$_s$ told my husband$_h$ that your dog chased me.
  c.   ✗ My sister$_s$ told my husband$_h$ that your dog chased her$_s$.
  d.   ✗ My sister$_s$ told my husband$_h$ that his$_h$ dog chased me.

That is, it must not be possible for a Nez Perce attitude complement to contain only an operator like OP_{AUTH}, as in (74a), or only an operator like OP_{ADDR}, as in (74b):

(74) a. $[\![\text{OP}_{\text{AUTH}}]\!]^{c,i,g} = \lambda p \in D_{<\kappa,\kappa t>} . p(i)(c^{author(i)/author}) = 1$
   b. $[\![\text{OP}_{\text{ADDR}}]\!]^{c,i,g} = \lambda p \in D_{<\kappa,\kappa t>} . p(i)(c^{addr(i)/addr}) = 1$

Such a restriction could be enforced in several ways, for instance, by banning such elements from the lexicon in favor of a single OP$_{\text{PERS}}$ shifter, or by a syntactic restriction forcing one element in (74) to be present in a CP whenever the other is. (We return to these choices in chapter 4.)

Second, note that when a second layer of clausal embedding is added, a new attachment site for shifty operators is introduced. This means that the predictions for indexicals that are not members of the same minimal attitude complement are somewhat more complex. Cases where two embedded indexicals of the same type are predicted to possibly fail to shift together can be visualized as in (75) and (76) (inspired by the diagrams used by Anand 2006). In (75), indexical ind$_1$, in CP$_1$, depends for its reference on the utterance context, as represented visually by a connecting line to the matrix clause.[38] Meanwhile, ind$_2$, which is also contained within CP$_1$, depends for its reference on the shifted contexts c_B introduced by an operator at the edge of CP$_2$. Suppose ind$_1$ and ind$_2$ are both first-person indexicals and that the shifty operator is OP$_{\text{PERS}}$. Then ind$_1$ will refer to the utterance author, *author(c_{utt})*, but ind$_2$ will refer to the author value introduced by attitude verb$_1$, *author(c_B)*.[39]

(75) ✓c_{utt} [subj verb$_0$ [$_{CP_1}$ ind$_1$ verb$_1$ [$_{CP_2}$ OP-c_B ind$_2$ ...]]]

In (76), indexical ind$_1$ depends for its reference on the shifted contexts c_A introduced by an operator at the edge of CP$_1$. Meanwhile, ind$_2$ continues to depend on shifted contexts c_B. In this case, if ind$_1$ and ind$_2$ are both first-person indexicals and the shifty operators are OP$_{\text{PERS}}$, ind$_2$ will again refer to the author value introduced by attitude verb$_1$, *author(c_B)*, but ind$_1$ will refer to the author value introduced by attitude verb$_0$, *author(c_A)*.

(76) ✓c_{utt} [subj verb$_0$ [$_{CP_1}$ OP-c_A ind$_1$ verb$_1$ [$_{CP_2}$ OP-c_B ind$_2$ ...]]]

What these considerations show is that the overall expected generalization about co-shifting effects is what we might call Local Determination:[40]

(77) *Local Determination*
An indexical *ind* of class Ψ has its reference determined by the closest shifty operator with scope over *ind* that manipulates contextual coordinate Ψ. If no operator has scope over *ind*, then *ind* has its reference determined by the utterance context.

Notice that Local Determination subsumes Shift Together as defined in (72), because shifty operators take scope over entire clauses. If a minimal attitude complement contains, on its edge, a shifty operator manipulating coordinate Ψ, then all indexicals of class Ψ within that complement will depend on the modified contexts introduced by the operator.

Local Determination is broader than Shift Together, as defined in (72), in its predictions for multiembedding structures. A pattern ruled out only by Local Determination may be visualized as shown in (78). Here indexical ind_2, in CP_2, depends for its reference on the utterance context value for Ψ, similar to ind_1 in (75). The difference is that ind_2 is in the scope of an operator that manipulates contextual coordinate Ψ. This pattern—in which ind_1 and ind_2 might both be first person, but ind_2 would refer to the utterance author, whereas ind_1 referred to the author value introduced by attitude $verb_0$ —is ruled out by the overwriting nature of context shift. Once the operator has introduced a shifty Ψ coordinate, the matrix value for that coordinate is not recoverable within its scope.

(78) ✗c_{utt} [subj $verb_0$ [$_{CP_1}$ OP-Ψ-c_A ind_1-Ψ $verb_1$ [$_{CP_2}$ ind_2-Ψ ...]]]

Likewise, in (79), ind_1 depends for its reference on the utterance context, exactly as it did in (75). The difference is that ind_1, a Ψ-class indexical, is now in the scope of a Ψ-shifting operator, which makes its presence felt by determining the Ψ-coordinate for the reference of ind_2. This pattern—in which ind_1 and ind_2 might both be first person, but ind_1 would refer to the utterance author, whereas ind_2 referred to the author value introduced by attitude $verb_0$—is also ruled out.

(79) ✗c_{utt} [subj $verb_0$ [$_{CP_1}$ OP-Ψ-c_A ind_1-Ψ $verb_1$ [$_{CP_2}$ ind_2-Ψ ...]]]

These predictions of Local Determination are borne out in Nez Perce. We begin with the cases correctly expected to be well-formed with two (non-minimally clausemate) indexicals of the same class failing to shift together. On the reading indicated by its translation, sentence (80a) exemplifies pattern (75), repeated in (80b): first-person indexicals in the medial clause are unshifted, whereas those in the most embedded clause are shifted by an operator at the edge of that clause.

(80) a. Katie   hi-neki-se-Ø   [$_{CP_1}$ 'in-lawtiwaa-nm
   Katie.NOM 3SUBJ-think-IMPERF-PRES [1SG-friend-ERG
   watiisx   hi-i-caa-qa   pro,   [$_{CP_2}$ kii meeywi
   1.day.away 3SUBJ-say-IMPERF-REC.PAST 1SG.ACC [this morning
   pro cikliitoq-tat'aa-sa-Ø   ]].
   1SG go.back-gonna-IMPERF-PRES]]
   Katie thinks that my friend$_f$ told me yesterday that he$_f$ is going to go home this morning.

   b. ✓c$_{utt}$ [subj verb$_0$ [$_{CP_1}$ ind$_1$ verb$_1$ [$_{CP_2}$ OP-c$_B$ ind$_2$ ...]]]

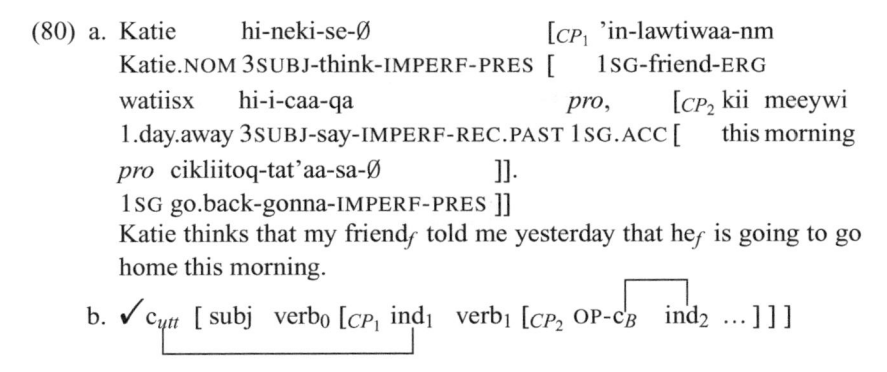

Likewise, on the reading indicated by its translation, (81a) exemplifies pattern (76): first-person indexicals in each clause are shifted by an operator local to the periphery of that clause.

(81) a. Caan   hi-neki-se-Ø   [$_{CP_1}$ watiisx   Sue-nim
   John.NOM 3SUBJ-think-IMPERF-PRES [1.day.away   Sue-ERG
   hi-i-caa-qa   pro,   [$_{CP_2}$ pro   taaqc   kine
   3SUBJ-say-IMPERF-REC.PAST 1SG.ACC [1SG same.day   here
   wek-u'   ]].
   be-PROSP]]
   John$_j$ thinks Sue$_s$ told him$_j$ yesterday that she$_s$ would be here today.

   b. ✓c$_{utt}$ [subj verb$_0$ [$_{CP_1}$ OP-c$_A$ ind$_1$ verb$_1$ [$_{CP_2}$ OP-c$_B$ ind$_2$ ...]]]

These cases contrast, as expected, with the patterns sketched in (78) and (79). Consider first (82), a baseline case, where there is no indexical shift (and indeed no indexicals) in the medial clause, and the first-person indexical in the innermost clause may have an unshifted reading. The test case is (83), where the medial clause contains a first-person indexical. If this indexical receives a shifty reading, then the indexical in the innermost clause must receive a shifty reading as well.

(82) Katie   hi-hi-ce-Ø   [$_{CP_1}$ pro
   Katie.NOM 3SUBJ-say-IMPERF-PRES [3SG.NOM
   hi-neki-se-Ø   [$_{CP_2}$ 'iin-k'u   wees   kine]].
   3SUBJ-think-IMPERF-PRES [1SG.NOM-too be.PRES here]]
   Possible reading: Katie$_i$ says she$_i$ thinks that I am also here.

(83) Katie   hi-hi-ce-Ø   [$_{CP_1}$ (OP) *pro*
    Katie.NOM 3SUBJ-say-IMPERF-PRES [1SG.NOM
    neki-se-Ø   [$_{CP_2}$ 'iin-k'u   wees   kine]].
    think-IMPERF-PRES [1SG.NOM-too be.PRES here]]
   a.   Katie$_i$ says she$_i$ thinks she$_i$ is also here.   (OP present)
   b.   Katie says I think I am also here.   (OP absent)
   c.   ✗ Katie$_i$ says she$_i$ thinks I am also here.
   d.   ✗ Katie$_i$ says I think she$_i$ is also here.

On the (a) reading, there is a person-shifting operator in CP_1, taking both indexicals in its scope. This operator is thus, for both indexicals, the closest shifty operator that manipulates the author coordinate, and so this operator determines the reference of both indexicals. On the (b) reading, the default clause of Local Determination is obeyed: there are no shifty operators in the structure. The missing readings in (c) and (d) are those that run afoul of Local Determination. Missing reading (c) exemplifies the scenario visualized in (78), repeated in (84); missing reading (d) exemplifies (79), repeated in (85).

(84) ✗c_{utt} [subj   verb$_0$ [$_{CP_1}$ OP-Ψ-c_A ind$_1$-Ψ   verb$_1$ [$_{CP_2}$ ind$_2$-Ψ ...]]]

(85) ✗c_{utt} [subj   verb$_0$ [$_{CP_1}$ OP-Ψ-c_A ind$_1$-Ψ   verb$_1$ [$_{CP_2}$ ind$_2$-Ψ ...]]]

In thinking about the full range of possibilities predicted for multiclausal structures, it should be noticed that (83) presents a simplifying factor: no additional referential possibility for the first person is generated if a second OP is included in the structure, on the edge of the innermost clause. This is because the medial verb has a first-person subject. Whenever a shifty operator is present on the edge of the medial clause (just below *Katie hihice* 'Katie says'), it will overwrite the author coordinate of context with *de se* counterparts of Katie. This produces reading (a). If a shifty operator were also present on the edge of the most embedded clause, the effect of this operator would be to overwrite the author coordinate of context for the most embedded clause with *de se* counterparts of *de se* counterparts of Katie. This certainly has no major effect on the perceived interpretation of indexical shift—for instance, it does not "undo" the higher shifter—and may have no effect at all, depending on how counterpart relations are understood.[41]

Further evidence of contextual overwriting in multiclausal cases comes from variants on base case (86), where (on the reading indicated by the translation) an operator is present on the edge of the most embedded clause, CP_2.[42]

The second-person indexical *'ee* in this clause depends on the shifted context determined by this operator.

(86) Caan   hi-neki-se-Ø   [$_{CP_1}$ Meeli-nm
     John.NOM   3SUBJ-think-IMPERF-PRES [Mary-ERG
     pee-Ø-n-e   Sue-ne   [$_{CP_2}$ OP 'ee   wees
     3/3-say-P-REM.PAST Sue-ACC [2SG.CL be.PRES
     qetu kuhet 'ip-nim-kin'ix]].
     more tall   3SG-OBL-from]]
     John$_j$ thinks that Mary told Sue$_s$ that she$_s$ is taller than him$_j$.

As we saw in the discussion of (73), a Nez Perce clause that contains shifty operators cannot shift only the addressee coordinate. Let us thus assume that the OP in (86) is OP$_{PERS}$.[43] As predicted by the shifty operator theory, it is not possible for a first-person indexical in the scope of this operator to draw its reference from an additional operator, OP′, on the edge of CP$_1$. Thus, the (a) reading of (87) is not possible: the author coordinate determined by OP′ in CP$_1$ is re-overwritten with the coordinate determined by OP in CP$_2$. Since OP is the closest operator that manipulates the author coordinate, this operator and no other can determine the reference of the first-person indexical in the most embedded clause.

(87) Caan   hi-neki-se-Ø   [$_{CP_1}$ (OP′) Meeli-nm
     John.NOM   3SUBJ-think-IMPERF-PRES [Mary-ERG
     pee-Ø-n-e   Sue-ne   [$_{CP_2}$ OP 'ee   wees
     3/3-say-P-REM.PAST Sue-ACC [2SG.CL be.PRES
     qetu kuhet 'iin-im-kin'ix]].
     more tall   1SG-OBL-from]]
     a. ✗ John$_j$ thinks that Mary told Sue$_s$ that she$_s$ is taller than him$_j$.
     b. ✓ John$_j$ thinks that Mary$_m$ told Sue$_s$ that she$_s$ is taller than her$_m$.

(88) ✗ c$_{utt}$ [subj verb$_0$ [$_{CP_1}$ OP-c$_A$ subj verb$_1$ [$_{CP_2}$ OP-c$_B$ ind$_1$ ind$_2$ ...]]]

(89) ✓ c$_{utt}$ [subj verb$_0$ [$_{CP_1}$ OP-c$_A$ subj verb$_1$ [$_{CP_2}$ OP-c$_B$ ind$_1$ ind$_2$ ...]]]

In terms of the generalizations with which this chapter began, these considerations highlight two distinctive predictions of the shifty operator approach—predictions that match the Nez Perce facts. One is that the behavior of shifty indexicals is distinguished from the behavior of bindable, anaphoric elements. This latter class obeys no Shift Together–like generalization on cobinding, as we saw in sentences such as (38). This is to be expected: two clausemate bindable elements may bear different binding indices, with the result that binding of one element has no effect on the reference of the other (as in (71)). Indexical elements are different in that they draw on a context, rather than a variable assignment—a much less data-rich formal object. Changes to the context produce the behaviors of co-shifting we have seen. The second generalization is that indexical shift operates on a whole-clause basis. This follows from the semantics of shifty operators (context coordinate overwriting) together with their syntax (attachment at the edge of a clause). The clause-level behavior of indexical shift is correctly expected to hold modulo those cases of multiple embedding where one indexical is more deeply embedded than another, and thus only the more deeply embedded indexical falls in the scope of a shifty operator.

2.2.4 Conclusion to the Case Study

This case study builds a foundation for the chapters to come, which augment and refine the basic architecture of the shifty operator view along several dimensions, both syntactic and semantic. One of its functions is thus to serve as a reminder of the empirical ground that will need to remain covered in any potential revision. As we have seen, central to the empirical picture is a set of four generalizations that tell in favor of the shifty operator theory of indexical shift:

1. Indexical shift is specific to speech and attitude reports.
2. It operates on a whole-clause basis (modulo differences in the level of embedding of clausemate indexicals).
3. It allows for the behavior of shifty indexicals to be distinguished from the behavior of bindable, anaphoric elements.
4. It is sensitive to the structure of the embedded clause.

The explanations now in hand for these patterns are as follows. Generalizations 1 and 4 directly reflect the syntax of shifty operators, in particular the fact that they attach very high inside certain types of CP. Generalization 2 reflects a combination of the syntax of the operators and their semantics—contextual overwriting. Generalization 3 reflects contextual overwriting and the relatively limited information store presented by contexts as opposed to variable assignments. As we move forward, the reader can confirm that these central aspects of the shifty operator view will remain in place and thus that the revisions to the theory that will be made in order to accommodate a predictive crosslinguistic typology (as well as further patterns of Nez Perce to be introduced in chapter 3) still allow us to get the basic details of Nez Perce right.

2.3 Epilogue: Operators beyond Nez Perce

The next chapter turns to the question of how patterns of indexical shift vary across languages. A preliminary question that might be asked in this respect is whether this chapter's four generalizations, characteristic of indexical shift in Nez Perce, are themselves subject to variation. I maintain that they are not, and therefore I conclude this chapter with a brief indication of the evidence for these generalizations crosslinguistically.

Indexical shift is specific to speech and attitude reports. This appears straightforwardly to be universal, in at least one clear sense: I am not aware of any language where indexical shift has been reported to be possible in clauses like (90a), yielding a reading like the bound reading available for (90b).[44]

(90) a. # Whenever Obama is speaking, I am a former president.
  b. Whenever Obama is speaking, the speaker is a former president.

Whether speech and attitude reports must always involve syntactic embedding under a lexical attitude verb (overt or covert) remains a topic of active discussion (see, e.g., Sharvit 2008, Spadine 2019, Thivierge 2019).

Indexical shift operates on a whole-clause basis (modulo differences in the level of embedding of clausemate indexicals). This co-shifting generalization reflects Local Determination, and its effects can be seen in data like Slave (Athabaskan) (91): either both embedded first persons shift or neither does.

(91) *Slave*
  [(OP) Sehlégé   segha   goníhkie rárulu   ] yudeli.
  [1SG.friend 1SG.for slippers 3SG.will.sew] 3SG.want.4SG
  a. She$_i$ wants her$_i$ friend to sew slippers for her$_i$.   (OP present)
  b. She$_i$ wants my friend to sew slippers for me.   (OP absent)
  c. ✗ She$_i$ wants my friend to sew slippers for her$_i$.
  d. ✗ She$_i$ wants her$_i$ friend to sew slippers for me.
  (Rice 1986, 56; Anand 2006, 99)

Obedience to a Shift Together constraint (a special case of Local Determination) is widely reported, e.g., for Farsi (Anvari 2019), Georgian (Thivierge 2019), Korean (Park 2016, section 2.3.1), Laz (Kartvelian; Demirok and Öztürk 2015, section 5), Tsez (Nakh-Dagestanian; Polinsky 2015, section 4.3), Uyghur (Turkic; Sudo 2012, 222), and Zazaki (Indo-Iranian; Anand 2006, section 2.5.1).[45] Evidence for Local Determination obedience in multiclausal structures has been reported for Zazaki (Anand and Nevins 2004; Anand 2006, section 2.5.2) and Korean (Park 2016, section 3.3).[46]

For the operator-based view, the special interest of multiple embedding structures lies in the fact that these structures facilitate the embedding of one indexical under a greater number of shifty operators than another. The indexical more likely to be shifty is the one that is lower in the structure—inside more CPs. If it were possible in a single-embedding structure for an indexical to move to the outermost edge of the embedded clause, beyond the attachment site of a shifty operator, the view predicts that the moved indexical will be unshifted while any indexicals remaining in the scope of the operator will be shifted. Thus indexical shift is predicted to operate on a whole-clause basis only insofar as an entire clause falls within the scope of a shifty operator (at LF). In Nez Perce, Korean, Laz, Tsez, and Zazaki, this detail seems to be safely overlooked: indexicals cannot be interpreted outside the scope of a shifty operator on the edge of their clause.

In Uyghur, however, indexicals may occupy multiple positions inside the attitude complement, such that they shift in the lower position but not the higher one.[47] Uyghur allows embedded subjects to be realized either in the nominative or the accusative case. Shklovsky and Sudo demonstrate that both types of subjects are base-generated inside the attitude complement and may be interpreted there. However, accusative subjects move into a higher position inside the attitude complement than nominative subjects do. Accusative (high) subject indexicals disallow shift, (92a), whereas nominative (low) subject indexicals require it, (92b).

(92) *Uyghur*
    a. Ahmet [**meni**   ket-ti   ] di-di.
       Ahmet [1SG.ACC leave-PAST.3] say-PAST.3
       Ahmet$_i$ said that I/✘he$_i$ left.
    b. Ahmet [**men**   ket-tim   ] di-di.
       Ahmet [1SG.NOM leave-PAST.1SG] say-PAST.3
       Ahmet$_i$ said that he$_i$/✘I left.
(Shklovsky and Sudo 2014, 386)

Likewise, any indexical to the left of (i.e., higher than) an accusative subject cannot shift, but any indexical to the right of (i.e., lower than) a nominative subject must shift. This is shown for second-person dative object *sanga* in (93).

(93) a. Ahmet Aygül-ge   [*sanga*   **meni**   xet   ewet-ti   ]
       Ahmet Aygül-DAT [2SG.DAT 1SG.ACC letter send-PAST.3]
       di-di.
       say-PAST.3
       Ahmet told Aygül$_i$ that I sent a letter to you/✘her$_i$.

b. Ahmet manga [**men** *sanga* xet ewet-tim]
Ahmet 1SG.DAT [1SG.NOM 2SG.DAT letter send-PAST.1SG]
di-di.
say-PAST.3
Ahmet$_i$ told me that he$_i$ sent a letter to me/✗you.
(Shklovsky and Sudo 2014, 395–396)

(Potentially similar facts obtain in Manambu [Ndu; Aikhenvald 2008].) As Sudo (2012) and Shklovsky and Sudo (2014) discuss, the pattern here follows from the syntactic location of the operators along with their scope-taking behavior. Operators sit at the edge of finite CPs. An indexical in the scope of a shifty operator must shift (provided the operator targets the relevant coordinate of context), but one that has moved outside the scope of any operator cannot. The possibility of scrambling past a clausemate operator makes it possible to observe deviations from the whole-clause pattern of indexical shift in cases like (94):

(94) Context: Ahmet told me "I like Aygül." I am telling Aygül what he said.
Ahmet [seni   OP *pro*   jaxshi kör-ymen   ] di-di.
Ahmet [2SG.ACC   1SG.NOM well   see-IMPERF.1SG] say-PAST
Ahmet said that he likes you.
(Sudo 2012, 221)

The interest of this case is that we have differences in the level of embedding, vis-à-vis operators, of two indexicals that nevertheless are contained in all of the same clauses. This is as predicted on the shifty operator approach for a language where indexicals may move to, and be interpreted in, a position higher than shifty operators.

Indexical shift allows for the behavior of shifty indexicals to be distinguished from the behavior of bindable, anaphoric elements. What is distinctive about context shift as opposed to binding is the way that it features overwriting of a limited store of information. An interesting case of a clearly overwriting-based logic, as opposed to the more expansive type of information storage permitted by binding, is found in syntactic contexts where indexical shift is obligatory. This is part of the pattern just discussed in Uyghur: except in cases where the indexical scrambles to the very edge of the embedded clause, it must shift. If we remove the complication of scrambling, this is also the pattern that Schauber (1979) reports for Navajo (Athabaskan), Munro et al. (2012) reports for Matses (Panoan), and Davies (1981) reports for Kobon (Madang). Navajo sentence (95) features only one first-person indexical, embedded under two indexical shifting verbs. This indexical may only refer to the most local attitude holder (Mary), not the matrix attitude holder (John) or the overall utterer.

(95) *Navajo*
Jáan [$_{CP_1}$ OP Mary [$_{CP_2}$ OP *pro* chidí nahideeshnih] nízin] ní.
John [Mary [1SG car 3.1.F.buy] 3.want] 3.say
John says Mary wants for Mary/✗John/✗me to buy a car.
(Schauber 1979, 22)

This fact is explained if shifty operators are obligatory in the complements of the attitude verbs *nízin* and *ní*, in keeping with Schauber's (1979, 25) claim that indexical shift is obligatory in these complements. The operator in CP_1 overwrites the author coordinate of context with counterparts of the matrix attitude holder (John); the operator in CP_2 subsequently re-overwrites this same coordinate with counterparts of the embedded attitude holder (Mary). In the scope of the operator in CP_2, the only value available for the shifted indexical is the "local" one—Mary. This exemplifies the overwriting nature of context shift: previous values, once overwritten, are no longer available.

Indexical shift is sensitive to the structure of the embedded clause. Evidence on this final factor is also available for a range of languages. A clear demonstration from Uyghur is provided in (96). The Uyghur verb *de* 'say' allows both finite and nonfinite (nominalized) complements. Indexical shift is possible only in complements that are finite.

(96) *Uyghur*
    a. Tursun Muhemmet-ke [*pro* xet jaz-ding] di-di.
        Tursun Muhemmet-DAT [2SG letter write-PAST.2SG] say-PAST.3
        Tursun told Muhemmet$_i$ that he$_i$ wrote a letter. (finite complement)
    b. Tursun Muhemmet-ke [*pro* xet jaz-ghan-lik-ing-ni]
        Tursun Muhemmet-DAT [2SG letter write-REL-NML-2SG-ACC]
        di-di.
        say-PAST.3
        Tursun told Muhemmet$_i$ that you/✗he$_i$ wrote a letter. (nonfinite complement)
(Shklovsky and Sudo 2014, 383)

Similar alternations are reported in Japanese (Sudo 2012, 238) and Tsez (Polinsky 2015, (29)). A related phenomenon holds in languages like Navajo. Individual Navajo verbs strictly require either finite or nonfinite (nominalized) complements; shifting is allowed only in those complements that are finite (Schauber 1979).[48] Korean, likewise, requires nominalized complements to the verb 'know', and indexical shift in this complement is ruled out (Yangsook Park, pers. comm.). Indeed I am not aware of any clear evidence that indexical shift is possible outside of simple CP embedding in any language.[49]

3 Shifty Asymmetries

A full theoretical or descriptive account of any particular instance of indexical shift requires attention to four components that vary across languages:

1. Which verbs are involved in shifting
2. Which indexicals shift (with which verbs)
3. How much optionality is permitted in indexical shift
4. Which indexicals must be read *de se* when shifted

These dimensions are listed in approximate descending order of the previous attention that has been paid to them. Dimension 1 is widely recognized as a point of crosslinguistic variation; dimensions 2 and 3 slightly less so; dimension 4 is not only scarcely recognized, but indeed contravenes the typical assumption that shifty indexicals simply belong under the heading of *de se* phenomena (Schlenker 1999, 2003, 2011, Anand 2006, Bittner 2014, Roberts 2015). In this chapter, I first assemble the evidence of variation along these four dimensions—evidence that reveals, in spite of significant variability, that substantial generalizations are nevertheless possible in these areas. Indeed, it will turn out that dimensions 2–4 are in fact regulated by the very same implicational hierarchy. In the second part of the chapter, I lay out an account of indexical shift that can account for these structured patterns of variation.

3.1 Dimensions of Variation

3.1.1 Which Verbs Are Involved in Shifting

Languages allowing indexical shift vary in which verbs allow indexicals to shift in their complements. A first split in this dimension falls between languages that allow shifting only with speech verbs, versus those that are more liberal. In the first class are languages like Zazaki (Anand 2006), Farsi (Anvari 2019), Kurmanji (Indo-Iranian; Koev 2013), and Dhaasanac (Afro-Asiatic;

Nishiguchi 2017), and perhaps also Somali (Afro-Asiatic; Nishiguchi 2017). The following Zazaki pair shows that the shiftiness of ɛz 'I' under va 'say' cannot be reproduced under tεɾmine 'think/believe':

(97) *Zazaki*
    a. Hɛseni va   [kɛ   ɛz dɛwletia   ].
        Hesen said [that I   be.rich.PRES]
        Hesen$_i$ said that I am/he$_i$ is rich.
    b. Hɛsen tεɾmine kɛno [kɛ   ɛz newɛsha   ].
        Hesen believe does [that I   be.sick.PRES]
        Hesen$_i$ believes that I am/✘he$_i$ is sick.
    (Anand and Nevins 2004)

Likewise, for Dhaasanac, Nishiguchi (2017) reports that shift is possible only in the complements of verbs meaning 'say', 'tell', and 'give news/report'.

In the second class are languages of two further types. In one, shift is limited to the complements of speech verbs and verbs of cognition, to the exclusion of verbs of knowledge. In Navajo, for instance, shift is possible in the complements of *ní* 'say', (98a), and *nízin* 'want/think',[1] (98b) (as well as *yó'ní* 'expect'), but not *shił bééhózin* 'know'.[2]

(98) *Navajo*
    a. Jáan [*pro* chidi nahałnii'] ní.
        John [1SG car   3.1.P.buy] 3.say
        John$_i$ says he$_i$ bought a car.
    b. Bíl [*pro* béégashii deeshłoh] nízin.
        Bill [1SG cow   3.1.F.rope] 3.think
        Bill$_i$ thinks he$_i$ will rope a cow.
    (Schauber 1979, 19)

Further examples of this class are Slave, where Rice (1986, 1989) demonstrates that shifting is possible under 'say', 'tell', 'ask', and two verbs glossed 'want/think', but not 'know'; Laz, where Demirok and Öztürk (2015) demonstrate that shifting is possible under 'say' and 'think', but not 'know'; Korean, where Park (2016) demonstrates shifting under 'say' and 'think', but where it is impossible under 'know' (Yangsook Park, pers. comm.; similar facts hold in Japanese, per Sudo 2012 and Yasu Sudo, pers. comm.); Matses, where Munro et al. (2012) demonstrate shifting under 'say', 'tell', and 'suppose mistakenly', but there is no dedicated verb 'know' (Fleck 2006, section 4); and plausibly also Uyghur, where Sudo (2012) demonstrates shifting under a large set of verbs, including those glossed as 'say', 'think', 'hear', 'brag', 'dream', and 'believe/know' (assuming, given the disjunctive gloss, that the last of these is not a dedicated verb of knowledge).³

In a final class of languages, indexical shift is possible in the complements of verbs of speech, thought, and also knowledge. As we saw in chapter 2, this is the case in Nez Perce, where shift occurs in the complements of *hi* 'say/tell', *neki* 'think', and *cuukwe* 'know':

(99) *Nez Perce*
 A.   { hi-hi-n-e   / hi-neki-se-Ø   /
 A.NOM { 3SUBJ-say-P-REM.PAST / 3SUBJ-think-IMPERF-PRES /
 hi-cuukwe-ce-Ø   } [*pro* taxc paay-no'   ].
 3SUBJ-know-IMPERF-PRES } [1SG soon arrive-PROSP]

 A$_i$ said/thinks/knows she$_i$ will soon arrive.

The Nez Perce verb *cuukwe* behaves like familiar knowledge verbs, e.g., English 'know', in several ways. First, it is factive; that is, it gives rise to an inference of veridicality for its complement even when embedded under entailment-canceling operators.⁴ Second, it is able to embed material that at least semantically corresponds to a question, with the meaning that the subject knows the true answer(s) to that question.⁵

These three language types should be contrasted with various logically possible options that are not attested. No language allows shift under verbs of thought and/or verbs of knowledge without also allowing it under verbs of speech. No language allows shift under verbs of knowledge without also allowing it under verbs of thought and speech. This is to say that the various possibilities form an implicational hierarchy. This hierarchy constitutes the first of three generalizations to be advanced in this chapter.

(G1) Implicational hierarchy of verbs

 Verbs of speech are more likely to allow indexical shift in their complement than are verbs of thought, which in turn are more likely to allow indexical shift in their complement than are verbs of knowledge.

	Shift takes place under verbs of:		
	Speech	Thought	Knowledge
Nez Perce	✓	✓	✓
Navajo, Slave, Uyghur	✓	✓	–
Dhaasanac, Zazaki	✓	–	–

Portions of this pattern, particularly the status of speech verbs with respect to other verbs, have been previously discussed by Anand (2006), Oshima (2006), and Sundaresan (2011, 2012, 2018).

3.1.2 Which Indexicals Shift (with Which Verbs)

Languages allowing indexical shift vary in which classes of indexicals shift. In this area the empirical basis for generalization is slightly narrower than for the previous dimension, as many studies of particular languages have not reported full data beyond person indexicals.[6] Given the state of the empirical literature, I will focus in this chapter on first-person, second-person, and locative indexicals, as data on these indexical types are available for relatively many of the languages for which indexical shifting has been most extensively described. Temporal indexicals will come back into the picture in chapter 4, in connection with an additional well-described indexical shifting language (Korean).

The shifting possibilities for locative and person indexicals conform to three basic patterns. First, some languages allow shifting of first-person, second-person, and locative indexicals such as 'here'. The following examples demonstrate these three indexical classes one by one for Zazaki.

(100) *Zazaki*
 Heseni va [kɛ ɛz newɛsha].
 Hesen.OBL said [that I be.sick.PRES]
 Hesen$_i$ said that he$_i$ was sick.
 (Anand 2006, 77)

(101) Heseni va Ali-ra [kɛ **ti** newɛsha].
 Hesen.OBL said Ali-to [that you be.sick.PRES]
 Hesen said to Ali$_i$ that he$_i$ was sick.
 (Anand 2006, 77)

(102) Waxto kɛ o London-de bime Pierri va [kɛ o **ita**
 when that he London-at be.PAST Pierre.OBL said [that it here
 rindɛka].
 be.pretty.PRES]
 When he was in London$_i$, Pierre said that it is pretty there$_i$.
 (Anand 2006, 80)

While Zazaki allows shift only in the complement of *va* 'say', the same range of shifting possibilities also obtains in languages allowing shift in further types of verb complements—for instance, Nez Perce, as we saw in chapter 2, as well as Matses (Munro et al. 2012).

The second possibility is more restricted: first- and second-person indexicals may shift, but locatives may not. This is the situation for verbs of communication in Uyghur (Sudo 2012). The following example shows that the same clause that allows shifting of *men* 'I' disallows shifting of *bu jer* 'here'.

(103) *Uyghur*
Context: This summer, I went to UCLA and met Muhemmet there. He told me, "I'm going to study here from this September." Now I'm back in Cambridge, MA, talking to Ahmet.
a. Men   UCLA-gha bar-dim.
   1SG.NOM UCLA-to   go-PAST.1SG
   I went to UCLA.
b. Muhemmet manga   [toqquzinji ay-din   bašla-p **(men)**
   Muhemmet 1SG.DAT [9th   month-from start-ing 1SG.NOM
   {u jer-de   / #**bu jer**-de} uqu-imen   ] di-di.
   {there-LOC / #here-LOC} study-IMPF.1SG] say-PAST.3
   Muhemmet told me that he would study there/#here from September.
(Sudo 2012, 244)

The same goes in Dhaasanac (Nishiguchi 2017), Laz (Demirok and Öztürk 2015), Tsez (Polinsky 2015), and potentially Navajo (Speas 2000)[7] (in each case without reported differences among embedding verbs that license shift). Languages such as Zazaki and Nez Perce, by contrast, show no similar prohibition on locative shifting either in general or in the company of a person indexical.[8]

The final possibility is even more restrictive. In complements in which only person indexicals shift, we find two patterns out of a logically possible three. One of these is exemplified by Uyghur complements in which both first and second persons are shiftable (Sudo 2012). We have seen first person shift in Uyghur (103); second person shift is exemplified in (104).

(104) Ahmet Aygül-ge [*pro* kim-ni   jaxshi kör-isen   ] di-di?
      Ahmet Aygül-DAT [2SG who-ACC well   see-IMPF.2SG] say-PAST.3
      Who did Ahmet tell Aygül$_i$ that she$_i$ likes?
      (Sudo 2012, 230)

In Slave, this same pattern is found in complements to *édedi* 'tell/ask': both first and second persons shift.

(105) *Slave*
   [Segha   ráwǫdí   ] sédįdi   yįlé.
   [1SG.for 2SG.will.buy] 2SG.tell.1SG PAST
   You told me to buy it for you.
   (Rice 1986, 51)

This behavior contrasts with a second class of complements in Slave, in which only first persons shift (Rice 1986). This pattern is found in complements to *hadi* 'say' and *yenįwę / hudeli* 'want/think'. I exemplify here for *hadi* 'say'; note that the second-person argument in the complement clause remains unshifted.

(106) Simon [rásereyineht'u] hadi.
    Simon [2SG.hit.1SG] 3SG.say
    Simon said that you hit him.
    (Rice 1986, 53)

Various other logical possibilities are not attested. There is no clear case of a language (or verb complement type within a language) in which locative indexicals shift but person indexicals do not.[9] There is no clear case of a language (or verb complement type within a language) in which second persons shift but first persons do not.[10] This suggests an implicational relationship between the shifting of locative indexicals and the shifting of indexical persons, and likewise between the shifting of second person and the shifting of first person. Locative shift occurs only if person is also shifted. Addressee shift occurs only if author is also shifted. These data support the following implicational generalization about shift by indexical class (to be expanded slightly later in this chapter and in chapter 4):

(G2) Implicational hierarchy of indexical classes   (preliminary version)
    The possibility of indexical shift is determined by the hierarchy 1st > 2nd > Loc. Indexicals of a certain class may shift only if indexicals of classes farther to the left shift as well.

	Shifty 1st	Shifty 2nd	Shifty Loc
Zazaki	✓	✓	✓
Uyghur, Slave 'tell'	✓	✓	–
Slave 'say'	✓	–	–
English	–	–	–

This hierarchy partially follows one formulated by Anand (2006, 110), as well as typological remarks by Oshima (2006, chapter 8). I return to Anand's particular implementation in section 4.3.

3.1.3 How Much Optionality Is Permitted in Indexical Shift

Languages allowing indexical shift vary in the extent to which indexical shift is optional.[11] This optionality extends along two closely related dimensions. First, languages differ in whether indexical shift is required when it is permitted by the verb. (This was previewed in connection with Navajo in section 2.3.) In Matses, for instance, Munro et al. (2012) document that indexical shift occurs in the complements of the verbs *que* 'say', *ca* 'tell', and *dan* 'suppose mistakenly'. In these complements, indexical shift is obligatory; nonshifted (and nonlocally shifted) interpretations for indexicals are unavailable.[12] Thus sentence (107) has only a (locally) shifted interpretation for indexicals *cun* 'my' and *nu* 'I'.[13]

(107) *Matses*
Cun papa [**cun** chido [debi [nid-**nu**] que-o-sh]
1GEN father [1GEN wife [Davy [go-INTENT:1] say-PAST-3]
que-o-sh] que-o-sh.
say-PAST-3] say-PAST-3
   a. ✓ My father$_f$ said that his$_f$ wife said that Davy$_d$ said that he$_d$ is going.
   b. ✗ My$_k$ father$_f$ said that my$_k$ wife$_w$ said that Davy$_d$ said that { I$_k$ am / (s)he$_{d/f/w/i}$ is } going.
   c. ✗ My$_k$ father$_f$ said that his$_f$ wife$_w$ said that Davy$_d$ said that { I$_k$ am / (s)he$_{f/w/i}$ is } going.
(Fleck 2003, 1173)

Similar facts have been noted for person indexicals in Laz (Demirok and Öztürk 2015), Navajo (Schauber 1979, Speas 2000), and Uyghur (Sudo 2012; see further discussion in chapter 2), and for indexicals of all classes in Kobon (Davies 1981). In Zazaki, by contrast, indexical shift is optional, and thus sentences like (108) have either of two distinct interpretations. Interpretation (a) involves indexical shift for ɛz 'I' and *to* 'you', whereas interpretation (b) does not. (In keeping with the approach taken for (59) in chapter 2, I will treat this optionality as reflective of a structural ambiguity.)

(108) *Zazaki*
Vɨzeri Rojda Bill-ra va [kɛ **ɛz to**-ra miradiša].
Yesterday Rojda Bill-to said [that I you-to angry.be-PRES]
   a. Yesterday Rojda$_i$ said to Bill$_j$ that she$_i$ is angry at him$_j$.
   b. Yesterday Rojda$_i$ said to Bill$_j$ that I am angry at you.
(Anand and Nevins 2004, (13))

Zazaki thus allows, internal to one language, the union of the indexical-shift possibilities presented by Matses and by standard English: either all indexicals shift (as in Matses) or none do (as in English). On a more fine-grained level, internal to Slave, the verbs *hadi* 'say', *yeṉıwę* 'want/think', and *hudeli* 'want/think' are distinguished by optionality in a parallel way: while these three verbs all shift only the first person, *hadi* 'say' does so obligatorily, whereas *yenịwę* 'want/think' and *hudeli* 'want/think' do so only optionally. Complements to *yenịwę* and *hudeli* thus show the union of the indexical-shift possibilities presented by complements to *hadi* and those presented by complements to verbs that disallow shift entirely (e.g., 'know', 'hear', 'teach', 'think/worry about', 'find out', Rice 1989, chapter 45).

One marked difference between Slave and Zazaki concerns the possibility of partial indexical shift, that is, shift of one type of indexical without shift of another. Crosslinguistic differences in this respect lead us to a second type of optionality-related variation. In this chapter we have seen initial cases of partial indexical shift in Uyghur, where person indexicals shift but locative indexicals do not (see (103)), and in Slave with *hadi* 'say', where first person shifts but second person does not (see (106)). The relationship between partial indexical shift and questions about optionality is particularly clear in languages where one kind of indexical shift determines the possibility of another kind of shift. This is the situation in Nez Perce, for instance, where (like in Zazaki) person and locative indexicals may optionally be shifted. The following examples, partially reprised from chapter 2, demonstrate optional shift of first person (109), second person (110), and 'here' (111).

(109) *Nez Perce*
Isii-ne$_2$ A.   hi-i-caa-qa
who-ACC A.NOM 3SUBJ-say-IMPERF-REC.PAST
[cewcewin'es-ki ***pro*** 'e-muu-ce-∅ t_2]?
[phone-with   1SG 3OBJ-call-IMPERF-PRES   ]
Who did A$_i$ say { she$_i$ / I } was calling?

(110) Manaa we'nikt   'u-us   haama-nm,   ke ko-nya$_1$ T.-nm
how   name.NOM 3GEN-be.PRES man-GEN   C RP-ACC T-ERG
pee-∅-n-e   R.-ne, [**'ee**   'o-opayata-yo'qa t_1] ?
3/3-say-P-REM.PAST R-ACC [2SG.CL 3OBJ-help-MODAL]
What is the name of the man that T told R$_i$ that { he$_i$ / you } should help?

(111) Talmaks-pa   *pro* hi-pe-hi-n-e   [*pro* weet'u **kíne**
Talmaks-LOC 3PL 3SUBJ-S.PL-say-P-REM.PAST [1PL   not   here
wisiinu'   kii k'ay'x-pa].
be.PROSP.PL this week-LOC]
They said at Talmaks$_i$ they won't be { there$_i$ / here } this week.

Yet as we saw in chapter 2, and in contrast to Zazaki, Nez Perce allows clauses in which person indexicals shift but *kine* 'here' does not. On the reading where the locative is not shifted, the pattern of indexical shift in (111) is as in Uyghur (103b) (given that the embedded subject is a shifted first-person pronoun). Notably, however, Nez Perce does not allow contra-Uyghur clauses, i.e., clauses in which *kine* 'here' shifts but person indexicals do not. If the shifted interpretation of a locative is held constant, shift of person indexicals becomes obligatory. To see this, consider baseline sentence (112), where the complement clause contains shifty *kine* 'here' but no person indexicals.

(112) Context: Taamsas is speaking.
'In-lawtiwaa-nm   Boston-pa   hi-nees-Ø-n-e   *pro*
1SG-friend-ERG   Boston-LOC   3SUBJ-O.PL-say-P-REM.PAST   3PL
[weet'u   kine   Taamsas   hii-wes   kii   kaa].
[NEG   here   Taamsas.NOM   3SUBJ-be.PRES   this then]
My friend in Boston$_i$ told them that Taamsas is not there$_i$ right now.

Since the embedded clause contains a shifty locative, it is not possible to replace the name *Taamsas* with a nonshifty first-person indexical *salva veritate*:

(113) Context: Same.
'In-lawtiwaa-nm   Boston-pa   hi-nees-Ø-n-e   *pro*
1SG-friend-ERG   Boston-LOC   3SUBJ-O.PL-say-P-REM.PAST   3PL
[weet'u   kine   *pro*   wees   kii   kaa].
[NEG   here   1SG   be.PRES   this then]
My friend$_i$ in Boston$_j$ told them that { he$_i$ is / ✗I am } not there$_j$ right now.

Likewise, in a sentence containing a nonshifted person indexical and an adverbial referring to the location associated with the matrix attitude eventuality, shifty *kine* 'here' cannot be added:

(114) Context: Harold is in Clarkston. I and my consultant are in Lapwai.
Pay's   Harold   hi-neki-se-Ø   [*pro*   wees
maybe Harold.NOM   3SUBJ-think-IMPERF-PRES   [1SG   be.PRES
Clarkston-pa   ].
Clarkston-LOC]
Maybe Harold thinks that I am in Clarkston.

(115) Context: same.
Pay's   Harold   hi-neki-se-Ø   [*pro*   wees   **kine**
maybe   Harold.NOM   3SUBJ-think-IMPERF-PRES   [1SG   be.PRES   here
Clarkston-pa   ].
Clarkston-LOC]
Intended: Maybe Harold thinks$_i$ that I am here$_i$ in Clarkston$_i$.
Consultant: "You could only say this if you were in Clarkston."

Nez Perce thus allows, internal to one language, the union of the indexical-shift possibilities presented by Matses, Uyghur, and standard English: either all indexicals shift (as in Matses), only person indexicals do (as in Uyghur), or none do (as in English).

The possibility of describing optionality effects in Zazaki, Slave, and Nez Perce in this way reveals a tight connection between variation across languages and within them: we see, for instance, that the pattern internal to Nez Perce reproduces the crosslinguistic implicational relationship between locative and person indexical shifting discussed in section 3.1.2. Such data suggest, in a familiar way, that within-language variation overall obeys the same basic generalization as crosslinguistic variation does; thus (G2) can be stated in a more explicit form as a generalization about indexicals both within and across languages. In the table in (116), the symbol → in a language column indicates the shifting patterns, by row, that occur in that language. Nez Perce, for instance, allows complements where first person, second person, and locatives shift (first row); complements where first persons and second persons shift but locatives remain unshifted (second row); and complements where no indexicals shift (bottom row).

(G2) Implicational hierarchy of indexical classes   (to be augmented)
Within and across languages, the possibility of indexical shift is determined by the hierarchy 1st > 2nd > Loc. Indexicals of a certain class undergo shift in a particular verbal complement only if indexicals of classes farther to the left undergo shift as well.

(116) Some patterns of within-language variation

Nez Perce	Slave	Zazaki	Shifty 1st	Shifty 2nd	Shifty Loc
→		→	✓	✓	✓
→	→		✓	✓	–
	→		✓	–	–
→	→	→	–	–	–

The core observation here is that languages allowing multiple patterns of indexical shift still remain within the overall class of possibilities attested on a crosslinguistic basis. The patterns that hold for whole languages also hold for individual verbal complements.

3.1.4 Which Indexicals Must Be Read *De Se* When Shifted

Languages allowing indexical shift vary in which classes of indexicals must receive *de se* interpretations when shifted. In making this claim some years after Schlenker (2003) and Anand (2006) put shifty indexicals firmly on the agenda of *de se* theorists (and vice versa), I contend that the empirical basis has grown sufficiently to permit us to discern significant generalizations both about the indexicals that must be read *de se* and about those that need not.

In Zazaki, shifty first-person indexicals impose a *de se* requirement, as we see in (117). What this example shows is that a first-person shifty indexical cannot be used in just any context in which the shifty indexical refers to a counterpart of the attitude holder. Rather, it must refer to an individual that the attitude holder *identifies* as herself or himself—which is the case in this example in context (a) but not context (b).

(117) *Zazaki*
Heseni va [kɛ ɛz newɛsha].
Hesen.OBL said [that I be.sick.PRES]
Hesen said that he was sick.
a. ✓ Hesen says, "I am sick today."
b. # Hesen, at the hospital for a checkup, happens to glance at the chart of a patient's blood work. Hesen, a doctor himself, sees that the patient is clearly sick, but the name is hard to read. He says to the nurse when she comes in, "This guy is really sick."
(Anand 2006, 79)

The same holds for shifty first person in Nez Perce: shift is rejected in a non–*de se* scenario.

(118) *Nez Perce*
Context: A woman was on a group tour and she wandered off from the group and went back to the bus to take a nap. People noticed she was missing and started searching for her. She woke up, got back off the bus, and noticed everyone searching around. Of course, she didn't know why they were searching. Someone said to her, "A woman is lost." So she joined the search party to look for that woman, without knowing it was herself![14]

'Aayat hi-nek-saa-qa [*pro*
woman.NOM 3SUBJ-think-IMPERF-REC.PAST [1SG
peeleey-ce-∅].
be.missing-IMPERF-PRES]
Intended: The woman$_i$ thought she$_i$ was missing.

Parallel data are reported for shifty first person in Amharic (Anand 2006, 79), Georgian (Thivierge 2019), Korean (Park 2016, (26)), and Uyghur (Sudo 2012, 224–225).[15]

In contrast with these data is the pattern in Dhaasanac, where Nishiguchi (2017) finds that no such requirement on shifty first person is imposed. Rather, she reports that shifty first person indexicals in Dhaasanac are acceptable both in *de se* contexts, such as (119a), and non–*de se* (*de re*) contexts, such as (119b).[16]

(119) *Dhaasanac*
    Baali   kiey-e   [sure-chu   he   jiet   hi
    Baali   say.3SG-PAST   [1SG.GEN-pants   COPULA   fire   RP
    konye   ].
    eat.3SG.PASS.PAST]
    Baali said his pants were on fire.
    (Nishiguchi 2017, 48)
    a.   ✓ Baali is looking at himself in a mirror. He recognizes himself and notices his pants are on fire. (He says, "My pants are on fire!")
    b.   ✓ Baali is looking at himself in a mirror. He does not recognize himself, but notices his pants are on fire. (He says, "That guy's pants are on fire!")

When we move past first person, variation of this type reemerges. Second-person shifty indexicals require addressee *de se* (*de te*) interpretations in Amharic (Anand 2006, 79), Japanese (Sudo 2012, 239), Korean (Park 2016, (27)), Nez Perce (Deal 2014, (38)), and Zazaki (Anand 2006, 80): shifty second person must refer to an individual that the attitude holder identifies as his or her addressee. A Zazaki example is provided in (120). Again, the sentence contains a shifty indexical and is acceptable in context (a) but not in context (b).

(120) *Zazaki*
    Heseni   va   Ali-ra [kɛ   ti   newɛsha   ].
    Hesen.OBL said Ali-to [that you be.sick.PRES]
    Hesen said to Ali that he was sick.
    a.   ✓ Hesen says to his patient Ali, "You are sick today."
    b.   # Hesen is examining two twins, Ali and Ali-baba, at the same time, though in different rooms. He walks into Ali's room to talk to him about his results, and starts explaining the results, but then thinks that he's actually in the wrong room, talking to Ali-baba. He apologizes, and just before leaving tells Ali, "Well, I shouldn't have told you all that, but, in summary, Ali is sick."

(Anand 2006, 80)

A Nez Perce example of this same restriction is shown in (121) (based on a context described by Anand 2006, 16). This context is akin to (120b) in that the attitude holder (Mary) does not correctly identify the person she is in fact addressing (John) as her addressee. Accordingly, the shifty second-person indexical is illicit.

(121) *Nez Perce*
Context: Mary is organizing a big dinner at a restaurant with waiters to help serve food. She hears that a certain waiter named John is being a nuisance. She tells the nearest waiter, "John should go home." Unbeknowst to her, she's talking to John.
Meeli-nm pee-Ø-n-e   Caan-e, ['ee
Mary-ERG 3/3-say-P-REM.PAST John-ACC [2SG.CL
cikliitoq-o'qa   ].
go.home-MODAL]
Literal: Mary told John$_j$ that you$_j$ should go home.
Consultant: "No! 'Cause she doesn't know she's talking to John."

These Zazaki and Nez Perce data are again in contrast to the pattern in Dhaasanac (Nishiguchi 2017), as well as in Uyghur (Sudo 2012). Indeed Sudo shows that the very same waiter context used in (121) allows shift of second person in Uyghur:

(122) *Uyghur*
Context: Muhemmet is hosting a party. He hears that a certain waiter named John is being a nuisance. Muhemmet tells the nearest waiter, "John should go home." Unbeknownst to him, he's talking to John.
Muhemmet John-gha [*pro* öy-ge   kit-sh-ing   kirek   ]
Muhemmet John-DAT [2SG home-DAT leave-GER-2SG should]
di-di.
say-PAST.3
Muhemmet told John$_i$ that he$_i$ should go home. (Sudo 2012, 225)

Recall, meanwhile, that only first- and second-person indexicals shift in Uyghur, and that first-person shifty indexicals impose *de se* requirements.

Variation also emerges in the sphere of locative indexicals. Just as for person indexicals, shifty locative indexicals require locative *de se* (*de hic*) interpretation in Zazaki (Anand 2006) and Korean (Park 2016, (28)): shifty 'here' must refer to a location that the attitude holder identifies as a counterpart of his or her location. A Zazaki example—again good in the (a) context, but bad in the (b) context—is provided in (123).

(123) *Zazaki*
Waxto kɛ o London-de bime Pierri va [kɛ o ita
when that he London-at be.PAST Pierre.OBL said [that it here
rindɛka].
be.pretty.PRES]
When he was in London, Pierre said that it is pretty there.
a. ✓ Pierre says in London, "It is pretty here."
b. # Pierre is walking around London, which is drab and rather disappointing. He says, "I wish I were in Londres. Londres is pretty."
(Anand 2006, 80)

The contrast in this case is with Nez Perce, in which no such requirement is imposed on shifty 'here' (Deal 2014). For the following context, we can specify three distinct locations: the utterance location (Lapwai), the thinker's location (Clarkston), and the thinker's self-ascribed location (Asotin). The shifty indexical refers to the thinker's actual location (Clarkston), not to the place that she takes as her location (Asotin).

(124) *Nez Perce*
Context (elicited in Lapwai): Costco is a prominent store in Clarkston. Everyone knows where it is.
'Aayat hii-wes Clarkston-pa,
woman.NOM 3SUBJ-be.PRES Clarkston-LOC
The woman is in Clarkston$_i$,
met'u *pro* hi-neki-se-Ø Asootin-pa,
but 3SG 3SUBJ-think-IMPERF-PRES Asotin-LOC
but she thinks (she is) in Asotin,
kaa *pro* hi-neki-se-Ø [Costco hii-wes kine].
and 3SG 3SUBJ-think-IMPERF-PRES [Costco 3SUBJ-be.PRES here]
and she thinks Costco is here$_i$.

Like in Uyghur, this behavior contrasts with that of other classes of indexicals internal to the language; as we have seen, first- and second-person shifty indexicals require *de se* interpretation in Nez Perce.

At this point I wish to make two conjectures. First, we will find other languages where shifty indexicals do not impose *de se* requirements.[17] That is to say that *de se* interpretation is not an inherent property of indexical shift.[18] Accordingly, the special behavior of Dhaasanac first and second person, Uyghur second person, and Nez Perce 'here' should not be chalked up to some special property of these elements themselves, as for instance on a potential analysis that treats them otherwise than as pure indexicals (perhaps à la Sudo 2012; see section 4.3). On an analysis of Nez Perce *kine* 'here' as an ordinary description ('the location of the speaker/thinker') rather than as an indexical, for instance, we would fail to account for the basic profile of unembedded indexicals reviewed in chapter 2. As we saw in that chapter, outside of attitude clauses, *kine* 'here' behaves exactly like its English counterpart: it must always refer to the utterance location and cannot be bound by a quantifier. In the following example, the consultant changes *kine* 'here' to *kona* 'there' in order to support a bound interpretation.[19]

(125) *Nez Perce*
Ke mine Obama hi-c'iiq-tetu-Ø, 'ilx̂nii-we
wherever Obama.NOM 3SUBJ-speak-HAB.SG-PRES many-HUMAN
kine hi-wsiix titooqan.
here 3SUBJ-be.PRES.PL person.NOM
Wherever Obama speaks, many people are here.
Consultant: "I don't think you say *kine* [here]... you're saying *ke mine*, 'wherever', so I think you have to say *koná* [there]."

Second, I conjecture that the cases of non–*de se* indexical shift that are already known are not arbitrarily distributed. In fact, the distribution of *de se* requirements seems to track the same implicational hierarchy that we found for variation in which classes of indexicals shift, within and across languages:[20]

(G3) Implicational hierarchy of *de se* requirements   (to be augmented)
Requirements for *de se* interpretation conform to the hierarchy 1st > 2nd > Loc. Indexicals of a certain class require *de se* interpretation only if indexicals of classes farther to the left require it as well.

	De se requirements are imposed on:		
	1st	2nd	Loc
Zazaki, Korean	✓	✓	✓
Nez Perce	✓	✓	–
Uyghur	✓	–	n/a
Dhaasanac	–	–	n/a

This hierarchy suggests that it is not an accident that it is second person that is free from *de se* strictures in Uyghur, rather than first person; likewise, it is no accident that 'here' is similarly liberated in Nez Perce, in contrast to person indexicals.

The ultimate status of these conjectures will have to be assessed by the fruits they bear, both in terms of crosslinguistic predictions and in terms of the insight afforded to the cases at hand. In the remainder of this chapter, I will lay out a theory of indexical shift that can at once predict the existence and the constrained distribution of non–*de se* shifty indexicals.

3.2 Deriving the Asymmetries

Having seen the case for an operator view of indexical shift (in chapter 2), along with patterns of shifty indexicality crosslinguistically (so far in this chapter), we now take up the core task of explaining the three generalizations laid out thus far. The project begins with two elaborations on the grammar of shifty operators, in the service of explaining the generalizations about indexicals (G2) and about verbs (G1). It rounds off with a new proposal about semantic variation in the field of shifty operators, in the service of explaining the generalization about *de se* (G3).

3.2.1 Regulating Which Indexicals Shift

We begin with our generalization about which indexical classes may shift in an attitude complement:

(G2) Implicational hierarchy of indexical classes
 Within and across languages, the possibility of indexical shift is determined by the hierarchy 1st > 2nd > Loc. Indexicals of a certain class undergo shift in a particular verbal complement only if indexicals of classes farther to the left undergo shift as well.

		Shifty 1st	Shifty 2nd	Shifty Loc
(a)	Matses	✓	✓	✓
(b)	Uyghur	✓	✓	–
(c)	Slave 'say'	✓	–	–
(d)	English	–	–	–

As we have seen, Nez Perce provides examples of rows (a), (b), and (d); Slave provides examples of rows (b), (c), and (d). For Slave, we may generalize that if an attitude complement has addressee shift, it has author shift. For Nez Perce, we may generalize that if an attitude complement has locative shift, it has person shift. In the latter case, for instance, this means that while some attitude complements in Nez Perce require the calculation of $[\![XP]\!]^{<author(i),\ldots,loc(c)>,i,g}$ (where c is the original utterance context, i is a bound index variable, g is a variable assignment, and XP is some embedded constituent), none require the calculation of $[\![XP]\!]^{<author(c),\ldots,loc(i)>,i,g}$. What accounts for this asymmetry?

We should first note that constraints on contexts (insofar as they are independently motivated) do not yield a full explanation. For instance, based on person asymmetries of the type in Slave, we might consider appealing to the fact that a shifted value is not always well-defined for the second person; thus, second-person shifting has a more constrained distribution than first-person shifting does (cf. Bittner 2014, 18). This type of explanation will not extend to the Nez Perce person/locative asymmetry, however. A shifted value is always well-defined for the locative indexical, since attitudes have locations, regardless of whether the person indexicals are shifted. Thus the mere definedness of shift does not account for why locative shift requires person shift.[21] Similarly, we must resist an explanation in terms of a blanket constraint against improper contexts, that is, contexts that do not correspond to any actual circumstance of utterance or attitude-holding (cf. Bittner 2014, 20). Partial indexical shift does exist and seems to require contexts of this type, for instance, those in which author is shifted but not addressee (as in Slave (106)) or in which author and addressee are shifted but not location (as in Uyghur (103) and Nez Perce (111)). Of course, it is relatively trivial to articulate a constraint on contexts tailor-made for the delivery of generalization (G2). Any such proposal should be evaluated against the proposal just below both on its ability to account for the present patterns and on how well it integrates into a larger picture of the workings of indexical shift. It is with this larger picture in mind that I propose an analysis based not on constraints on contexts but rather on the meaning and grammar of shifty operators.

We begin with variation inside a single language. Let us suppose that a language like Nez Perce contains not one but three shifty operators—OP_{LOC}, OP_{ADDR}, OP_{AUTH}—each responsible for a simple modification of context:

(126) Nez Perce shifty operators (to be revised)
    a. $[\![\text{OP}_{\text{AUTH}}]\!]^{c,i,g} = \lambda p \in D_{<\kappa,\kappa t>}.p(i)(c^{author(i)/author})$
    b. $[\![\text{OP}_{\text{ADDR}}]\!]^{c,i,g} = \lambda p \in D_{<\kappa,\kappa t>}.p(i)(c^{addr(i)/addr})$
    c. $[\![\text{OP}_{\text{LOC}}]\!]^{c,i,g} = \lambda p \in D_{<\kappa,\kappa t>}.p(i)(c^{loc(i)/loc})$

Insofar as it allows for multiple distinct operators within the lexicon of a single language, this proposal follows Anand (2006). Unlike Anand's operators, however, those in (126) make noninteracting changes to the context against which their complement is evaluated. To model shift of both person and locative indexicals, multiple operators must occur together at the edge of the finite clause.

This raises a structural question. Shifty operators are functional elements, that is, elements of a type that decades of syntactic research has found to occupy rigid "functional sequences" requiring that one type of element asymmetrically command another type of element (Zamparelli 1995, Rizzi 1997, Cinque 1999, inter alia). Given the prevalence of these sequences throughout the grammar, we should expect shifty operators to fit into one, in particular one that articulates the periphery of finite attitude complements. It could, in principle, universally be the case that OP_{ADDR} occurs higher than OP_{AUTH} when the two co-occur, or vice versa; this is an empirical question concerning the functional sequence.

It is precisely generalizations like (G2) that allow such questions to be adjudicated. It has long been known about the syntax of embedded clauses that complement clauses come in different sizes (e.g., CP vs. TP [vs. vP], or in earlier work $\tilde{\text{S}}$ vs. S; see Bresnan 1972, Rochette 1988, and much following work). Furthermore, clause size variation is generally monotonic; the difference is where in the sequence of projections upward the embedded clause ends (Rizzi 2005). Given that T occurs higher than v in the functional sequence, a clause may end at vP, including v and everything lower in the sequence (127a); it may end at TP, including T and everything in vP (127b); it cannot mix and match from different parts of the clause, containing TP but omitting v or vP, as in (127c), for example.[22]

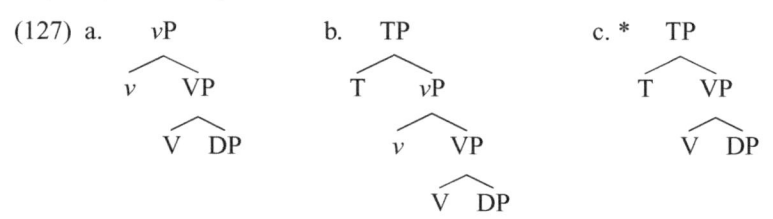

(127) a. vP
          / \
         v VP
             / \
            V   DP

b. TP
    / \
   T vP
       / \
      v VP
          / \
         V   DP

c. * TP
     / \
    T   VP
        / \
       V   DP

Similarly, in the realm of shifty operators, we expect that a clause projected only up to OP_α will show shift only with respect to α, whereas a clause projected past OP_α up to OP_β will show shift both with respect to α and with respect to β. This is the pattern reported in (G2), where α is author and β is addressee and likewise where α is addressee and β is location. I conclude, therefore, that OP_{ADDR} occupies a higher position than OP_{AUTH} and likewise that OP_{LOC} occupies a higher position than OP_{ADDR} (and, accordingly, OP_{AUTH} as well).[23]

Shifty Asymmetries

The implicational relationship between shifting of different classes of indexicals falls out from these syntactic facts together with variation in the precise size of the embedded clause. Given the operators in (126), an attitude complement may come in any of four varieties, differing in the extent to which they enforce indexical shift on material inside TP. (I use an ellipsis mark in these structures to abstract away, temporarily, from the position of C.)

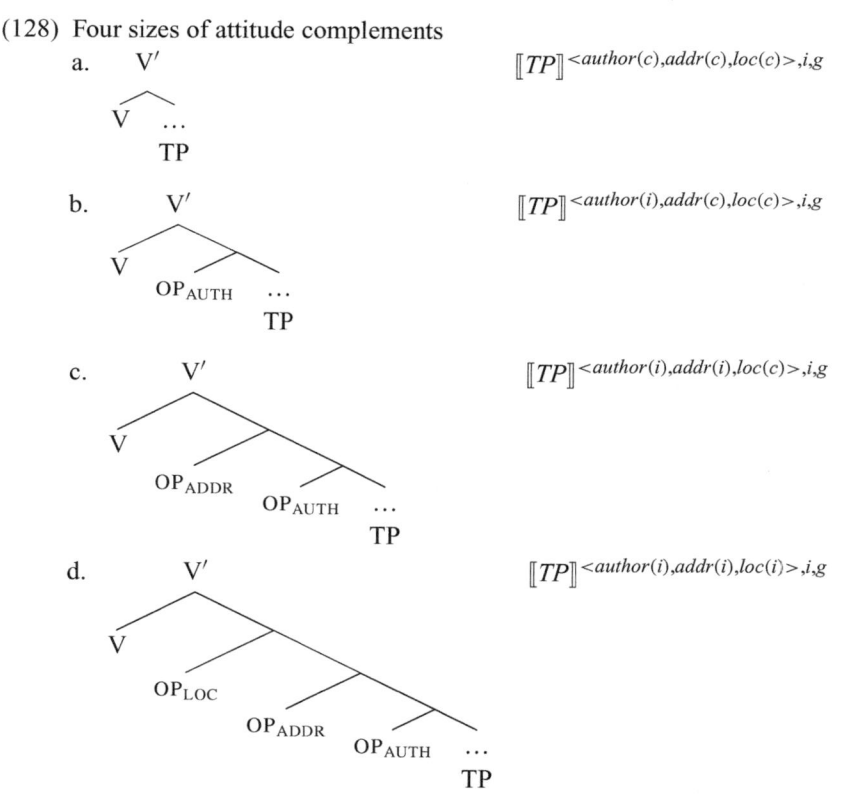

(128) Four sizes of attitude complements

a. V′ → V … TP $[\![TP]\!]^{<author(c),addr(c),loc(c)>,i,g}$

b. V′ → V OP$_{AUTH}$ … TP $[\![TP]\!]^{<author(i),addr(c),loc(c)>,i,g}$

c. V′ → V OP$_{ADDR}$ OP$_{AUTH}$ … TP $[\![TP]\!]^{<author(i),addr(i),loc(c)>,i,g}$

d. V′ → V OP$_{LOC}$ OP$_{ADDR}$ OP$_{AUTH}$ … TP $[\![TP]\!]^{<author(i),addr(i),loc(i)>,i,g}$

Both within and across languages, it is possible for attitude complements to include a full suite of operators, yielding total indexical shift (as found in Zazaki and Matses) in structure (128d). It is also possible for attitude complements to include OP$_{ADDR}$ and OP$_{AUTH}$ only, yielding shift of person indexicals but not locatives, (128c).[24] This is the only option allowed in Uyghur finite clauses (recalling that Uyghur allows indexicals to avoid shift by moving outside the scope of shifting operators, as discussed in chapter 2). In Nez Perce, this is a possibility that coexists with structures (128d) and (128a). An additional possibility is that attitude complements include OP$_{AUTH}$ only, yielding shift of first-person indexicals only, (128b). In Slave, this is a possibility that coexists with structure (128c) (the choice being regulated, as discussed in the section 3.2.2, by verb). The final option is simply one where no indexicals shift whatsoever, (128a).

By contrast, it is not possible (for instance) for attitude complements to include OP_{LOC} only, without any operators lower in the sequence. Similar remarks apply to further combinations involving the person shifters OP_{ADDR} and OP_{AUTH}. A shifter may only be present in a structure if those lower than it in the sequence are also present. This yields the hierarchy effect regarding which indexicals shift.

(129) *A structure in violation of functional sequencing:*[25]

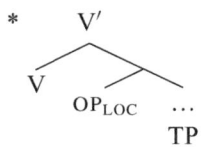

```
   *     V′
        /  \
       V    \
          OP_LOC  ...
                  TP
```

3.2.2 The Effect of Verbs

One implication of the operator-stacking view is that clauses with different degrees of indexical shift (including none at all) constitute syntactic objects of different sizes—or, equivalently, different categories. A clause with full indexical shift is an $\text{OP}_{\text{LOC}}\text{P}$; one with person shift only is an $\text{OP}_{\text{ADDR}}\text{P}$. To explain the effect of verb choice on indexical shift, we will put this together with Rice's (1986) proposal that variation by verb is a side effect of verbal subcategorization. Verbs that select for larger structures will allow a greater degree of indexical shift in their complements (Anand 2006, Sundaresan 2011, 2012, 2018). Given the hierarchy effect described in (G1), this suggests that verbs of speech must allow the syntactically largest complements, followed by verbs of thought, followed by verbs of knowledge. (Such a state of affairs could perhaps be motivated functionally by the fact that speech complements are able to echo the subject's own words more directly than are verbs of thought, leading to a more main clause–like structure, and verbs of thought in turn are able to do so more directly than are verbs of knowledge.)

(G1) Implicational hierarchy of verbs

Verbs of speech are more likely to allow indexical shift in their complement than are verbs of thought, which in turn are more likely to allow indexical shift in their complement than are verbs of knowledge.

	Shift takes place under verbs of:		
	Speech	Thought	Knowledge
Nez Perce	✓	✓	✓
Navajo, Slave, Uyghur	✓	✓	–
Dhaasanac, Zazaki	✓	–	–

A partial corresponding hierarchy of syntactic complement sizes is explicitly proposed by Sundaresan (2011, 2012), drawing on various types of typological findings. Finite complements, for instance, are generally taken to be syntactically larger than nonfinite ones or nominalizations,[26] and finite complementation does not occur with verbs of knowledge unless it also occurs with verbs of speech and thought. English allows finite complements for *say*, *think*, and *know*; Korean allows finite complements only for 'say' and 'think' but requires nominalization for 'know' (Yangsook Park, pers. comm.); no language requires nominalized or otherwise nonfinite complements for 'say', while allowing full finite complementation for 'think' and/or 'know'. Relatedly, the distribution of logophoric pronouns follows an identical hierarchy, favoring verbs of speech over verbs of thought, and verbs of thought over verbs of knowledge (Stirling 1993; Speas 2004; Oshima 2006, 208). Supposing that logophors require binding by operators in the left periphery, as Koopman and Sportiche (1989) and many others have proposed, this effect, too, suggests a hierarchy of complement size—a line of thinking pursued in influential work by Speas (2004). Speech complements are most likely to support indexical shift, finiteness, and logophoric elements because they are syntactically largest. As the syntactic size of the complement decreases, the likelihood of indexical shift, finiteness, and logophoric binding decreases accordingly.

The possible and impossible language types outlined by (G1) may thus be modeled as follows. In Nez Perce, verbs of speech, thought, and knowledge all take complements large enough to constitute finite clauses containing indexical shifting operators. Accordingly, indexical shift is possible in complements of all three types.

(130) a. SAY [OP [TP
 b. THINK [OP [TP
 c. KNOW [OP [TP

In Navajo, only verbs of speech and thought have complements large enough to host shifty operators; verbs of knowledge do not.

(131) a. SAY   [OP [TP
     b. THINK [OP [TP
     c. KNOW   [TP

In Zazaki, only verbs of speech have complements large enough to host shifty operators.

(132) a. SAY   [OP [TP
     b. THINK   [TP
     c. KNOW   [TP

By contrast, it is not possible (for instance) for a language to permit indexical shift only in complements of thought verbs without also allowing it in complements of speech verbs:

(133) Impossible pattern
     a. SAY   [TP
     b. THINK [OP [TP
     c. KNOW   [TP

A language of this last type would need to allow thought complements to be systematically syntactically larger than speech complements—an option that language does not allow.[27,28]

3.2.3 Back to the *De Se*

Before we move on, let us take stock by considering what can now be said about speech reports in three indexical-shifting languages: Nez Perce, Uyghur, and Zazaki. Zazaki, as we have seen, allows both person and locative indexicals to shift under 'say'. This suggests the LF in (134) for Zazaki speech reports. An LF of this type will give rise to the calculation of $[\![TP]\!]^{<author(i),addr(i),loc(i)>,i,g}$, where i is an index variable bound by modal quantification.

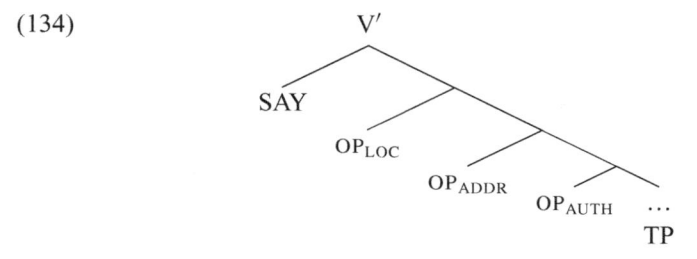

(134)
```
            V'
           /  \
         SAY   \
              OP_LOC
                   \
                 OP_ADDR
                       \
                     OP_AUTH  ...
                             TP
```

Uyghur, by contrast, does not allow locative indexicals to shift. This suggests that speech reports in Uyghur have a slightly less articulated LF than their Zazaki counterparts, giving rise to the calculation of $[\![TP]\!]^{<author(i),addr(i),loc(c)>,i,g}$, where i is a bound index variable and c is the utterance context.

(135)

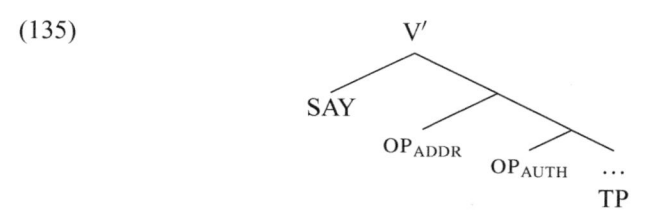

```
        V'
       / \
     SAY   \
          / \
       OP_ADDR \
              / \
           OP_AUTH ...
                  TP
```

Finally, Nez Perce presents two options: either both person and locative indexicals shift or only person indexicals do. This suggests that Nez Perce allows the union of the possibilities allowed by the other two languages—both (134) and (135) are well-formed Nez Perce LFs.[29]

It is useful to begin with this range of possibilities as we move to a final dimension of variation in indexical shift, namely variation in requirements of *de se* interpretation. For the particular languages just exemplified, there are two instances of semantic undergeneration that remain to be explained. On the basis of the semantics for shifty operators presented in chapter 2 (following Anand and Nevins 2004, Anand 2006, Sudo 2012), we expect that the only possible shifted value for an indexical should be a *de se* value. (We review the details of this prediction just below.) This prediction is welcome for Zazaki and for a subset of the indexicals of Uyghur and Nez Perce. Something must be done, however, to explain the rest of the data, in particular the availability of Uyghur shifty second-person indexicals and Nez Perce shifty locative indexicals in scenarios that do not support *de se* readings, and whatever is done about these particular cases must be connected back to generalization (G3).

(G3) Implicational hierarchy of *de se* requirements
Requirements for *de se* interpretation conform to the hierarchy 1st > 2nd > Loc. Indexicals of a certain class require *de se* interpretation only if indexicals of classes farther to the left require it as well.

	De se requirements are imposed on:		
	1st	2nd	Loc
Zazaki, Korean	✓	✓	✓
Nez Perce	✓	✓	–
Uyghur	✓	–	n/a
Dhaasanac	–	–	n/a

This is to say that any full account will need to provide both an analysis of individual non–*de se* shifty indexicals and a source for the hierarchy effect in their distribution. The hierarchy effect in particular suggests that the source of non–*de se* shifty indexicals should in some way be connected to the hierarchy of shifty operators in the clause periphery. This connection is at the heart of the analysis I will propose.

Let us first remind ourselves in more depth how the account as presented in chapter 2 imposes *de se* requirements. One part of the explanation comes from the nature of attitudinal quantification; the other comes from the semantics of shifty operators. On the former count, modal quantification in attitude reports is quantification over centered tuples (indices), which pair a possible world with various coordinates that determine a perspectival center. On the latter count, given the semantics of shifty operators, it is elements of these tuples that are used to overwrite coordinates of context. As laid out in chapter 2, the quantificational component in an attitude report comes from the attitude verb itself, as in (136), and shifty operator semantics are as exemplified in (137).

(136) $[\![SAY\ \alpha]\!]^{c,i,g} = \lambda x. \forall i' \in R_{say}(x,i) [\![\alpha]\!]^{c,i',g}$
where $i' \in R_{say}(x,i)$ iff
  a. $w(i')$ is compatible with what x says at i
  b. $author(i')$ is an individual in $w(i')$ that x identifies at i as herself
  c. $addr(i')$ is an individual in $w(i')$ that x identifies at i as her addressee
  d. $loc(i')$ is a location in $w(i')$ that x identifies at i as her spatial location
  e. $time(i')$ is a time in $w(i')$ that x identifies at i as her temporal location

(137) $[\![\text{OP}_{\text{AUTH}}]\!]^{c,i,g} = \lambda p \in D_{<\kappa,\kappa t>}.p(i)(c^{author(i)/author})$

In the scope of attitudinal quantification, coordinates of the index are thus always *de se* coordinates. If only these *de se* coordinates can be used to determine contextual values, shifty indexicals cannot avoid *de se* interpretations. On the other hand, if contextual values could be overwritten with something *other* than a coordinate of the index, escaping the centering requirements imposed by attitudinal quantification, a non–*de se* shifty indexical would result. This would be the case, in particular, if shifty values could be drawn from information about the attitude event itself.

Implementing this type of picture requires a closer look at the composition of attitude complements. In this regard I follow a trail that has been blazed by Hacquard (2006) and Anand and Hacquard (2008) (as well as in closely related terms by Kratzer 2006 and Moulton 2009, 2015). These authors capitalize on the idea that attitudes are a special type of eventuality, which is associated with propositional content. The content of a saying event is the set of (centered) worlds compatible with what is said. The content of a thinking state is the set of (centered) worlds compatible with what is thought. An attitude clause overall must introduce an eventuality, identify what type of attitude it is, provide its various arguments, and quantify over its content. Some of these types of information are more lexically variable than others: different types of attitude verbs introduce different types of eventualities, but the core modal quantification of attitude complements does not vary with the choice of attitude verb. This suggests that modal quantification may actually be contributed not by the attitude verb itself, but by a more fixed element in attitude report composition, for instance, the finite complementizer. The semantics of attitude verbs themselves then becomes quite slim, much of the work having moved to the interpretation of C^0:

(138) $[\![say]\!]^{c,i,g} = \lambda e.saying(e)$
(139) $[\![think]\!]^{c,i,g} = \lambda e.thinking(e)$
(140) $[\![C^0 \, \alpha]\!]^{c,i,g} = \lambda e. \forall i' \in \mathrm{RCON}(e) [\![\alpha]\!]^{c,i',g}$
where $i' \in \mathrm{RCON}(e)$ iff
a. $w(i')$ is a member of the content of e
b. $author(i')$ is an individual in $w(i')$ that $\mathrm{EXT}(e)$ identifies in e as herself
c. $addr(i')$ is an individual in $w(i')$ that $\mathrm{EXT}(e)$ identifies in e as her addressee, if any; otherwise $addr(i')$ is $\emptyset$
d. $loc(i')$ is a location in $w(i')$ that $\mathrm{EXT}(e)$ identifies in e as her spatial location
e. $time(i')$ is a time in $w(i')$ that $\mathrm{EXT}(e)$ identifies in e as her temporal location

Here $\mathrm{EXT}(e)$ is a function that applies to an event and yields its external argument (roughly: agent or experiencer). Attitudes vary in whether they have addressees in addition to external arguments. Therefore, in view of the role of the addressee coordinate of the index in determining *de te* interpretation, any proposal for a single C head present in the complements of both speech and thought verbs must allow for an addressee coordinate of the index to receive a normal value in some cases but not others. Accordingly, in (140), I treat the *addr* coordinate as receiving defective value $\emptyset$ when there is no addressee, leading to trivial truth or falsehood for sentences containing pronouns referencing this value. (See chapter 4 for applications of this idea to Nez Perce and Uyghur.)

This picture does not perturb the analysis of *de se* shifty operators from chapter 2, provided the operators in question attach in the scope of C. Along with the author shifter in (137), we can posit a *de hic* shifter of this type for languages like Zazaki and a *de te* shifter of this type for languages like Nez Perce.

(141) Zazaki locative shifter
$[\![\mathrm{OP_{LOC}}]\!]^{c,i,g} = \lambda p \in D_{<\kappa,\kappa t>}.p(i)(c^{loc(i)/loc})$

(142) Nez Perce addressee shifter
$[\![\text{OP}_{\text{ADDR}}]\!]^{c,i,g} = \lambda p \in D_{<\kappa,\kappa t>}.p(i)(c^{addr(i)/addr})$

What would happen if a shifty operator attached outside the scope of C? In this environment, information about the attitude cannot be recovered from the index, but it can be recovered from the event argument. I propose, therefore, that non–*de se* shifters directly use the event argument associated with the attitude to overwrite the context. For the proposals in (143)–(144), let *l* be the type of eventualities; let LOC and ADDR be predicates that combine with an event argument and retrieve, respectively, the associated location or addressee.[30,31]

(143) Nez Perce locative shifter (non–*de se*)
$[\![\text{OP}_{\text{LOC}}]\!]^{c,i,g} = \lambda P \in D_{<\kappa,<\kappa,lt>>}.\lambda e.P(i)(c^{\text{LOC}(e)/loc})(e)$

(144) Uyghur addressee shifter (non–*de se*)
$[\![\text{OP}_{\text{ADDR}}]\!]^{c,i,g} = \lambda P \in D_{<\kappa,<\kappa,lt>>}.\lambda e.P(i)(c^{\text{ADDR}(e)/addr})(e)$

Because these shifters draw directly on the attitude event, they impose no requirement of *de se* identification.[32] In the scope of locative shifter (143), a locative indexical will refer to a counterpart of the attitude location, regardless of whether the attitude holder self-locates there.[33] Likewise, in the scope of addressee shifter (144), a second-person pronoun will refer to a counterpart of the addressee of the embedding attitude, regardless of whether the attitude holder identifies this individual as such. This makes for a contrast with the corresponding shifters in (141) and (142), which overwrite only with *de se* location and addressee values as determined by the restriction on quantification in (140).

The hierarchy effect in *de se* requirements arises as a consequence of the way the two types of operator denotations relate to the contribution of C. C, as defined in (140), introduces both the attitude event argument and quantification over centered indices. In order to have access to the indices quantified over, *de se* shifters must occur below C. (Above it, they are vacuous.) In order to have access to the event argument, non–*de se* shifters must occur above C. (Below it, they pose a type mismatch.) If C sits in the middle of the sequence of operators, all those below it will impose *de se* requirements, but none of those above it will. For Nez Perce, this suggests that C is located between OP_{LOC} and OP_{ADDR} in a maximally articulated attitude complement. The structure in (145) gives rise to the calculation of $[\![TP]\!]^{<author(i),addr(i),\text{LOC}(e)>,i,g}$, where *i* is an index variable bound by centered modal quantification and *e* is an event variable restricted by the attitude verb.

(145)
```
        V'
       / \
      V   \
         OP_LOC
           \
            C
             \
            OP_ADDR
                \
               OP_AUTH  TP
```

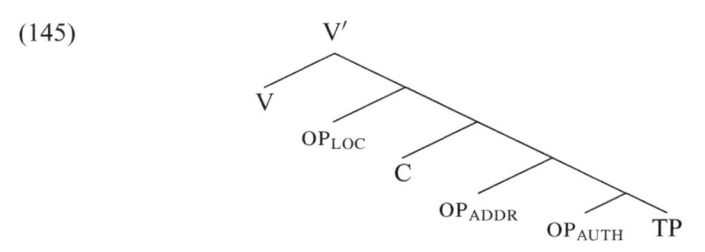

Thus shifty locatives in a Nez Perce attitude report need not be read *de se*, but their person indexical counterparts must. For Uyghur, second-person shifty indexicals need not be read *de se*, but first-person ones must. So, C must be located between OP$_{\text{ADDR}}$ and OP$_{\text{AUTH}}$ in this language:

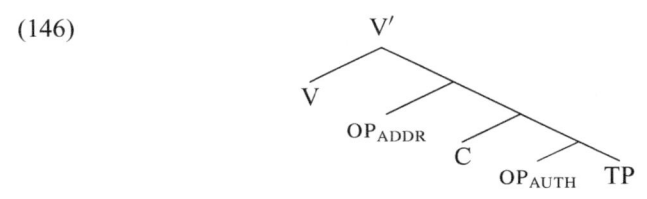

(146)
```
        V'
       / \
      V   \
         OP_ADDR
            \
             C
              \
             OP_AUTH  TP
```

This structure gives rise to the calculation of $[\![TP]\!]^{<author(i),\text{ADDR}(e),loc(c)>,i,g}$, where i is an index variable bound by centered modal quantification, e is an event variable restricted by the attitude verb, and c is the utterance context. By interleaving C between two distinct shifty operators in Uyghur, the theory succeeds in modeling the language's three-way distinction among indexical types: first persons shift and require *de se* interpretations (since OP$_{\text{AUTH}}$ is projected below C), second persons shift but do not require *de te* interpretations (since OP$_{\text{ADDR}}$ is projected above C), and locatives do not shift (since OP$_{\text{LOC}}$ is not projected).

Finally are the cases of Zazaki and Dhaasanac. In Zazaki, all shifty indexicals require *de se* interpretation, meaning all shifters occur below C. Structure (147) gives rise to the calculation of $[\![TP]\!]^{<author(i),addr(i),loc(i)>,i,g}$, where i is an index variable bound by centered modal quantification.

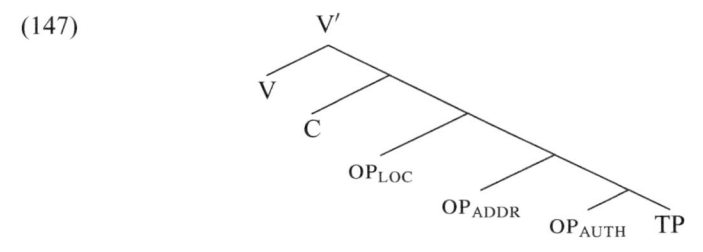

(147)
```
        V'
       / \
      V   \
          C
           \
          OP_LOC
             \
            OP_ADDR
                \
               OP_AUTH  TP
```

For Dhaasanac, in contrast, neither first- nor second-person shifty indexicals need to be read *de se* and locative indexicals do not shift (as in Uyghur). So, C must be located very low in this language—below both OP$_{ADDR}$ and OP$_{AUTH}$ in maximally articulated attitude complements. Structure (148) gives rise to the calculation of $[\![TP]\!]^{<\text{AUTH}(e),\text{ADDR}(e),loc(c)>,i,g}$, where e is an event variable restricted by the attitude verb and c is the utterance context.

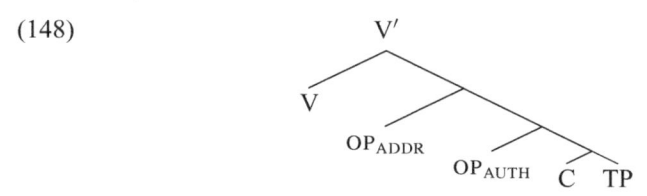

(148)

```
            V'
           / \
          V   \
             OP_ADDR
              /    \
           OP_AUTH  \
                   C  TP
```

The pattern in these four languages demonstrates that C may appear anywhere in the sequence of shifters OP$_{LOC}$ > OP$_{ADDR}$ > OP$_{AUTH}$. It appears in Zazaki above OP$_{LOC}$, in Nez Perce between OP$_{LOC}$ and OP$_{ADDR}$, in Uyghur between OP$_{ADDR}$ and OP$_{AUTH}$, and in Dhaasanac below OP$_{AUTH}$. All shifters below C impose *de se* requirements—index coordinates, bound by centered quantification, overwrite context—and all shifters above C do not—event parameters overwrite context, free of any such constraint.

A syntactic consequence of this analysis concerns the status of C. If C (as defined in (140)) is a head in the functional spine of finite clauses, we might not expect it to remain present in clauses where the next head down in the functional sequence is absent, in keeping with the monotonicity of structural impoverishment. Yet various languages that allow indexical shift also allow for attitude complements without any indexical shift at all (e.g., Japanese, Nez Perce, Zazaki), and in such complements, the semantic contribution of C remains necessary for sentence interpretability. One intriguing possibility compatible with these facts is that the C element defined in (140) is, in syntactic terms, an adjunct, according it more flexibility in its placement across languages and a greater ability to survive impoverishment of its complement. On this view the obligatoriness of C would result not from its syntax but from its semantics— attitude complements lacking C would be grammatical but uninterpretable. An alternative possibility is that C as defined in (140) should be treated in a way parallel to how Rizzi (1997) treats Topic; he posits Topic projections on both sides of a Focus projection, meaning the order of Topic and Focus is effectively free. Parallel remarks extend to Cinque's (1999) treatment of agreement heads, which he claims may appear anywhere in the functional sequence of adverb-related projections.

4 Extending the Theory

The account now before us regulates variation in terms of three interrelated dimensions:

(149) Dimensions of variation
    a. Which operators are present in the language
    b. Where C fits into the sequence of operators
    c. Which structures particular verbs select for

Independent of any particular language, dimension (a) is constrained by the hierarchy of operators, $\text{OP}_{\text{LOC}} > \text{OP}_{\text{ADDR}} > \text{OP}_{\text{AUTH}}$; dimension (b) is totally free; and dimension (c) is constrained by the hierarchy of complement size. Internal to a particular language, behaviors along different dimensions are constrained by one another in straightforward ways. A language that lacks shifty operators (such as standard English) cannot contain verbs that select for them. A language lacking OP_{LOC} (such as Uyghur) cannot contain verbs selecting for $\text{OP}_{\text{LOC}}\text{P}$ nor require that C sit above OP_{LOC}. In terms of operator denotations, a language where C sits below OP_{ADDR} cannot make use of a *de te* addressee shifter as in (150), and likewise a language where C sits above OP_{ADDR} cannot make use of a non–*de te* addressee shifter as in (151).

(150) $[\![\text{OP}_{\text{ADDR}}]\!]^{c,i,g} = \lambda p \in D_{<\kappa,\kappa t>}.p(i)(c^{addr(i)/addr})$
    [repeated from (142)]

(151) $[\![\text{OP}_{\text{ADDR}}]\!]^{c,i,g} = \lambda P \in D_{<\kappa,<\kappa,lt>>}.\lambda e.P(i)(c^{\text{ADDR}(e)/addr})(e)$
    [repeated from (144)]

Shifty operators themselves vary in two different ways (as highlighted, in part, by (150) and (151)): in terms of which coordinate of context they modify and in terms of how they make this modification.

In this chapter, I make a case for an expanded inventory of shifty operators, building on the theory developed in the previous chapter in two ways. The first addition concerns temporal indexical shift and draws directly on the analytical tools of chapter 3. Temporal indexicals, I will propose, are shifted by an operator that occurs lowest in the functional sequence. The overall sequence of shifty operators proposed in this book is thus as shown in (152).

(152) The hierarchy of shifty operators (final version)

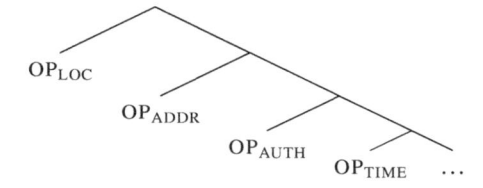

$$
\begin{array}{c}
OP_{LOC} \\
\quad OP_{ADDR} \\
\qquad OP_{AUTH} \quad OP_{TIME} \quad \ldots
\end{array}
$$

Partly on the basis of this expanded hierarchy, I then put forward a third and final way that shifty operators vary across languages. I will propose (building on ideas from Anand 2006) that operators may vary in how many coordinates of context they modify. The recognition of this final dimension of variation will allow for an account of the variable behavior of second-person pronouns in complements of verbs of cognition (a point of variation highlighted by Sudo 2012), as well as a series of facts about temporal and locative indexicals in Korean (as highlighted by Park 2016), building on the treatment of temporal indexical shift laid out in section 4.1. The chapter concludes with a brief comparison to the view from Anand (2006), followed by a look at the overall set of predictions made by the theory in its full form.

4.1 Temporal Indexicals

One piece missing from the picture as developed in chapter 3 is a treatment of temporal indexicals. Temporal elements in embedded clauses are extremely well-studied insofar as they constitute tense systems; yet the connection of embedded tenses to indexical shift is at best murky, given the availability of binding-based analyses of embedded tenses (e.g., Ogihara 1989, von Stechow 1995, Abusch 1997, Kusumoto 2005, Ogihara and Sharvit 2012, Bochnak, Hohaus, and Mucha 2019, among many others).[1] Independent temporal adverbials, like their counterparts in the locative domain, furnish an alternative source of evidence on temporal indexical shift—provided, that is, that we can rule out nonindexical analyses for *these* items.

This turns out to be a much more pressing issue crosslinguistically than in the case of indexical persons, because pairs of temporal adverbial translation equivalents across languages are not always identical in terms of indexicality.[2] As we saw in chapter 2, for instance, the Nez Perce temporal adverbial *watiisx* is typically translated with an English indexical element, 'yesterday' or

Extending the Theory 79

'tomorrow'. Yet *watiisx* behaves sharply differently from these elements, and more in line with nonindexical translation 'the next/previous day', in the scope of temporal quantification, (153). Similar remarks apply to other Nez Perce temporal adverbials, such as *kii taaqc* 'today/the same day', featured in (154).[3]

(153) *Nez Perce*
Ke-x mawa *pro* capaakayx-tato-Ø 'aatamoc, kaa **watiisx**
C-1 when 1SG wash-HAB.SG-PRES car.NOM then 1.day.away
hi-weeqi-yo'qa.
3SUBJ-rain-MODAL
Whenever I wash my car, the next day (#tomorrow) it rains.   = (37b)

(154) Ke-m kaa *pro* 'ew-'nii-se-Ø laqaas-na
C-2 then 2SG 3OBJ-give-IMPERF-PRES mouse-ACC
cicyuk'iisin' k'aɬk'aɬ, kaa *pro* hi-wewluq-o'qa qahasnim wee'ikt
cookie.NOM then 3SG 3SUBJ-want-MODAL milk.NOM
kii taaqc.
same.day
When you give a mouse a cookie, he wants some milk that same day
(#today).   = (36b)

This behavior suggests that *watiisx* and *kii taaqc* are not indexical elements, but rather (contain) bindable temporal anaphors. Why are they translated with indexicals in English, then? Pragmatic competition in English furnishes an explanation. In English, simplex expression *tomorrow* blocks complex expression *the next day* from referring to $t_c + 1$ in matrix contexts. Speakers wishing to refer to $t_c + 1$ must therefore use *tomorrow* and not *the next day* in English, even when translating from a language that lacks competition of this type. Thus *watiisx* receives a 'tomorrow' translation in (155), for instance, even though 'the next day' is more true to the Nez Perce original.[4]

(155) **Watiisx** *pro* ciq'aamqal-niin 'itamyaanwas-x pe-k-yu'.
1.day.away 1SG dog-with town-to S.PL-go-PROSP
Tomorrow I'm going into town with my dog.   = (37a)

The upshot, empirically, is that languages vary in whether they contain truly indexical temporal adverbials, and methodologically, is that translation with an indexical element furnishes a poor diagnostic for indexicality. The fact that a word is translated as 'today' or 'tomorrow' does not mean it is actually indexical.

These concerns have the consequence of significantly narrowing the range of evidence available on temporal indexical shift across languages. Evidence bearing on the existence and location of an OP$_{\text{TIME}}$ head can only come from languages where we can confirm that temporal adverbials are truly indexical.

Two contributions that meet this criterion come from recent work on Korean and on a dialect of (American) English.[5] These studies provide initial evidence that temporal indexicals do indeed shift in natural language, while at the same time allowing us to pinpoint the location of OP$_{TIME}$ in the functional sequence. In notable contrast to OP$_{LOC}$, this element occupies a very low position in the sequence, one below even OP$_{AUTH}$. Shifting of temporal indexicals is therefore possible even when person indexicals do not shift, and in complements of verbs that do not support other types of indexical shift.

A first example comes from work on Korean by Park (2016). Park demonstrates that a class of temporal expressions in this language cannot be bound by temporal quantifiers, as we expect for true indexicals. Thus *cikum* 'now' contrasts with *palhwa sikaney* 'at the speech time', (156); similar contrasts obtain for other temporal expressions such as *ece* 'yesterday' (vs. *palhwail cen nal* 'the day before the day of speech'), *onul* 'today' (vs. *palhwa tangil* 'the day of speech'), *nayil* 'tomorrow' (vs. *palhwail taumnal* 'the day after the day of speech').

(156) *Korean*
     Obama-ka   malhal ttyaymyun,
     Obama-NOM speaks when
     When Obama speaks, ...
    a. manhun salamtul-i   palhwa sikan-ey pakswuchinta.
        many   people-NOM speech time-at clap
        ... many people clap at the speech time.
    b. # manhun salamtul-i   cikum pakswuchinta.
        many   people-NOM now   clap
        ... many people clap now.
     (Park 2016, 14)

Yet these elements can optionally shift in attitude complements, including those that are clearly not clausal quotations. (In (157), for instance, the embedded *wh*-word has matrix scope.)

(157) Context: It is January 8th.
     Cinan   cwu-ey   Mary-ka   [nwuka   nayil   ttenanta-ko]
     Last   week-in   Mary-NOM [who-NOM tomorrow leave-C   ]
     malhayss-ni?
     said-Q
     Who did Mary say a week ago would leave on January {2nd/9th}?
     (Park 2016, (19b))

Korean temporal indexicals obey Shift Together, as predicted on the shifty operator approach:[6]

(158) Context: It is June 25. We are discussing Bob's strange work schedule. I consulted Bob's supervisor, John, on June 18, and am sharing with you the information I got from him.
Cinan cwu-ey John-i   [Bob-i   onul-pota   nayil   te
Last week-in John-NOM [Bob-NOM today-than tomorrow more
il-ul   (manhi) hal-geora] malhayess-ta.
work-ACC (a.lot) do-C.FUT] said-DECL
Literal: Last week John said that Bill work[FUT] more tomorrow than today.
   a. ✓ The plan was for Bob to work more on June 19 than on June 18.
   b. ✓ The plan was for Bob to work more on June 26 than on June 25.
   c. ✗ The plan was for Bob to work more on June 19 than on June 25.
   d. ✗ The plan was for Bob to work more on June 26 than on June 18.

And Korean temporal indexicals must be interpreted *de nunc* (temporal *de se*):

(159) John-i   cinancwu welyoil-ey [Mary-ka   onul   ttenanta-ko]
      John-NOM last.week Monday-on [Mary-NOM today leave-C   ]
      malhayssta.
      said
      John said last Monday$_i$ that Mary would leave that day$_i$.
   a. ✓ Last Monday John said, "Mary is leaving today."
   b. # John knew that Mary was going to leave on Monday last week. On that day, John somehow thought it was Sunday rather than Monday, and said, "Mary leaves tomorrow, on Monday."
(Park 2016, 29)

These facts suggest that the language contains an OP$_{TIME}$ operator that sits inside the scope of C. Further clues to the relative location of this operator come from the selectional behavior of verbs. Verbs of speech in Korean allow not only temporal indexical shift, (157), but also person shift:

(160) Mary-ka   [nwuka na-lul coahanta-ko] malhayss-ni?
      Mary-NOM [who   I-ACC like-C   ] said-Q
      Who did Mary$_i$ say likes {me/her$_i$}?
      (Park 2016, (18a))

Yet verbs of thought allow only temporal indexicals to shift, (161), not person indexicals, (162).

(161) Context: It is January 8th.
 Cinan   cwu-ey   Mary-ka   [nwuka   nayil   ttenanta-ko]
 Last   week-in Mary-NOM [who-NOM   tomorrow   leave-C   ]
 sayngkakayss-ni?
 thought-Q
 Who did Mary think a week ago would leave on January {2nd/9th}?
 (Park 2016, fn. 10)

(162) Mary-ka   [nwuka na-lul coahanta-ko] sayngkakayss-ni?
 Mary-NOM [who   I-ACC   like-C   ] thought-Q
 Who did Mary$_i$ think likes {me/✗her$_i$}?
 (Park 2016, (30b))

The availability of temporal indexical shift but not person indexical shift in the complement of *sayngkakayss* 'think' suggests that the complements to this verb may contain OP$_{TIME}$ but no other shifters. This means that the hierarchy of shifty operators should be articulated as in (163) (previewed in (152)), where OP$_{TIME}$ occupies the bottom-most position.

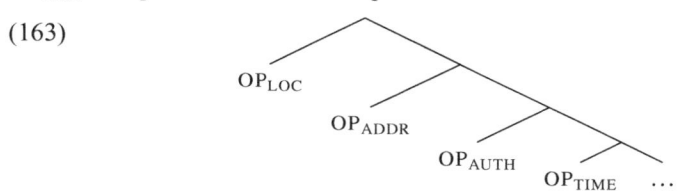

(163)
          OP$_{LOC}$
              OP$_{ADDR}$
                  OP$_{AUTH}$ OP$_{TIME}$ ...

Additional evidence for the low position of OP$_{TIME}$ comes from work on an indexical-shifting dialect of English by Anderson (2015). Based on both consultant judgments and numerous examples from corpora, Anderson reports a pattern wherein temporal adverbials cannot be bound by a temporal quantifier, (164), but nevertheless can shift in (nonquoted) attitude complements, for instance, (165). I will refer to the dialect that permits these patterns as "Anderson English."[7]

(164) # Whenever you wash your car, it rains tomorrow.
(165) % When I saw Kate a week ago, she said that she'd seen *Star Wars* yesterday. (acceptable in Anderson English)
 (Standard English paraphrase: When I saw Kate a week ago, she said that she'd seen *Star Wars* the previous day.)

In this dialect, as in standard English, person and locative embedded indexicals remain unshifted (Anderson 2015). Like complements to the Korean verb *sayngkakayss* 'think', shifty attitude complements in Anderson English must therefore contain OP$_{TIME}$ but no other shifters. This possibility is made available by the very low position of OP$_{TIME}$ in the functional sequence.

Anderson English also provides a final example of shifty indexicals that need not be interpreted *de se* and, in so doing, provides new evidence that C may appear anywhere in the functional sequence of shifty operators. We saw in chapter 3 that shifty first person in Dhaasanac imposes no *de se* requirement, revealing that C may appear below OP_{AUTH}.[8] In Anderson English, C may appear even lower—below OP_{TIME}—giving rise to shifty temporals without a *de nunc* requirement:

(166) Context: John is confused on Thursday and thinks the date is the 23rd, when it is really the 24th. On Thursday, John tells Sarah, "I'm coming on the 25th." But he doesn't show up until Saturday. A week later, Sarah is telling Bill what happened. She says:

% Last Thursday, John said that he was going to come over tomorrow, but he showed up on Saturday instead! (acceptable in Anderson English)

The absence of a *de nunc* requirement calls for a treatment of shifty attitude complements in this dialect where C attaches below the bottom-most shifter (the only shifter projected in this grammar):

(167)

```
        V
       / \
  OP_TIME  \
           / \
          C   TP
```

Anderson English thus adds new support for the existence of indexical shift without *de se* requirements, together with the hierarchy effect on *de se* requirements captured in generalization (G3).

4.2 Lexical Bundling

We now turn to a second extension on the core theory proposed in chapter 3, this time concerning the question of lexical bundling—that is, the question of whether languages may contain single lexical items that correspond semantically to more than one basic shifty operator, or alternatively, to both a shifty operator and some other material (e.g., C). I will suggest that both possibilities are instantiated in natural languages.

4.2.1 Verbs of Cognition and the Second Person

It is a common observation that verbs' selectional behavior is at least in part correlated with their meaning. In a theory where selectional behavior determines the possibilities for indexical shift in verbal complements, this observation suggests a potential constraint on selection by verbs of cognition. Cognition, unlike conversation, is at most a one-participant state; verbs of thinking and knowing lack addressees. This makes it reasonable to expect such verbs to select for a constituent containing no shifters beyond OP_{AUTH} (and OP_{TIME}). Given that there is no addressee, OP_{ADDR} (if present) would cause the addressee coordinate of context to be overwritten with ∅ (see (140))—an outcome that serves no plausible communicative goal.

This expectation is borne out in Slave. In the complement of *yeniwe̜* 'want/think' or *hudeli* 'want/think', first person optionally shifts, while second person always remains unshifted (Rice 1989, 1280–1289). This indicates that OP_{AUTH} is optionally present in these complements, but that OP_{ADDR} is not permitted; the complement of 'want/think' is at most (modulo CP^9) an $\text{OP}_{\text{AUTH}}\text{P}$.[10]

(168) *Slave*
[Sacho̜   nínaohjá   ] yeniwe̜.
[tomorrow 1SG.OPT.return] 3.want
Shifted interpretation: She wants to come back tomorrow.
(Rice 1989, 1281)

(169) Denexare [woji̜   ] yeniwe̜.
sister   [2SG.OPT.sing] 3.want
Sister wants you to sing.
(Rice 1989, 1281)

Yet a rather different pattern is attested in Nez Perce. In this language, on one hand, first-person arguments optionally shift in the complement of *neki* 'think', suggesting that OP_{AUTH} is optionally present:

(170) *Nez Perce*
Kii   hii-wes   'iniit   yox̂$_1$ ke   Jack
this.NOM 3SUBJ-be.PRES house.NOM RP.NOM   C   Jack.NOM
hi-neki-se-∅   ['iin   hani-∅-ya t_1].
3SUBJ-think-IMPERF-PRES [1SG.NOM make-P-REM.PAST]
This is the house that Jack$_j$ thinks { I / he$_j$ } built.

On the other hand, first-person shifting becomes impossible when a second-person pronoun is present within the complement.

(171) Lori   hi-neki-se-∅   ['ee   wees   qetu kuhet
Lori.NOM 3SUBJ-think-IMPERF-PRES [2SG.CL be.PRES more tall
'in-im-x   ].
1SG-OBL-from]
Lori$_l$ thinks that you are taller than { me / ✗her$_l$ }.

This pattern suggests (contrary to the expectation outlined above, but in keeping with the pattern from chapter 2) that a Nez Perce 'think' complement contains

OP$_{\text{AUTH}}$ iff it also contains OP$_{\text{ADDR}}$. In a 'think' complement that lacks any second persons, such as (170), the work of OP$_{\text{ADDR}}$ may take place with no harm done; the addressee coordinate of context is set to a defective value, but this value is not invoked. When a second person is present, though, as in (171), it is crucial that OP$_{\text{ADDR}}$ *not* be present, to avoid the defective value. Given the biconditional relationship between OP$_{\text{AUTH}}$ and OP$_{\text{ADDR}}$, this means that author shift must be avoided as well.

How can we model this relationship between OP$_{\text{ADDR}}$ and OP$_{\text{AUTH}}$ in Nez Perce and the difference between Nez Perce and Slave? The work could be done by selectional fiat, though at a cost. That is, the lexicon of Nez Perce could simply declare, as a matter of selectional features recorded in the verb's lexical entry, that the complement of *neki* 'think' either contains OP$_{\text{ADDR}}$ or it contains no shifters at all. Slave is different in that its verbs of cognition select at most OP$_{\text{AUTH}}$. The cost of this approach is that we give up on verb meaning as a functional source of constraint in determining selectional features. In Nez Perce, the OP$_{\text{ADDR}}$ head does nothing but create a defective contextual value in the complement of *neki* 'think'—but the verb selects for it all the same.

A more promising approach to these facts models the relationship between different types of person indexicals by adopting a central piece of Anand's (2006) shifty operator view. Instead of distinct OP$_{\text{ADDR}}$ and OP$_{\text{AUTH}}$ heads, we might treat Nez Perce as containing a unified OP$_{\text{PERS}}$ operator, optionally present in the complement of the verb *neki* 'think' (Deal 2014). The denotation for this operator reflects function composition of OP$_{\text{AUTH}}$ and OP$_{\text{ADDR}}$:

(172) $[\![\text{OP}_{\text{PERS}}]\!]^{c,i,g} = \lambda p \in D_{<\kappa,\kappa t>}.p(i)(c^{author(i)/author, addr(i)/addr})$

The data in (170)–(171) fall out if *neki* 'think' optionally selects this single operator. If the complement contains a second person, the operator must be absent, in order to avoid the defective value. In this case neither first nor second person shifts. If the complement does not contain a second person, on the other hand, the operator may be present and facilitate first person shift. Indeed, it is its ability to shift the author coordinate that presumably justifies the presence of the operator in the complement of 'think' in the first place. Shifting of the addressee coordinate is a side effect that comes from the fact that OP$_{\text{ADDR}}$ and OP$_{\text{AUTH}}$ have been bundled together in one lexical item.

These observations suggest that crosslinguistic variation in the semantics of shifty operators extends to *how many* coordinates of context a single operator shifts—that is, the extent of lexical bundling. Shift of first-person, second-person, and locative indexicals in Nez Perce is accomplished with two operators, OP$_{PERS}$ and OP$_{LOC}$, rather than three. As a lexical bundle of OP$_{ADDR}$ and OP$_{AUTH}$, OP$_{PERS}$ presumably inherits its position in the functional sequence from its more primitive components; it sits below OP$_{LOC}$. This accounts for the fact that locative shift requires person shift in Nez Perce, but that person shift does not require locative shift (as we saw in section 3.1.3): a clause may be projected up to OP$_{PERS}$P, shifting only person indexicals, or up to OP$_{LOC}$P, shifting both persons and locatives.

This first example of lexical bundling features two shifty operators bundled together. Could shifty operators be bundled together with other types of material—in particular, with C? This possibility offers a ready analysis of a pair of distinctive facts about indexical shift in Uyghur noted by Sudo (2012) and Shklovsky and Sudo (2014). In this language, on the proposal in (146), C sits between a *de se* OP$_{AUTH}$ head and a non–*de te* OP$_{ADDR}$ head. Let us now suppose that the Uyghur lexicon bundles these three pieces together into a single piece—call it COP. Appealing again to function composition for the meaning of a lexical bundle, $[\![\text{COP}]\!] = [\![\text{OP}_{ADDR}]\!] \circ [\![\text{C}]\!] \circ [\![\text{OP}_{AUTH}]\!]$, and thus syncategorematically (where $\mathbb{RCON}$ is defined as in (140)):

(173) $[\![\text{COP } \alpha]\!]^{c,i,g} = \lambda e. \forall i' \in \mathbb{RCON}(e) [\![\alpha]\!]^{c^{Author_{i'}/Author, ADDR(e)/Addr}, i', g}$

Given the semantic necessity of C (in the sense defined in chapter 3) in an attitude complement, this lexical bundling explains why indexical shift is obligatory in Uyghur (modulo scrambling, as seen in section 2.3): since the contribution of C is semantically obligatory, shifty operators are obligatory, too. At the same time, it accounts for a curious constraint on Uyghur verbs of cognition: second-person pronouns in the complements of these verbs are unacceptable. As Sudo (2012, 231) writes, "It should be emphasized here that the second-person pronouns in [(174b) and similar examples] are completely infelicitous/ungrammatical, and there is no felicitous interpretation where they are construed as the current hearer or somebody else." Thus (174b) lacks the interpretation 'Who does Ahmet believe that you like?'.

(174) *Uyghur*
    a.   Ahmet [*pro* kim-ni   jaxshi kör-imen   dep] bil-du?
         Ahmet [1SG who-ACC well   see-IMPF.1SG C] believe-IMPF.3
         Who does Ahmet believe that he likes?
    b. * Ahmet [*pro* kim-ni   jaxshi kör-isen   dep] bil-du?
         Ahmet [2SG who-ACC well   see-IMPF.2SG C] believe-IMPF.3
    (Sudo 2012, 231)

These facts are as expected in a language where not just OP$_{ADDR}$ and OP$_{AUTH}$, but also C, are bundled together. Since C is part of the bundle, the language does not have the option of simply omitting all context-shifting material when a second-person pronoun is present in a cognition complement. (The contrast here is Nez Perce (171), where the shifter can [and must] be omitted.) The result is that second-person pronouns are simply not interpretable in these complements. Context shift is obligatory both for first person and for second person—regardless of whether this forces second person to receive a defective value—as a consequence of lexical bundling.[11]

4.2.2 Temporal/Locative Bundling in Korean

These observations on lexical bundling in Nez Perce and Uyghur allow for two initial generalizations about lexical bundles to be made. First, as seen in Uyghur, a lexical bundle is obligatory if any notional part thereof is necessary for semantic composition. Since C is semantically obligatory, any bundle whose meaning subsumes it is obligatory as well. Second, as seen in Nez Perce, the attachment site of a lexical bundle in the functional sequence is inherited from the attachment sites of its semantic parts. Since OP_{ADDR} and OP_{AUTH} attach below OP_{LOC}, the lexical bundle containing these two pieces attaches below OP_{LOC} as well. These observations could be thought of as semantic and syntactic aspects of the same generalization: lexical bundles inherit their properties from their semantic parts.

This generalization constrains the way we might think about the behavior of lexical bundles of operators that do not occupy structurally adjacent positions in hierarchy (163).[12] Suppose, for instance, OP_{LOC} and OP_{TIME} were lexically bundled in a particular language; we might call the bundle OP_{ADV}. Where would this element attach? If its behavior is inherited from its semantic parts, either a very high position (inherited from OP_{LOC}) or a very low position (inherited from OP_{TIME}) could be justified. If OP_{ADV} could freely attach in either location, we expect a language containing it to demonstrate a pattern rather different from the Nez Perce pattern of person and locative indexicals discussed in section 3.1.3. In Nez Perce, locative shift requires an OP_{LOC} head which is present only if OP_{PERS} is also present; OP_{LOC} always attaches higher than OP_{PERS}. In an OP_{ADV} language, on the other hand, locative shift could be accomplished in clauses without any person shift (if OP_{ADV} were associated to in its low position) and person shift could be accomplished in clauses without any locative shift (if OP_{ADV} were associated to its high position).

This is precisely the pattern of indexical shift that Park (2016) documents in Korean. Her observations come against a backdrop of co-shifting effects between locative and temporal indexicals in Korean, suggesting that both are indeed sensitive to the same shifty operator (OP_{ADV}):

(175) *Korean*
Context: John and Mary are having a conversation in Boston on July 3rd. John says:
Tom-i   ece   cenyek New York-eyse
Tom-NOM yesterday night   New York-at
[Sue-ka   ece   yeki-ey wassta-ko] malhayssta.
[Sue-NOM yesterday here-at came-C] said
Literal: Tom said in New York last night that Sue came here yesterday.
a.   'here' = Boston, 'yesterday' = July 2nd   (no shift)
b.   'here' = NY, 'yesterday' = July 1st   (both shift)
c. ✗ 'here' = NY, 'yesterday' = July 2nd   (location shift only)
d. ✗ 'here' = Boston, 'yesterday' = July 1st   (time shift only)
(Park 2016, (25))

Reading (a) arises if OP$_{ADV}$ is absent, leaving both *ece* 'yesterday' and *yeki* 'here' to draw on the utterance context; reading (b) arises if OP$_{ADV}$ is present, shifting coordinates of context relevant to both indexicals; readings (c) and (d), if OP$_{LOC}$ and OP$_{TIME}$ cannot be projected independently, cannot be derived. Given this reasoning, this bundling effect immediately explains why example (176), containing both a person and a locative indexical, is ambiguous in four ways, rather than just three:

(176) Context: John and Mary are having a conversation in Seoul. John says:
Tom-i   New York-eyse [nay-ka yeki-eyse thayenassta-ko]
Tom-NOM New York-at   [I-NOM here-at   be.born-C   ]
malhayssta.
said
Literal: Tom said in New York that I was born here.
a.   'I' = John, 'here' = Seoul   (no shift)
b.   'I' = John, 'here' = New York   (location shift)
c.   'I' = Tom, 'here' = Seoul   (person shift)
d.   'I' = Tom, 'here' = New York   (both shift)
(Park 2016, (32))

Park argues independently for a bundled OP$_{PERS}$ shifter in Korean, parallel to that proposed for Nez Perce earlier in this chapter; I adopt this proposal here. In these terms, reading (a) arises if no shifter is present; reading (b) arises if only OP$_{ADV}$ is present (occupying a low position); reading (c) arises if only OP$_{PERS}$ is present (OP$_{ADV}$ having been postponed until its higher attachment site); reading (d) arises if both OP$_{PERS}$ and OP$_{ADV}$ are present (in either order). Full four-way ambiguity follows here because OP$_{ADV}$ may associate to a position either above or below OP_{PERS}, having derived its attachment site from the union of those of its semantic pieces OP_{LOC} and OP_{TIME}. Internal to Korean, lexical bundling thus provides a unified explanation for temporal/locative co-shifting effects as in (175) and locative/person independence as in (176); crosslinguistically, it explains the difference between Korean (where person and locative shift are independent of one another) and Nez Perce (where locative shift implies person shift).

4.3 Remarks on Single-Operator Analyses

As noted in section 4.2.1, the recognition of lexical bundling among shifty operators makes the theory presented here similar in certain key respects to the theory of indexical shift outlined by Anand (2006). Instead of stacking shifty operators, shifting of multiple coordinates of context is accomplished on Anand's account by individual operators with increasing control over contextual coordinates:

(177) a. $[\![OP_{AUTH}]\!]^{c,i,g} = \lambda p \in D_{<\kappa,\kappa t>}.p(i)(c^{author(i)/author})$
b. $[\![OP_{PERS}]\!]^{c,i,g} = \lambda p \in D_{<\kappa,\kappa t>}.p(i)(c^{author(i)/author, addr(i)/addr})$
c. $[\![OP_\forall]\!]^{c,i,g} = \lambda p \in D_{<\kappa,\kappa t>}.p(i)(c^{author(i)/author, addr(i)/addr, loc(i)/loc, time(i)/time})$

Of course, the denotations for these operators are precisely those that would be obtained via lexical bundling of the independently projectable operators defended here.[13] The difference? While the present view *allows* for lexical bundling, it does not *require* it; languages vary in the extent to which they bundle operators together, and the behavior of bundled operators reflects the behavior of their lexical subcomponents with respect to the functional sequence (as we saw in particular in the case of locative and temporal indexicals in Korean). On Anand's view, by contrast, at most one shifty operator is present on the edge of a clause with indexical shift, and there is no functional hierarchy among shifters. Given this, the hierarchy in (G2) must ultimately follow from a constraint on the lexicon: a language may simply not contain an operator that shifts location, for instance, without that same operator also shifting person. (The formulation of (G2) given here has been updated to include temporal indexicals.)

(G2) Implicational hierarchy of indexical classes (final version)
Within and across languages, the possibility of indexical shift is determined by the hierarchy Time > 1st > 2nd > Loc. Indexicals of a certain class undergo shift in a particular verbal complement only if indexicals of classes farther to the left undergo shift as well.

The following must be impossible lexical items:

(178) a. $[\![\text{OP}_{\text{ADDR.ONLY}}]\!]^{c,i,g} = \lambda p \in D_{<\kappa,\kappa t>}.p(i)(c^{addr(i)/addr})$
   b. $[\![\text{OP}_{\text{LOC.ONLY}}]\!]^{c,i,g} = \lambda p \in D_{<\kappa,\kappa t>}.p(i)(c^{loc(i)/loc})$

The "single-operator" approach might be thought to present conceptual advantages over the operator-stacking view by avoiding questions about the etiology of the syntactic mechanisms to which I have appealed. While I have stated a hierarchy for indexical shifters, viz. (163), I have not explained why the hierarchy should be this way. Fair enough; but we must remind ourselves that the problem is much more general. Both in the clausal domain and in the nominal domain, as a scientific community, we do not know *why* functional sequences exist, but we know that they *do* exist. The absence of a known explanation for the known facts should be met with a research project, not with empirical denial. Indeed, significant work has begun on the ultimate explanation for functional sequences (e.g., Hacquard 2006; Ramchand and Svenonius 2014; Scontras, Degen, and Goodman 2017; Ramchand 2018) which can be expected to prove fruitful well into the future. Similar remarks may be made in response to the same objection in the case of the hierarchy of verb complement sizes, where functional explanations are under development (e.g., Cristofaro 2003, and references there). Thus this objection strikes me as premature.

Where the theories are more directly comparable is in empirical domains, and here the advantages of the operator-stacking view come into focus. Among the relevant empirical dimensions is the possibility of variation in the range of permissible indexical shift on a verb-by-verb basis ("mixed indexical shift by verb"): the operator-stacking approach, but not the single-operator view, predicts that a language that allows shift in the complement of both speech and thought verbs may allow more shifty coordinates with speech verbs than with thought verbs, but not vice versa. This follows on the operator-stacking view because an increase in syntactic structure facilitates an increase in operators, which in turn increases the number of shifty coordinates. We have seen evidence for this situation in Korean in section 4.1: while verbs of speech allow both person and adverbial indexicals to shift, verbs of thought allow only adverbial shift:

(179) *Korean*
Context: It is January 8th.
Cinan cwu-ey   Mary-ka   [nwuka   nayil   ttenanta-ko]
Last   week-in Mary-NOM [who-NOM tomorrow leave-C   ]
sayngkakayss-ni?
thought-Q
Who did Mary think a week ago would leave on January {2nd/9th}?
(Park 2016, fn. 10)

(180) Mary-ka   [nwuka   na-lul   coahanta-ko]   sayngkakayss-ni?
Mary-NOM   [who   I-ACC   like-C   ]   thought-Q
Who did Mary$_i$ think likes {me/✗her$_i$}?
(Park 2016, (30b))

While the single-operator view can stipulate such patterns via arbitrary lexical selection, it cannot make a connection to other respects in which the complements of speech verbs are syntactically larger than those of verbs of thought. This means that it also does not provide a straightforward explanation for the absence of the opposite pattern of mixed indexical shift by verb, where speech complements allow fewer types of shift than thought complements do.

The single-operator view as outlined by Anand (2006) also differs empirically from the operator-stacking approach defended here in that it disallows non–*de se* shifty indexicals (which, after all, have been discovered after 2006). While revisions might be made to the single-operator view in this respect, these do not point to a straightforward explanation for (G3) (updated here to include temporal indexicals):

(G3) Implicational hierarchy of *de se* requirements   (final version)
Requirements for *de se* interpretation conform to the hierarchy Time > 1st > 2nd > Loc. Indexicals of a certain class require *de se* interpretation only if indexicals of classes farther to the left require it as well.

For the contrast between Uyghur second person and its necessarily *de te* counterpart in Zazaki and Nez Perce, for instance, Sudo (2012, section 18.4) appeals to semantic variation in the meaning of second-person pronouns: in Zazaki and Nez Perce they are pure indexicals, but in Uyghur they are concealed definite descriptions. A version of this proposal for Uyghur second-person pronoun *sen* versus Nez Perce second-person pronoun *'iim* is shown in (181).[14]

(181) a. Uyghur: $[\![sen\ \text{'2sg'}]\!]^{c,i,g}$ = the individual that $author(c)$ is talking to in $w(i)$
b. Nez Perce: $[\![\ 'iim\ \text{'2sg'}]\!]^{c,i,g} = addr(c)$

By localizing the source of non–*de se* indexicality in the shifty elements themselves, this proposal opens the door to non–*de se* readings of potentially any type of indexical in any language. In particular, it predicts that a language may have non–*de te* second person but fully shiftable *de hic* locative indexicals, in violation of (G3). Similar remarks apply on the proposal from Pearson (2015), which is aimed at accounting for non–*de se* readings of logophoric pronouns. Pearson proposes that an inherently *de se* element (a logophor, in her study) may occur as the argument of a concept generator variable (Percus and Sauerland 2003a), giving rise to a *de re* reading rather than a *de se* reading. If applied to shifty indexicals, this type of mechanism predicts even greater freedom in which indexicals receive *de se* interpretations, as two indexicals of the same type in the same clause could potentially differ in whether they are read *de se* or *de re*.[15] Finally, no greater constraint would be imposed by a picture that ties variation in *de se* requirements to variation in the "centeredness" of attitudinal quantification, for instance by treating Uyghur $[\![C]\!]$ as imposing no *de te* requirement:[16]

(182) $[\![C^0\ \alpha]\!]^{c,i,g} = \lambda e.\forall i' \in \mathrm{RCON}_{Uyghur}(e) [\![\alpha]\!]^{c,i',g}$

where $i' \in \mathrm{RCON}_{Uyghur}(e)$ iff
a. $w(i')$ is a member of the content of e
b. $author(i')$ is an individual in $w(i')$ that $\mathrm{EXT}(e)$ identifies in e as herself
c. $addr(i')$ is an individual in $w(i')$ **who is a counterpart of the addressee of** e
d. $loc(i')$ is a location in $w(i')$ that $\mathrm{EXT}(e)$ identifies in e as her spatial location
e. $time(i')$ is a time in $w(i')$ that $\mathrm{EXT}(e)$ identifies in e as her temporal location

This style of change in the modal accessibility relation can in principle be made for any coordinate(s) of the index, with no prediction that non–*de te* second persons should in any way correlate with the interpretations available to other shifty indexicals. (G3), again, remains unexplained.

These remarks serve to illustrate how the core proposals of this book rest, fundamentally, on empirical claims. The argumentation just given can be defeated, empirically, by the demonstration of non–*de se* shifty indexicals which, in the context of the full set of indexicals in their language, fail to obey the hierarchy in (G3). Likewise, the argument for operator stacking can be defeated, empirically, by the demonstration of a language where indexicals do not shift in finite clauses with a richer left periphery but do shift in those with a more impoverished left periphery.

4.4 Summary of Predictions

The theory now before us makes several novel, testable predictions highlighted at the end of section 4.3, as well as various others of crosslinguistic scope that we may now put forward. These draw from the initial generalizations of section 3.1 as refined by the investigations of sections 4.1 (on time) and 4.2 (on lexical bundling), and are in addition to those laid out in chapter 2 (e.g., specificity to speech and attitude reports; Shift Together / Local Determination; sensitivity to the structure of the embedded clause).

First, indexical shift is constrained by (G1):

(G1) Implicational hierarchy of verbs
Verbs of speech are more likely to allow indexical shift in their complement than are verbs of thought, which in turn are more likely to allow indexical shift in their complement than are verbs of knowledge.

The structural explanation for this generalization predicts that syntactic diagnostics of complement size will correlate with the shiftability of indexicals. Clauses that allow more embedded root phenomena (cp. Heycock 2006) will be more likely to allow indexical shift in the first place, and more willing to allow multiple types of indexicals to shift, than their counterparts that allow fewer embedded root phenomena or disallow these phenomena altogether.

Second, indexical shift is constrained in three different ways by the functional hierarchy of shifty operators (183). (Two of these ways are initially articulated in (G2) and (G3).)

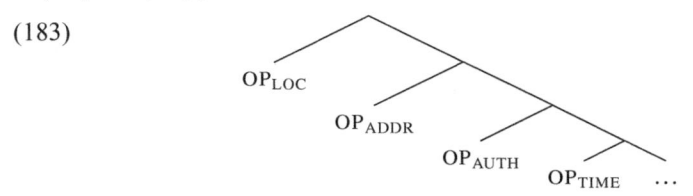

(183) OP_{LOC}
          OP_{ADDR}
            OP_{AUTH} OP_{TIME} ...

The first effect of the hierarchy concerns co-shifting effects among classes of indexicals. Within and across languages, indexicals of a certain class undergo shift only if indexicals of classes further down on the hierarchy defined by (183) undergo shift as well, (G2).

(G2) Implicational hierarchy of indexical classes

Within and across languages, the possibility of indexical shift is determined by the hierarchy Time > 1st > 2nd > Loc. Indexicals of a certain class undergo shift in a particular verbal complement only if indexicals of classes farther to the left undergo shift as well.

Apart from cases in which indexicals differ in their level of embedding (as discussed for Nez Perce and Uyghur in chapter 2), exceptions may arise only in case of lexical bundling of nonadjacent operators (e.g., OP_{LOC} and OP_{TIME}); any such case should be diagnosable by co-shifting effects between indexicals of the relevant types, as shown for Korean in (175). Thus a language with shifty author indexicals and shifty temporal indexicals will always have temporal shift in clauses with author shift, except if temporal indexicals are required to shift together with addressee or locative indexicals.[17]

The second effect of the hierarchy concerns requirements of *de se* interpretation, (G3).

(G3) Implicational hierarchy of *de se* requirements

Requirements for *de se* interpretation conform to the hierarchy Time > 1st > 2nd > Loc. Indexicals of a certain class require *de se* interpretation only if indexicals of classes farther to the left require it as well.

Within a particular language, the range of shifty indexicals that are required to have *de se* interpretations can be picked out only by a contiguous portion of hierarchy (183) that begins from the bottom. Thus a language may impose this requirement on temporal indexicals only; on temporal and author indexicals only; on temporal, author, and addressee indexicals only; or on all indexicals.[18] It is not possible for a language to impose the requirement on a noncontiguous segment of the hierarchy or on a segment that does not begin from the bottom. Thus a language with both temporal and author indexicals may not impose *de se* requirements only on author indexicals but not on temporals.

This prediction differs from its counterpart regarding co-shifting effects in that no caveat regarding lexical bundling is necessarily in order, on the assumption that bundled elements may be given unified (i.e., unambiguous) denotations while nevertheless inheriting their attachment site from the attachment sites of their semantic parts. Consider now the case of a hypothetical language where shifty person indexicals but not shifty temporal indexicals require interpretation *de se*. To account for this via lexical bundling, we would need to posit structure (184a), where temporal indexicals are shifted by an OP_{ADV} head in a high position. Because lexical bundles inherit their attachment sites from both ingredients to the bundle, such a language should also allow structure (184b), where OP$_{ADV}$ occupies its low position. Yet no unified denotation for OP$_{ADV}$ is possible here. It must be index-based (*de se*) in (184b), but event-based (non–*de se*) in (184a). If shifty operators within individual languages are not ambiguous in this way, then lexical bundling will not offer a way around the generalization about the hierarchy effect in *de se* interpretation.

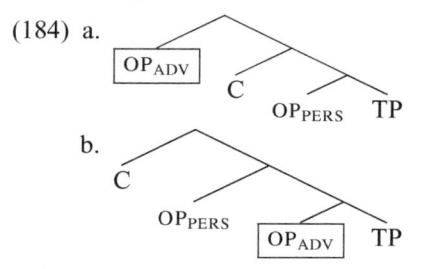

(184) a.

```
        OP_ADV
              C
                OP_PERS  TP
```

b.

```
    C
      OP_PERS
              OP_ADV  TP
```

A third way the hierarchy constrains indexical shift relates to the interactions among co-shifting effects, optionality, and interpretation *de se*. If the meanings of lexical bundles are derived by function composition, then *de se* and non–*de se* shifters are not suitable for bundling: where OP$_1$ is an event-based (non–*de se*) shifter, and OP$_2$ is an index-based (*de se*) shifter, $[\![\text{OP}_1]\!] \circ [\![\text{OP}_2]\!]$ is not well-formed.[19] These elements may only be bundled together if C is also part of the bundle; this predicts that the bundle should not be optional.[20] Thus languages with a co-shifting requirement between indexical class α and indexical class β, where shift of α and β is optional, will always be uniform in the imposition of *de se* requirements across these classes. If one must be interpreted *de se*, both must be.[21]

In general, the role of a functional hierarchy in constraining indexical shift predicts that the same type of constraints discussed herein will extend to any new type of indexical shift beyond those discussed thus far—for example, shift of a "judge" coordinate, as in McCready (2007) and Deal and O'Connor (2011), building on Lasersohn (2005) and Stephenson (2007), or shift of an "origo" coordinate, as in Korotkova (2016). (For some comments on the implications of these proposals, especially Korotkova's, see appendix A.) Shift of any new type raises the immediate question of where the corresponding operator should sit in the functional sequence. Particular hypotheses in this regard will now yield immediate predictions regarding verb subcategorization, co-shifting effects, and *de se* interpretation across the range of indexicals present in a given language.

5 Beyond Indexical Shift

At the heart of the proposals of this book is a reduction of the facts on indexical shift to more general (and more familiar) facts in the theory of grammar. The patterns concerning which indexicals shift, and with which verbs, reduce to a familiar type of functional sequencing effect, coupled with familiar variation in the size of the complements that attitude verbs allow. The pattern concerning *de se* interpretation ties back to the role of event arguments in grammar, together with an independently proposed style of analysis for the finite complementizer. Resting on these foundations, the theory provides a set of predictions, summarized in the previous chapter, which together delimit a constrained typology for indexical shift across languages. In this chapter I turn to the question of how this typology can be further tested on new languages and data sets beyond those discussed thus far, primarily by investigating the question of which particular phenomena in fact instantiate indexical shift (and which are best analyzed in some other way). As we will see, several types of factors may give the impression of indexical shift while nevertheless showing distinctive characteristics of other types of phenomena. I will sort these into two general categories: those that feature indexicals, but not indexical *shift*, and those that do not feature indexicals at all.

Indexicals that are not shifted may nevertheless show shiftlike behavior in cases of quotation—a phenomenon that gives rise to characteristic demonstrative or iconic behaviors (such as the use of expressive phonology that portrays a reported speaker) as well as opacity for phenomena such as *de re* ascription, *wh*-movement, and NPI licensing. On the basis of these behaviors, I argue for a quotation-based analysis of two phenomena that have been analyzed as indexical shift by some previous authors. The first is Free Indirect Discourse, found in written and especially in literary registers of many familiar languages; in analyzing this phenomenon as a form of (mixed) quotation, I follow Maier (2014b, 2015, 2017). The second is the phenomenon of Role Shift in French Sign Language (LSF) and American Sign Language (ASL), where my adoption of a quotation analysis follows Davidson (2015) and Maier (2018).

Any test of proposals about indexical shift requires attention to what is actually indexical. For adverbials, we have seen variation in this respect even among translation equivalents in comparing Nez Perce and English temporal adverbials in chapter 2. Locative adverbials are ripe for exploration along similar lines: a language where locatives seemingly shift but person indexicals do not (and where locative and temporal elements do not show the co-shifting requirement noted for Korean in section 4.2.2) may well be a language in which locative adverbials are not indexical. We are well-acquainted with nonindexical locative adverbials in the form of items like English *there*. As discussed in connection with (155), the caution is that elements that are translated by speakers with indexical words like English *here* may nevertheless have bindable, nonindexical meanings.

In the second part of this chapter I consider additional types of indexical shift-like phenomena where, I argue, the characteristic semantics of indexicality is likewise simply absent; these involve not adverbials but pronouns and/or agreement. The first is the (aptly named) phenomenon of "fake indexicality," where, under binding by a focus operator, indexical meaning is either not present at all semantically (von Stechow 2003, Kratzer 2009, Sudo 2012, inter alia) or else not present on the focus dimension (Jacobson 2012, Sauerland 2013, inter alia). The second subsumes a group of phenomena described in the literature under various names, including *first person logophoricity* (Curnow 2002), *egophoricity* (Coppock and Wechsler 2018), *local logophoricity* (Anand 2006), and *indexiphoricity* (Deal 2018b). Following Anand (2006) and Deal (2018b), I argue that distinguishing this type of nonindexical element from true first-person indexicals requires careful attention to multiclause embedding and to the syntactic position of nominals that are read *de re*.

5.1 From Mixed Quotation to Free Indirect Discourse

A potential confound in testing the predictions laid out in section 4.4 concerns quotation—in particular partial or "mixed" quotation, that is, quotation of material other than a full clause. In (185), for instance, only the embedded verb is quoted, and in (186) only the embedded object is; extensive discussion of similar cases can be found in Cappelen and Lepore (1997, 2017), De Brabanter (2010), and Maier (2014a, forthcoming), among many others.

(185) Bush is saying that you and I "misunderestimated" him yesterday.
(186) He now plans to make a new, more powerful absinthe that he says will have "a more elegant, refined taste than the one I'm making now." (Cumming 2003)

The challenge of such cases is that they (partially) resist application of the opacity diagnostics discussed in chapter 2. So long as it is not within the quotation itself, material in the same clause as the quotation is clearly not opaque for phenomena such as Ā-movement; in (186), for instance, the subject of the complement clause under 'say' is relativized, but the object is quoted. Meanwhile, cases of mixed quotation may contain indexicals either outside (185) or inside (186) the quotation, in the latter case potentially giving the impression of indexical shift.

Mixed quotation of the type shown in (185) and (186) is commonplace in the written register of English and other familiar languages, especially in journalistic prose. In speech, it is much more marked, often coming with distinctive gestures (e.g., "air quotes") or marked prosody (Kasimir 2008). Studies of this prosodic behavior have emphasized that prosodic cues are primarily used not to indicate boundaries of quotation, but rather in connection with the imitative, iconic component that all quotation shares: Sams (2010), for instance, writes that "speakers use prosodic cues as tools for conveying to their recipients how these words could or would have been said instead of as a cue to the onset of a quotation." In an example like (185), if the speaker adopts a special affect for the pronunciation of the word *misunderestimated*, this affect is understood as representing Bush in some way. This nonlinguistic representational prosody in turn indicates, in spoken language, the mixed quotation status of (185). Just as for full clausal quotation, this effect is not explained if partial quotation is itself modeled in terms of pure context shift, at least given a standard understanding of contextual coordinates (Maier 2016).

These considerations are relevant in assessing the extension of indexical shift analyses to Free Indirect Discourse (FID), as proposed by Schlenker (1999, 2004, 2011), Sharvit (2008), Eckardt (2014), and Reboul, Delfitto, and Fiorin (2016). These analyses are motivated by the well-known phenomenon of temporal and locative adverbial indexicals behaving in FID as though shifty:

(187) John pondered all that had transpired in the past year. After the move, he thought they'd be happy in Tulsa, but he'd been wrong, terribly wrong. Living **here**, in this house, was part of the problem! **Now** he had to reconsider all their options.

(lightly modified from Roberts 2015)

I will contend that this pattern represents not a true case of indexical shift, but rather a quotation-based look-alike phenomenon. It should be noted that, like the examples in (185) and (186), FID possesses a mix of quotative and nonquotative properties. Its primary nonquotation-like behaviors concern pronouns and tenses, which show their standard behavior from indirect discourse.

Thus in (188), the attitude holder is referred to with a third-person pronoun (*him*) and the simple past tense that would be used in a quotation is replaced with a pluperfect:

(188)   He was flaming mad. They had treated him like a total outsider yesterday.

But FID also behaves like quotation in several ways that are quite striking from the perspective of the indexical shift phenomena explored in the previous chapters of this book. First, like other types of quotations, but in contrast to the behavior of indexical shift, FID clauses do not allow descriptions to be read *de re* (Banfield 1973, Schlenker 2004, Sharvit 2008). Thus (189) cannot describe a situation where John does not believe that the person who likes him is the dean (for instance, because he mistakenly thinks this individual is the provost):

(189)   The dean liked him today(, thought John).
           (Sharvit 2008)

This contrasts with the behavior for indexical shift we have seen for Nez Perce, for instance, where a shifty indexical may readily be clausemate with a description read *de re*:

(190)   *Nez Perce*
           Context: Beth told me she met Harold. She doesn't know he is a teacher. When we are in class, I say to someone else:
           Beth-nim hi-hi-n-e   pro   [*pro*
           Beth-ERG 3SUBJ-say-P-REM.PAST 1SG.ACC [1SG
           'e-wewkuny-Ø-e   sepehitemenew'etuu-ne].
           3OBJ-meet-P-REM.PAST teacher-ACC   ]
           Beth told me she met the teacher.

Parallel data are reported for indexical shift in Georgian (Thivierge 2019), Navajo (Speas 2000), and Tsez (Polinsky 2015): shifted indexicals may be clausemates with descriptions read *de re*.

Second, Schlenker (2004, 2011) notes that FID clauses must be "faithful to the words used," to the extent that (191a,b) are not mutually entailing:

(191)   a.   Tomorrow Peter or Sam would come, Ann thought.
           b.   Tomorrow Sam or Peter would come, Ann thought.

There is no such verbatim requirement imposed on clauses containing indexical shift, as we have seen for examples such as (192):

(192) *Nez Perce*
Context: On day 1, Mary says:
Fido-nm hi-ken'ip-Ø-e *pro*.
Fido-ERG 3SUBJ-bite-P-REM.PAST 1SG.ACC
(Fido bit me.)

On day 2, I say to you:
a. ✓ Meeli hi-i-caa-qa
   Mary.NOM 3SUBJ-say-IMPERF-REC.PAST
   [hi-ken'ip-Ø-e *pro* Fido-nm].
   [3SUBJ-bite-P-REM.PAST 1SG.ACC Fido-ERG]
   Literal: Mary said, bit me Fido.
b. ✓ Meeli hi-i-caa-qa [ciq'aamqal-nim
   Mary.NOM 3SUBJ-say-IMPERF-REC.PAST [dog-ERG
   hi-ken'ip-Ø-e *pro*].
   3SUBJ-bite-P-REM.PAST 1SG.ACC]
   Literal: Mary said, the/a dog bit me.

Parallel data on paraphrase are reported for Zazaki (Anand 2006, 88) and Matses (Munro et al. 2012). Indeed, it is expected that such manipulations are possible in any language with indexical shift, given the evidence against verbatim requirements demonstrated with the help of NPI licensing or Ā-extraction for the many languages discussed throughout this book.

Third, Sharvit (2008) and Maier (2014b, 2017) show that FID may demonstrate extralinguistic aspects of an original thought or utterance, just as quotation classically does. Phonological features of a speaker's accent are seen in (193); hesitations and pauses are seen in (194); and (195) displays a range of dialectal features in prosody, segmental phonology, and syntax.

(193) Ah well, her fathaire would shoorly help her out, she told John in her thick French accent. (Maier 2014b)

(194) Err.... yes... ahhmm... yes she would be delighted(, she muttered as she shook his hand).
(Sharvit 2008)

(195) Most of the great flame-throwers were there and naturally, handling Big John de Conquer and his works. How he had done everything big on earth, then went up tuh heben without dying atall. Went up there picking a guitar and got all de angels doing the ring-shout round and round de throne.
(Z. N. Hurston, *Their Eyes Were Watching God*, 187; Maier 2014b)

While this type of effect is commonplace in quotation, data of this type are not standardly reported in indexical shift.

These types of facts reveal the same sort of iconicity and representational use of language in FID as in straightforward quotation, whether of a full clause or a subclausal component. Accordingly, on the analysis developed by Maier (2014b, 2015, 2017), FID is, essentially, quotation; it is distinguished from more standard types of quotation only in that pronouns and tenses are unquoted, motivated by pragmatic "attraction" to the prominent character and time of the story.[1] Unquotation of these elements means that FID is in fact a species of mixed quotation. Quotation of all material other than pronouns and tenses results in the three ways we have just reviewed in which FID differs from the indexical shift phenomena this book has been concerned with:[2]

(196) Contrasting indexical shift, FID, and quotation

	Indexical shift	FID	Quotation
De re descriptions possible?	Yes	No	No
Verbatim requirement?	No	Yes	Yes
Reproduction of extralinguistic factors?	No	Yes	Yes

Cases of apparently "shifty" locative and temporal indexicals in FID, as in (187), result simply because these elements remain within the scope of the quotation. But first-person indexicals do not shift in FID, because these elements are unquoted; Maier (2017) hypothesizes that this unquotation results because the speaker prefers to use indexicals that relate to the most salient speech act participants.

(197) Charlene was sitting in front of me. She looked at me uneasily. Would I hire her? Did she make a good impression?
(Eckardt 2014, 181)

The complex pragmatics required to effect this mix of quotation and unquotation presumably explain why FID is confined to a written, literary style, given the distinctive pragmatics of that genre. If this hypothesis is correct, it means that FID is unlikely to provide a compelling analysis for a hypothetical newly discovered linguistic pattern found outside of similar confines of genre. FID is a potential confound for a putative case of indexical shift found in a literary corpus more so than for a putative case found in the commonplace spoken (or signed) language of a human group.

5.2 Sign Language Role Shift

An additional indexical shift-like phenomenon potentially best analyzed as quotation shows the distinctive demonstrative or iconic component found in FID without its particular partial-quotation character. This is the case most prominently in certain well-studied sign languages for the Role Shift construction, "in which the signer breaks eye gaze with the addressee and may move his/her body slightly to signal that the words used belong to somebody else" (Davidson 2015, 478). While sign linguists have often analyzed Role Shift in ways parallel to analyses of quotation in written and spoken language (e.g., as "constructed dialogue"; see Liddell and Metzger 1998 and discussion in Lillo-Martin 2012, Davidson 2015, Maier 2018), analyses in terms of indexical shift are proposed by Quer (2005, 2011) and Schlenker (2017a,b).

Strong evidence in favor of the quotative analysis, at least for LSF and ASL, comes from two sources. First, the quotative analysis readily accommodates the behavior of extralinguistic gesture and affect in role shift: nonlinguistic material (such as a happy face) produced while signing a Role Shift clause is obligatorily attributed to the reported attitude holder, rather than just the overall utterer/signer (Schlenker 2017b; on the nongrammaticized status of this material, see Liddell and Metzger 1998). This is parallel to the interpretation of nonstandard linguistic features in quotation in examples like (185). Second is a set of facts showing the characteristic opacity of clausal quotes: in LSF, Role Shift clauses are opaque for *wh*-movement, NPI licensing, and *de re* readings, and require that all indexical expressions be evaluated against the reported context. The ASL data are similar overall, though the status of *wh*-extraction remains controversial. (Schlenker's consultant accepts it, though Lillo-Martin's [1995, 164–165] *wh*-data are different, and evidence on dislocation from Lee et al. 1997 likewise suggests opacity of Role Shift clauses.) If we set aside the empirically disputed case of *wh*-extraction in ASL, this overall body of facts is readily accounted for if Role Shift clauses in LSF and ASL are full (i.e., not mixed) clausal quotations.[3] No wonder, then, that the patterns in these languages differ from those of languages with indexical shifting regarding descriptions *de re* and NPI licensing, as well as perhaps *wh*-extraction.

It should be noted that the case for a pure indexical shift analysis of Role Shift could possibly be better in other sign languages, such as Catalan Sign Language (Quer 2005, 2011, 2013), Danish Sign Language (Engberg-Pedersen 1995), or German Sign Language (Herrmann and Steinbach 2012, Hübl 2013, Hübl, Maier, and Steinbach 2019), given that not all elements must shift to the perspective of the reported speaker in these languages. Quer's (2013) data are of particular interest in connection with the present proposal, in that he reports that certain temporal adverbs shift in Catalan Sign Language if and only if they are in non-clause-final position. This observation is reminiscent of the effect that Shklovsky and Sudo (2014) document in Uyghur (as reviewed in chapter 2), assuming that movement to the clause periphery is rightward in sign language, rather than leftward, in line with observations from *wh*-movement (Cecchetto, Geraci, and Zucchi 2009). Note, though, that various controls are needed to confirm this analysis: for instance, it has yet to be shown that relevant adverbials in Catalan Sign Language are indeed indexical, rather than anaphoric, with movement to the periphery interfering with binding rather than with context shift. Alternatively, the facts that Engberg-Pedersen (1995) describes in Danish Sign Language are reminiscent of "unquotation," as discussed by Shan (2010) and Maier (2014a) for spoken language; on this approach see Maier (2017, 2018). It is clear overall that further research is needed into Role Shift in sign languages of this class.

5.3 Fake Indexicals

We have now seen two types of phenomena for which a quotation-based analysis appears superior to one featuring indexical shift. While these cases involve elements that are indeed semantically indexical, they do not involve indexical *shift*. We next turn to two types of phenomena which, in spite of an initial similarity to cases of indexical shift, show signs of lacking semantically indexical elements at all.

The first is the well-studied phenomenon of "fake indexicality" in languages such as English and German, exemplified in (198) and (199). Of interest here is the interpretation of the second instance of *I* in each example.

(198) I'm the only one around here who will admit that I could be wrong.
(Partee 1989)

(199) Only I got a question that I understood.
(Kratzer 1998a, citing unpublished work by Heim)

On a prominent reading, sentence (199) (for instance) reports that no person x, apart from the speaker, got a question that x understood. Notably, on this gloss, the embedded *I* is translated not as an indexical element referring to the context author, but rather as a variable bound by the quantification introduced by *only*.

The distribution of fake indexicals is markedly different from the distribution of shifty indexicals in at least four ways. First, fake indexicals but not shifty indexicals readily occur outside of speech and attitude reports, as in cases like (199). Second, fake indexicals require an antecedent: for instance, the bound reading of *I* is not possible without a first-person element elsewhere in the structure.[4]

(200) Only Jack got a question that I understood.
   Cannot mean: Jack is the only x such that x got a question x understood.

There is no such requirement on shifty indexicals, as we see in familiar cases like (201).

(201) *Nez Perce*
   Kii   hii-wes   'iniit   yox̂$_1$ ke   Jack
   this.NOM   3SUBJ-be.PRES   house.NOM   RP.NOM   C   Jack
   hi-hi-ce-Ø   ['iin   hani-Ø-ya t_1].
   3SUBJ-say-IMPERF-PRES   [1SG.NOM make-P-REM.PAST   ]
   This is the house that Jack$_i$ says he$_i$ built.

Third, fake indexicals occur only in cases of quantification with focus-sensitive operators. They are not licensed by ordinary quantifiers such as *every* or *no*. There is no similar requirement for a focus-sensitive operator for shifty indexicals.

(202) No friend of mine got a question that I understood.
   Cannot mean: there is no friend of mine x such that x got a question x understood.

Fourth and last, fake indexicals readily give rise to "mixed" readings, wherein some pronominal elements but not others receive standard indexical meanings. Example (203), for instance, has a reading according to which no one else recommends your books to their librarian, as well as a reading according to which no one else recommends their own books to your librarian. This is in contrast to the Shift Together behavior for shifty indexicals reviewed in chapter 2.[5]

(203) Only you recommend your books to your librarian. (Kratzer 2009)
   a. You are the only x such that x recommends x's books to x's librarian.
   b. You are the only x such that x recommends your books to your librarian.
   c. You are the only x such that x recommends your books to x's librarian. (Mixed reading 1)
   d. You are the only x such that x recommends x's books to your librarian. (Mixed reading 2)

In view of these facts, it is perhaps not surprising that analyses of fake indexicality have typically differed substantially from analyses of indexical shift (with a few exceptions, in particular von Stechow 2003, Cable 2005, Roberts 2015, and, for a limited subset of cases, Kratzer 2009). Rather, this empirical situation has lent itself to three prominent styles of analysis which have in common that they each identify a way in which *I* lacks standard indexical meaning in (198) and (199). Let us briefly review these analyses, with the aim of elucidating a variety of theoretical ways in which a morphologically first- or second-person element may fail to be semantically indexical.

The first approach posits a morphology–semantics mismatch: the most embedded subject has the morphology of first person, but not the semantics. For von Stechow (2003) and Reuland (2010), the mismatch is attributable to feature deletion under binding: embedded *I* bears an indexical first-person feature in the syntax, and this determines its morphological form, but this feature is deleted at LF due to binding by the higher quantifier. Kratzer (1998a, 2009) takes the opposite approach, positing that the embedded subject bears no first-person feature in the syntax; the feature responsible for its morphological realization as *I* is transmitted postsyntactically, i.e., at PF. The feature-transmission view is taken up by Rullmann (2004), Heim (2008), Landau (2016), and Wurmbrand (2017). Both on the feature-transmission view and the feature-deletion view, there is an absolute sense in which *I* is a nonindexical element in (198) and (199): at the point of semantic interpretation, there is simply no first-person feature associated to this element.

A second approach maintains a basic analysis of embedded *I* as a semantically first-person element, but relaxes the connection between first person and indexicality. For Sudo (2012) and Podobryaev (2014, 2017), pronouns bear a complex index, which is a pair of a natural number and a person feature.[6] Thus the embedded *I* could bear, for instance, the index $< 244, ①>$ (the second element of the pair being a person feature). Sudo and Podobryaev propose that indexicality of first person arises from a constraint on assignments for such indices that crucially holds *only at the utterance level*: an utterance of a sentence is felicitiously evaluated with respect to an assignment and a context only if that assignment maps all indices $< n, ①>$ to *author*(*c*). But binding, as in (198) and (199), modifies assignments used at a subsentential level. Thus *only I* in (199) may introduce a binder with index 244 (assuming this is the first coordinate of the index on embedded *I*), leading to quantification over assignments that provide a variety of values for this index and accordingly a variety of values for the embedded *I*. None of these assignments are required to meet the condition that indices including a first person coordinate are in fact mapped to *author*(*c*). This conception of first person features makes it possible for the embedded *I* to be first person in terms of its syntax, semantics, and morphology, but without an actual indexical semantics in cases like (198) and (199).

A third and final view identifies a more limited sense in which the element *I* may be nonindexical, building on the observation that fake indexicality is a phenomenon closely tied to focus operators such as *only*. For Jacobson (2012), what (198) and (199) show is that indexical person features are ignored in the focus dimension. While the ordinary semantic value of a first person indexical is always the author of the context, the focus semantic value is much less restricted. Accordingly, as Jacobson (2012, 319) writes, "the effect of the features being uninterpreted is tied only to the computation of the focus value." Versions of this view are taken up by Sauerland (2013), Bassi and Longenbaugh (2018), and Charnavel (2019).

One general conclusion to be drawn from the analysis of fake indexicality is that appearances can be deceiving: even elements with the clear morphological appearance of first- or second-person pronouns may lack a truly indexical semantics. This, of course, does not require giving up the claim that many cases of morphological first- and second-person pronouns (or indeed *all* such cases, if we adopt the focus-based view) are indeed to be treated as ordinary Kaplanian indexicals.

5.4 Indexiphors

A final look-alike phenomenon also concerns shiftlike behaviors for what might appear to be first- or second-person elements—in particular, in many cases, apparent first- or second-person verbal agreement. Let us begin with a subcase that features a look-alike for first person only. Of interest here are patterns such as those found in the Dogon language Donno Sɔ or the Tibeto-Burman language Kathmandu Newari, which have been described in the literature as showing "first person logophoricity" (Culy 1994) and "egophoricity" (Hargreaves 2018, Coppock and Wechsler 2018), respectively. These languages each possess verbal inflections which, if attention were limited to simple matrix declaratives, might well be identified as first-person verb agreement. In Donno Sɔ, for instance, matrix sentences with a first-person subject feature a nasal suffix on the verb (-$ŋ$ for Heath 2016, -m for Culy 1994; I gloss this element -N), which is absent when the subject is third person.

(204) *Donno Sɔ*
    a. (Mi) bojɛ-m.
        1SG go-N
        I'm going.
    b. (Wo) bojɛ.
        3SG go
        He/she is going.
    (Culy 1994, 122)

In attitude reports, however, this type of inflection on the embedded verb occurs only when the embedded subject is the attitude holder. (As Culy writes, "first person inflection acts as logophoric inflection when it occurs in indirect discourse" [1994, 123].)

(205) a. Oumar [ma jɛmbɔ paza boli] miñ tagi.
Oumar [1SG sack.DEF drop left] 1SG.OBJ informed
Oumar informed me that I had left without the sack.
b. Oumar [inyemɛ jɛmbɔ paza bolu-m] miñ tagi.
Oumar [LOG sack.DEF drop left-N] 1SG.OBJ informed
Oumar$_i$ informed me that he$_i$ had left without the sack.
(Culy 1994, 123)

If the inflection in question is identified as a first-person indexical, or a reflex of agreement with such an element, then sentences like (205b) would be cases of indexical shift.

Cause to question an indexical analysis comes from several sources. First, -*N* appears to reflect agreement with a logophor in (205b), rather than with a (shifted) first-person nominal element. The use of a logophoric pronominal form, however, is not essential to the appearance of -*N* (Heath 2016); so long as the embedded subject refers to the attitude holder, -*N* appears. This suggests that -*N* is not agreeing with an indexical first-person feature on the embedded subject, nor (as Sundaresan 2018 proposes) is it agreeing with an abstract first-person element with which agreement is possible only in cases where the subject is a logophor. (Note that the examples that follow are taken from Heath 2016 and reflect his transcription.)

(206) Sé:dù [ǹjèmɛ́ / wó yɛ̀l-lì-ŋ́] gì-ỳ.
Seydou [LOG / 3SG.NOM come-PFV.NEG-N] say-PFV
Seydou$_i$ said that he$_i$ didn't come.
(Heath 2016, 303)

Moreover, first-person pronominal indexicals never shift in Donno Sɔ, even when a clausemate with -*N*, as we see in the most embedded clause of (207).[7]

(207) Sé:dù [ú wà [*pro* mì=ŋ́ dà-dá:-dɛ̀-ŋ́]
Seydou [2SG QUOT.SUBJ [2SG 1SG=ACC AUGM-kill-IMPF-N]
gì-ỳ] gì-y.
say-PFV] say-PFV
Seydou said you said that you will kill me.
(Heath 2016, 304)

Accordingly, Heath (2016, 303) describes -*N* as "transpersonal logophoric subject" marking, rather than as first-person inflection.

The case against an indexical analysis is perhaps even clearer for a related pattern in Kathmandu Newari. This language contains a set of verbs which, in typical matrix declaratives, take a special inflection (past tense -$\bar{a}$, nonpast tense -e; Hargreaves 2018) only when the subject is first person; in attitude reports, like in Donno Sɔ, this inflection indicates that the embedded subject is the attitude holder. Also required is that the attitude report be interpreted *de se* (Zu 2018, 175). Following Hargreaves, I gloss the relevant inflection 'ego'.

(208) *Kathmandu Newari*
 Jĩ: a:pwa twan-ā.
 1.ERG much drink-PAST.EGO
 I drank a lot. (Hargreaves 2018, (1))

(209) a. Syām-ā [wã: a:pwa twan-ā dhakā:] dhāl-a.
 Syam-ERG [3.ERG much drink-PAST.EGO C] SAY-PERF
 Syam$_i$ said he$_i$ drank too much.
 (Hargreaves 2018, (11))
 b. Wã: [jĩ: a:pwa twan-a dhakā:] dhāl-a.
 3.ERG [1.ERG much drink-PERF C] say-PERF
 He$_i$ said I$_j$ drank a lot.
 (Hargreaves 2018, 7)

Could 'ego' inflection be indicative of a first-person indexical, undergoing indexical shift in (209a)? Numerous factors suggest the contrary. First, as Hargreaves (2018) and Zu (2018) discuss, the relation between first person and ego inflection is complex in Kathmandu Newari: first-person matrix subjects fail to control -$\bar{a}$/-e inflection in questions, in the presence of inferential evidentials, and in the presence of adverbs such as *macāeka* 'unwittingly'. These effects are unexpected if -$\bar{a}$/-e simply reflects agreement with an indexical first-person subject. Moreover, like in Donno Sɔ, first-person pronominal indexicals never shift in Kathmandu Newari. And a final challenge arises in questions, where the inflectional system shows "interrogative flip": the -$\bar{a}$/-e inflection is typically controlled by second-person subjects, rather than by first-person ones as in declaratives.

A promising path toward a nonindexical analysis of the Kathmandu Newari and Donno Sɔ data is provided by Coppock and Wechsler (2018). Focusing on Kathmandu Newari, their analysis does not treat -$\bar{a}$/-e inflection as (reflective of) an indexical element and therefore does not invoke indexical shift. Rather, relative to an index i, their analysis suggests that Kathmandu Newari 'ego' inflection involves reference to *author(i)*.[8] Let us suppose that the relevant inflection reflects syntactic agreement with a subject bearing a meaningful feature. I assume this feature is of a standard type of presuppositional feature found on DPs (Heim 2008, Kratzer 2009), and name it simply [AUTH-I]. Whenever the subject bears this feature, it will denote *author(i)*, and the verb will be inflected in agreement. The agreement, in Kathmandu Newari, is *-ā/-e*; in Donno Sɔ, it is *-N*. I will refer to this inflection, which directly references information from the index, as *indexiphoric*.[9]

(210) $[\![\text{AUTH-I}]\!]^{c,i,g} = \lambda x : author(i).x$

In a matrix clause, modulo quantification of some type, values for the index are identical to those of the context, as discussed in chapter 2. This follows on the definition of truth in a context we have adopted from Kaplan:

(211) A sentence α is true at a context c and assignment g iff $[\![\alpha]\!]^{c,c,g} = 1$

Accordingly, if the subject must denote *author(i)*, this will be equivalent in a simple matrix clause to requiring that it denote *author(c)*, as a first-person indexical would. This is why Donno Sɔ and Kathmandu Newari indexiphoric inflection might appear, in matrix clauses, to indicate first person. (Of course, matrix clauses with certain evidentials, adverbs, or question operators may involve quantification over indices, breaking this apparent connection.)

In an embedded clause, values for *author(i)* and *author(c)* routinely diverge. Attitude complements involve quantification over values for the index that have *de se* counterparts of the attitude holder as *author(i)* coordinates. The analysis of attitude verbs and complementizers below is repeated from chapter 3.

(212) $[\![say]\!]^{c,i,g} = \lambda e.saying(e)$
(213) $[\![C^0\ \alpha]\!]^{c,i,g} = \lambda e.\forall i' \in \mathbb{RCON}(e)[\![\alpha]\!]^{c,i',g}$

    where $i' \in \mathbb{RCON}(e)$ iff
    a. $w(i')$ is a member of the content of e
    b. *author*(i') is an individual in $w(i')$ that EXT(e) identifies in e as herself
    c. *addr*(i') is an individual in $w(i')$ that EXT(e) identifies in e as her addressee, if any; otherwise *addr*(i') is ∅
    d. *loc*(i') is a location in $w(i')$ that EXT(e) identifies in e as her spatial location
    e. *time*(i') is a time in $w(i')$ that EXT(e) identifies in e as her temporal location

Embedded under C^0 as in (213), a subject that is required to denote *author(i)*, as in (214a), must denote a *de se* counterpart of the attitude holder. If there is no context shift in Kathmandu Newari or Donno Sɔ, however, *author(c)* will always pick out the overall speaker. Indexiphoric inflection is lacking in (214b) because, relative to the index and context against which the embedded clause is interpreted, the embedded subject denotes *author(c)* but not *author(i)*.

(214) *Kathmandu Newari*
    a. Syām-ā [wã: a:pwa twan-ā   dhakā:] dhāl-a.
       Syam-ERG [3.ERG much drink-PAST.EGO C   ] SAY-PERF
       Syam$_i$ said he$_i$ drank too much.
       (Hargreaves 2018, (11))
    b. Wã: [jĩ: a:pwa twan-a   dhakā:] dhāl-a.
       3.ERG [1.ERG much drink-PERF C   ] say-PERF
       He$_i$ said I$_j$ drank a lot.
       (Hargreaves 2018, 7)

This account captures two central respects in which indexiphoricity differs from indexical shift. First, "mixed" readings of pronouns and clausemate agreement are readily derived; for instance, in (215), an indexiphoric subject (referring to the addressee) is clausemate with an indexical first-person object (referring to the speaker). Because such examples do not contain two first-person indexicals, they contrast with the Shift Together behavior we have seen for indexical shift.

(215) *Donno Sɔ*
    Sé:dù [ú   wà   [*pro* mì=ŋ́ dà-dá:-dɛ̀-ŋ̀   ]
    Seydou [2SG QUOT.SUBJ [2SG 1SG-ACC AUGM-kill-IMPF-N]
    gí-ỳ   ] gì-y.
    say-PFV] say-PFV
    Seydou said you said that you will kill me.
    (Heath 2016, 304)

Second, indexiphoricity shows a distinctive behavior in multiclause embedding. Given that every attitude complementizer quantifies over the index used for the interpretation of its complement, overwriting previously assigned values, indexiphoric agreement in a doubly embedded clause will occur only when the subject of the doubly embedded clause denotes (a *de se* counterpart of) the most local attitude holder. In (216), for instance, for the interpretation of the most embedded clause, *author(i)* values range over counterparts of Shyam, not the policeman.

(216) *Kathmandu Newari*
Thanedara   dhāl-a   [ki Shyam-a   swikareyat-a [ki wa
policeman.ERG say-PERF [C Shyam-ERG admit-PERF [C 3SG
daa   kuy-ā   ]].
money steal-PAST.EGO]]
The policeman$_i$ said Shyam$_j$ admitted that he$_j$ / ✗he$_{i,k}$ stole the money.
(Zu 2018, 139)

(217) *Donno Sɔ*
Sé:dù   [ú   wà   [*pro* yɔ́gù wɔ̀-ŋ̀] gí-ỳ   ]
Seydou [2SG QUOT.SUBJ [nasty be-N] say-PFV]
gì-y.
say-PFV
Seydou$_i$ said you said that {you are/✗he$_i$ is } nasty.
(Heath 2016, 304)

In contrast, many languages with indexical shift allow long-distance shifting. In Korean example (218), for instance, *na-lul* 'me' may find an antecedent two clauses up (among other possibilities discussed by Park 2016):

(218) *Korean*
John-i   Seoul-eyse [$_{CP}$ Bill-i   yeki-eyse [$_{CP}$ Mary-ka   na-lul
John-Nom Seoul-at   [Bill-Nom here-at   [Mary-NOM I-ACC
cohahanta]-ko malhayssta]-ko malhayssta.
like]-C   said]-C   said
John$_j$ said in Seoul that Bill said {here / in Seoul} that Mary likes him$_j$.
(Park 2016, (53))

A language with indexical shift will show a full pattern of locality like (216) and (217) only if shifty operators are obligatorily present at the edge of every embedded clause. One consequence is that first-person reference to the original speaker is ruled out, as we see in Navajo (219). (Contrast this with the behavior of first persons in Donno Sɔ (215) and Kathmandu Newari (214b).)

(219) *Navajo*
Jáan [Mary [*pro* chidí nahideeshnih] nízin   ] ní.
John [Mary [1SG car   3.1.F.buy   ] 3.want] 3.say
John says Mary wants for Mary/✗John/✗me to buy a car.
(Schauber 1979, 22)

In a language with indexiphoricity, no such obligatoriness need be stipulated, and no parallel restriction on the reference of first-person indexicals is expected. The locality of indexiphors arises automatically from the nature of quantification expressed by attitude complementizers.[10]

Evidence for indexiphors in the form of mixed readings and locality requirements may be found in several additional languages (many described in some previous literature as showing indexical shift); these include Amharic (Semitic; Anand 2006), Mishar Tatar (Turkic; Podobryaev 2014), and Tamil (Dravidian; Sundaresan 2012, 2018), for which both mixed readings as well as locality requirements have been documented, as well as perhaps Late Egyptian (Afro-Asiatic; Kammerzell and Peust 2002), Mutki Zazaki (Indo-Iranian; Akkuş 2018), varieties of Turkish (Özyıldız 2012, Akkuş 2018), and various Trans-New Guinea languages (Evans 2006). In the remainder of this section, I review four additional observations concerning indexiphoricity that arise from this larger crosslinguistic sample.

A first concerns the morphological relationship between indexiphoric agreement and agreement for first person. In Donno Sɔ and Kathmandu Newari, the morphology of agreement is different in these two cases; for example, in Donno Sɔ, -*N* inflection occurs only in agreement with an [AUTH-I] feature, not due to agreement simply with first person. By contrast, in Amharic, this distinction is collapsed by the verbal morphology: the verb form is the same under agreement with an indexiphor and agreement with a first-person indexical. This is to say that, in Amharic, both indexiphors and first-person indexicals control agreement/clitics on the verb from the same "first-person" series. Note that (220) exemplifies a mixed reading in a simple case; (221) shows the locality effect. In both examples, the most embedded clause contains an indexiphor and a first-person indexical, each controlling "first-person" agreement/clitics.

(220) *Amharic*
John [*pro*$_{subj}$ *pro*$_{obj}$ al-ɨttazzəzə-ññ   ] alə.
John [NEG.1S-obey.MKIMPERF-1SO] say.PERF.3SM
John$_i$ says he$_i$ will not obey me.
(Leslau 1995)

(221) Bill [John [*pro*$_{subj}$ *pro*$_{obj}$ al-ɨttazzəzə-ññ   ]
Bill [John [NEG.1S-obey.MKIMPERF-1SO]
alə   ] alə.
say.PERF.3SM] say.PERF.3SM
Bill$_b$ says John$_j$ says he$_j$/✗he$_b$ will not obey me.
(Anand 2006, 101)

A plausible hypothesis regarding this type of pattern concerns the syntactic feature makeup of first-person indexicals and *author(i)* indexiphors. These elements have in common, semantically, an *auth* function; they differ in whether this function is applied to context or index. We might suppose, then, that in parallel to the [AUTH-I] feature posited for indexiphors, the first-person feature is represented as [AUTH-C]:

(222) a. $[\![$ [AUTH-C] $]\!]^{c,i,g} = author(c) =$ "first person"
      b. $[\![$ [AUTH-I] $]\!]^{c,i,g} = author(i)$

In common to these two features is the subfeature [AUTH]. It is this subfeature, I will propose, that is realized by all cases of "first-person" morphology in Amharic. Accordingly, the system does not distinguish in terms of inflectional morphology between mere indexiphors and first-person indexicals. The two categories are syncretic.[11] Beyond Amharic, this pattern holds for verbal inflection in Mishar Tatar (Podobryaev 2014) and Tamil (Sundaresan 2012, 2018), as well as in other languages that may feature indexiphoricity such as Late Egyptian (Kammerzell and Peust 2002), Mutki Zazaki (Akkuş 2018), and Turkish (Özyıldız 2012, Akkuş 2018).[12]

A second additional observation comes from a contextualization of indexiphoricity in the wider space of dedicated *de se* devices. Anand (2006) divides these into two classes: shifted indexicals (for which he pursues an analysis in essential respects parallel to the one defended here), and bound elements, including logophors, bound pronouns, and PRO. He observes that a distinctive behavior of bound *de se* elements, in contrast to shifted indexicals, is that they cannot be c-commanded by certain expressions read *de re*. For clarity, I will refer to the elements forbidden from c-commanding bound *de se* elements as "*de re* competitors."

An initial illustration of this pattern can be seen in Yoruba (Niger-Congo). This language contains two third-person pronouns, *ó* (possessive form *rẹ̀*) and *òun*; *òun*, but not *ó/rẹ̀*, must be read *de se* (Adesola 2006, 2081; Anand 2006, 56). Notably, *òun* is ruled out when it is c-commanded by a pronoun that refers to the matrix subject *de re*, (223). Reversing or removing the c-command relation between *òun* and its *de re* competitor obviates the effect, (224). (Similar data can be found for bound *de se* pronouns in English dream reports; see Percus and Sauerland 2003b.)

(223) *Yoruba*

Olú$_i$ sọ pé ó$_{j,*i}$ rí bàbá òun$_i$.
Olu say that he(weak) see father his(strong)
Olu$_i$ said that he$_j$/✗he$_i$ saw his$_i$ father.
(Adesola 2005, 185)

(224) a. Olú$_i$ sọ pé òun$_i$ ti rí ìwé rẹ̀$_{i,j}$.
Olu say that he(strong) ASP see book his(weak)
Olu$_i$ said that he$_i$ has seen his$_{i,j}$ book.
(Adesola 2005, 200)
b. Olú$_k$ sọ pé [bàbá rẹ̀$_{k,j}$] ti rí [ìyá òun$_k$].
Olu say that [father his(weak)] ASP see [mother his(strong)]
Olu$_k$ said that his$_{k,j}$ father has seen his$_k$ mother.
(Adesola 2005, 199)

Anand observes that an effect much like this holds for indexiphors in Amharic. In (225), as with the excluded reading of Yoruba (223), the embedded subject refers to the attitude holder *de re*. It functions as a *de re* competitor, ruling out an indexiphor lower in the embedded clause.

(225) *Amharic*

Context: John has a valuable rare book library. Recently, he has experienced a spate of thefts where the thief pretends to be a restorer coming to pick up a book; in many cases, the clerk at the desk simply hands the book over. In order to prevent this, John has invited a consultant to come in and change security policies. In order to test them, the consultant arranges for a mock-thief to come in and vet the system, asking for a rare folio of *Hamlet*. The following day, John reviews security camera footage from the mock-theft. John [as a clerk] is actually one of the participants, though the video angle prevents identification of the clerks. When the video gets to him, he notices that the thief is being met with some skepticism. He says to the consultant, "The thief will not be able to get his hands on *Hamlet* now."

Question: How can the consultant report this to his mock-thief?

John [*pro* [*pro* meSɨhaf-e] ay-səTT əTəh]
John [3SG [**xphor** book-1SG] NEG.3SG-give-2SMO]
alə.
say.PERF.3SM
Intended: John said that he would not give you his book.
(Anand 2006, 103)

The effect of c-command by *de re* competitor expressions extends to an additional type of case in Amharic as well, Anand notes. In (226), repeated from (220), both the embedded subject and the embedded object control [AUTH] agreement. To avoid a Principle B violation, one must be an indexiphor while the other is an indexical. The choice of which element occupies which syntactic position is not free: the indexiphor may occupy the subject position, as in parse (a), but not the object position, as in parse (b). This is parallel to the behavior of Yoruba bound *de se* pronoun òun in (223) and (224a), and suggests that an (unshifted, *de re*) indexical functions as a *de re* competitor for an indexiphor.

(226) John [pro_{subj} pro_{obj} al-ɨttazzəzə-ññ   ] alə.
John [NEG.1S-obey.MKIMPERF-1SGO] say.PERF.3SM

    a. ✓ John$_i$ says he$_i$ will not obey me.
    b. ✗ John$_i$ says I will not obey him$_i$.
(Anand and Nevins 2004, (46)ff.; Anand 2006, 101)

As expected, just as in Yoruba (224b), if the c-command relation between the indexiphor and its *de re* competitor is broken, the restriction against indexiphors in object position ceases to hold:[13]

(227) John [[pro_{poss} lɨj-e   ]$_{subj}$ pro_{obj} ay-ɨttazzəzə-ññ   ]
John [[son-1SG]   NEG.3S-obey-1SGO]
alə.
say.PERF.3SM

    a. John$_i$ says my son will not obey me.
    b. John$_i$ says his$_i$ son will not obey me.
    c. John$_i$ says my son will not obey him$_i$.
    d. John$_i$ says his$_i$ son will not obey him$_i$.
(Anand 2006, 101)

Overall, the Amharic data suggest that indexiphors must not be c-commanded by either of two types of *de re* competitors: those that refer *de re* to a counterpart of the same individual referred to by the indexiphor (as in (225); compare with Yoruba (223)), and those that control [AUTH] agreement (as in (226)).[14]

Sensitivity to *de re* competitors—what Anand dubs "the *De Re* Blocking effect"—suggests, in Anand's typology, that indexiphors are a type of bound *de se* element. Shifted indexicals do not show the *De Re* Blocking effect (Anand 2006, 111); the fact that indexiphors do makes them like logophors and like pronouns that may be bound to yield dedicated *de se* readings. These data could be taken to suggest that the composition of attitude complementizers with their complements is mediated not by Intensional Function Application (Heim and Kratzer 1998; see chapter 2, (52)) but rather by syntactically instantiated binding operators that bind index-sensitive elements.

A closing comment on the *De Re* Blocking effect is that it opens up a path to the diagnosis of indexiphoricity in additional languages. For instance, Evans (2006) discusses a type of mixed reading in a group of New Guinea languages including Dani (Bromley 1981), Dom (Tida 2006, cited in Aikhenvald 2008),

Gahuku (Deibler 1976), Golin (Loughnane 2005), and Usan (Reesink 1993). These languages pattern like Amharic in showing the asymmetry in (226). As Evans writes, "person deixis is calculated absolutely for the object slot and relatively for the subject slot" (2006, 101). That is, the subject may be an indexiphor while the object is an indexical, but not vice versa.

(228) *Gahuku*
Leliq nemoqz *pro* [mota *pro*$_{subj}$ *pro*$_{obj}$ li-m-it-ove   ]
ours it.is.but 3SG [now   XPHOR 1SG   1PL.OBJ-give-FUT-1SG.SUBJ]
l-oka-ke.
say-3SG-SS
It is ours, but after he said that he would give it to us now.
(Deibler 1976, 115)

Akkuş (2018) reports a similar pattern in effect among Turkish speakers who allow mixed readings, as well as for speakers of Mutki Zazaki and Kurmanji (in the latter case citing unpublished work by Songül Gündoğdu).[15] [16]

The Amharic data discussed by Anand (2006) also point to a third observation regarding indexiphoricity: indexiphoricity and indexical shift may coexist in the same grammar. Anand shows this in two ways. First, Amharic allows a classic pattern of indexical shift for second person, as in (229); note that here a second-person element is clausemate with a *wh*-expression interpreted in a higher clause (a pattern that would be unexpected under clausal quotation of the most embedded clause).

(229) *Amharic*
Pro   [*pro*$_{subj}$ *pro*$_{obj}$ [*pro*   mɨm   amt'-a   ]
1SG   [3SG   1SG   [2SG   what   bring.IMPER-2M]
ɨnd-al-ə-ññ   ]   al-səmma-hu-mm.
COMP-say.PERF-3M-1SO]   NEG-hear.PERF-1S-NEG
I didn't hear what he told me to bring.
(Leslau 1995, 779)

Evidence that this pattern involves indexical shift, rather than an element making reference to *addr(i)* (which we might call an "*addr(i)* indexiphor"), comes from Shift Together effects. The absence of mixed readings for elements controlling second-person agreement/clitics is shown in (230). (The absence of mixed readings here is in direct contrast with (227). In the earlier example, [AUTH] agreement/clitics could be controlled either by an indexiphor or by an indexical, giving rise to mixed readings.)

(230) John Bill [[*pro* lɨj-ɨh   ]*subj* *pro*ₒbⱼ ay-ɨttazzəzə-ɨh   ]
     John Bill [[2SG son-2SG]   2SG   NEG.3S-obey-2SGO]
     alə-w.
     say.PERF.3SM-3SMO
   a. John said to Bill your son will not obey you.
   b. John said to Bill_b his_b son will not obey him_b.
     (John said to Bill_b [OP 2SG's son will not obey 2SG].)
   c. ✗John said to Bill_b your son will not obey him_b.
   d. ✗John said to Bill_b his_b son will not obey you.
   (Anand 2006, 101)

We expect, given (G2), that a language allowing second-person indexicals to shift should also allow first-person indexicals to shift. Evidence that this is so in Amharic comes from cases of multiple embedding such as (231), repeated in part from (221). In this example, the most embedded clause contains two elements controlling [AUTH] agreement/clitics. Readings where both are indexical will violate Principle B. It is possible, as we have seen, for the embedded clause to contain an indexiphor subject and an unshifted indexical object, as shown in reading (a). Given the locality of indexiphoricity, the indexiphor subject can only refer to (a *de se* counterpart of) John, not Bill, excluding reading (b). Evidence for indexical shift comes from the felicity of a third reading, shown in (c): here the subject continues to be an indexiphor, referring to the local attitude holder, but the object indexical is shifted to refer to Bill (showing the familiar possibility of long-distance indexical shifting). This suggests that a shifty operator may be present in the complement of the higher instance of 'say'.

(231) Bill [John [*pro*_subj *pro*_obj al-ɨttazzəzə-ññ   ]
     Bill [John [NEG.1s-obey.mkimperf-1sO]
     alə   ] alə.
     say.PERF.3sm] say.PERF.3sm
   a.   Bill_b says John_j says he_j will not obey me.
        (Bill says [John says [XPHOR will not obey 1SG]].)
   b. ✗ Bill_b says John_j says he_b will not obey me.
        (indexiphoric parse violates locality)
   c.   Bill_b says John_j says he_j will not obey him_b.
        (Bill says [OP John says [XPHOR will not obey 1SG]].)
   (Anand 2006, 101)

Beyond Amharic, cases of indexical shifting co-occuring with indexiphoricity are plausibly found in Mutki Zazaki and some varieties of Turkish (Akkuş 2018).

The fourth and final observation about indexiphoricity to be reviewed here involves a limitation to first-person-like elements, which has been in place throughout the discussion of this section. As we just saw, for Amharic, there is reason to think that the language extends its "first-person" agreement paradigms (properly, [AUTH] agreement paradigms) to both first-person indexicals and nonindexical elements referring to $author(i)$—but that similar flexibility does not obtain for second person. That is, second-person agreement in Amharic reflects not a general [ADDR] feature, referring either to $addr(c)$ or $addr(i)$, but rather a classic indexical feature [ADDR-C]:[17]

(232) $[\![$ [ADDR-C] $]\!]^{c,i} = addr(c) =$ "2nd person"

This asymmetry between first and second person in terms of the level of morphological specialization/syncretism is not universal. In the variety of Turkish documented by Akkuş (2018), for instance, "second-person" pronoun and agreement morphology may reflect either $addr(i)$ or $addr(c)$—that is, these forms reflect a general syncretized [ADDR] category, much like the [AUTH] category of Amharic. These forms are used in (233) as an indirect object and as a possessor of the direct object. The morphology leaves open several lexical possibilities: both the indirect object and the possessor may be second-person indexicals, yielding reading (a); both may be $addr(i)$ indexiphors, yielding reading (b); or the indirect object, which is the syntactically higher of the two, may be an $addr(i)$ indexiphor while the possessor is a second-person indexical, yielding reading (c). Note that this possibility is exactly the type of mixed reading expected from a system with indexiphors. It should be constrasted with a final potential parse, where the higher pronoun is an indexical while the lower one is an indexiphor, as in (d); this violates *De Re* Blocking.[18]

(233) *Turkish*
Tunç Ayşe-'ye [ben$_{subj}$ san-a$_{IO}$ [pro$_{poss}$
Tunç Ayşe-DAT [AUTH.XPHOR 2SG/ADDR.XPHOR [2SG/ADDR.XPHOR
resmi-in-i   ]$_{DO}$ nere-de göster-eceğ-im] de-miş?
picture-2POSS-ACC]   where   show-FUT-1SG] say-PAST

   a. (?) Where did Tunç$_t$ say to Ayşe$_a$ that he$_t$ would show you your picture?
   b. Where did Tunç$_t$ say to Ayşe$_a$ that he$_t$ would show her$_a$ her$_a$ picture?
   c. ? Where did Tunç$_t$ say to Ayşe$_a$ that he$_t$ would show her$_a$ your picture?
   d. ✗ Where did Tunç$_t$ say to Ayşe$_a$ that he$_t$ would show you her$_a$ picture?
(Akkuş 2018, 19)

Similar encoding of a general [ADDR] feature, as opposed to a specifically indexical [ADDR-C] feature, is found in Mishar Tatar, where "second-person" elements likewise give rise to mixed readings (Podobryaev 2014).

This finding raises a typological question. Both Turkish (as documented by Akkuş 2018) and Mishar Tatar show a syncretism across both "first-person" and "second-person" morphology: only the very general subfeatures [ADDR] and [AUTH] are encoded morphologically, rather than more specific features that require reference to either the context or the index. In Amharic, as we saw, the syncretism is limited to [AUTH]. Might there be languages with a syncretism only for [ADDR]? In such a language, elements with first-person morphology would show standard indexical behavior, but elements with "second-person" morphology might be either second-person indexicals or *addr*(*i*) indexiphors. While information on languages of this type is limited, several potential cases are noted by Nikitina (2012b) (all of them in west Africa); these include Adioukrou (Kwa; Côte d'Ivoire), Obolo (Cross River; Nigeria), Wan (Mande; Côte d'Ivoire), Mundang (Adamawa; Chad and Cameroon), and Akɔɔse (Bantu; Cameroon), as well as perhaps Engenni (Kwa; Nigeria) and Aghem, Ngwo, and Babungo (all Narrow Grassfields Bantoid, Cameroon). (Nikitina's description is less complete regarding languages in this second group.) In these languages, first-person indexicals rigidly refer to *author*(*c*); there is no indexical shift. (Some of the languages in question make use of logophors to refer to reported speakers; some simply use third-person pronouns, as in English.) Nikitina's description suggests that, by contrast, "second-person" pronouns and agreement are used for either *addr*(*i*) or *addr*(*c*). Unfortunately, the available documentation on these languages is quite slim regarding *addr*-based elements. I will simply note that if the diagnosis of these languages as containing *addr*(*i*) indexiphors and a syncretized [ADDR] morphological category is correct, a suite of testable expectations falls into place. First, we expect to find mixed readings, wherein a single clause contains both an *addr*(*i*) indexiphor and an *addr*(*c*) indexical. In such cases, second, we expect to see a *De Re* Blocking effect: the indexiphor may c-command the indexical, but not vice versa. Third, we expect locality: an *addr*(*i*) indexiphor should be possible only with reference to (*de te* counterparts of) the addressee of the most local attitude report. It is to be hoped that these predictions will be tested in future work on languages of this interesting class.

5.5 Closing Remarks

Progress in the further study of indexical shift depends in large part on new data, both from languages previously reported to allow shifting (including those discussed in this book) and from those for which shifting patterns have yet to be reported. Any new case of potential indexical shift bears on the generalizations discussed in the previous chapters to the extent that it indeed features indexicals and these indexicals indeed shift. This chapter has aimed to cast light on a variety of ways in which each of these diagnoses may, in practice, be nontrivial. Distinguishing shift from quotation requires attention both to iconicity and to quotational opacity, keeping in mind the possibility of mixed quotation. Distinguishing indexicals from the broad range of similar though nonindexical elements requires attention to binding by adverbial quantifiers, to focus operators, to multiclause embedding, and to the effect of elements read *de re*. Without attention to these matters, reports of shiftlike patterns will remain unclassifiable in terms of the typological space explored in this chapter and this book.

6 Conclusions

In this book, I have put forward a theory of indexical shifting that synthesizes ideas from the semantic literature on embedded clauses—namely, that these clauses may host operators that overwrite contextual coordinates (Anand and Nevins 2004, Anand 2006, Sudo 2012, Deal 2014, Shklovsky and Sudo 2014, Park 2016), and that modal quantification is contributed by C (Kratzer 2006, Anand and Hacquard 2008)—with ideas from the syntactic literature on universals and variation—namely, that natural languages draw from a restricted set of contentful primitives, constrained by functional sequences (Rizzi 1997, Cinque 1999, and much work following), that languages vary in how they bundle these primitives together into lexical items (Bobaljik and Thráinsson 1998, Pylkkänen 2008, Grashchenkov and Markman 2008, Harley 2013), and in general that variation in the functional lexicon constitutes the primary, if not only, source of variation in grammar (Borer 1984, Ouhalla 1991, Chomsky 1995).

At the heart of the proposal is a functional sequence of operators that shift locative, addressee, author, and time coordinates of context:

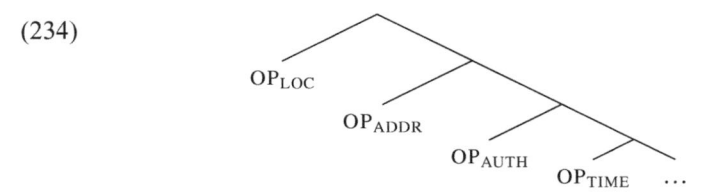

(234)

$$\text{OP}_{\text{LOC}} \quad \text{OP}_{\text{ADDR}} \quad \text{OP}_{\text{AUTH}} \quad \text{OP}_{\text{TIME}} \quad \ldots$$

The operators that form this sequence change the context against which their complement is interpreted. They may do so in two ways, as exemplified in (235) for locative shifters. I have argued that the choice among the two meanings for a given shifty operator is determined by the position, relative to the sequence in (234), of a meaningful C head.

(235) Locative shifters
   a. $[\![\text{OP}_{\text{LOC}}]\!]^{c,i,g} = \lambda p \in D_{<\kappa,\kappa t>}.p(i)(c^{loc(i)/loc})$
      (Zazaki)
   b. $[\![\text{OP}_{\text{LOC}}]\!]^{c,i,g} = \lambda P \in D_{<\kappa,<\kappa,lt>>}.\lambda e.P(i)(c^{\text{LOC}(e)/loc})(e)$
      (Nez Perce)

I have shown in chapters 3 and 4 that this sequence and the meanings of the operators in it provide the grounding for our understanding of a series of implicational universals that touch on several distinct aspects of the grammar of embedding: verb selection, co-shifting requirements, and interpretation *de se*.

(G1) Implicational hierarchy of verbs

Verbs of speech are more likely to allow indexical shift in their complement than are verbs of thought, which in turn are more likely to allow indexical shift in their complement than are verbs of knowledge.

(G2) Implicational hierarchy of indexical classes

Within and across languages, the possibility of indexical shift is determined by the hierarchy Time > 1st > 2nd > Loc. Indexicals of a certain class undergo shift in a particular verbal complement only if indexicals of classes farther to the left undergo shift as well.

(G3) Implicational hierarchy of *de se* requirements

Requirements for *de se* interpretation conform to the hierarchy Time > 1st > 2nd > Loc. Indexicals of a certain class require *de se* interpretation only if indexicals of classes farther to the left require it as well.

In capturing these generalizations, the theory is able to account for indexical shift patterns in a wide range of languages (e.g., Korean, Matses, Navajo, Nez Perce, Slave, Uyghur, and Zazaki) while also delineating clear predictions for language types that could not be attested. Should further work bear these predictions out, we stand to gain a substantial example of ways that apparently purely semantic or even pragmatic variation may ultimately connect with variation in grammar.

A Remarks on Shift Together

Shift Together is a generalization about the meanings available for certain attitude complements containing more than one indexical element. In chapter 2, I proposed the following statement of the pattern:

(236) *Shift Together*
If one indexical of class Ψ picks up reference from context c, then all indexicals of class Ψ within the same minimal attitude complement must also pick up reference from context c.
(The following are classes of indexicals: first person, second person, locative, temporal.)

As stated, Shift Together applies only to indexicals that share the same minimal attitude complement. The broader generalization, also as noted in chapter 2, is what I have called Local Determination:

(237) *Local Determination*
An indexical *ind* of class Ψ has its reference determined by the closest shifty operator with scope over *ind* that manipulates contextual coordinate Ψ. If no operator has scope over *ind*, then *ind* has its reference determined by the utterance context.

If two indexicals of class Ψ are members of the same minimal attitude complement, they fall in the scope of all of the same shifty operators (if any are present). Since both must have their reference determined by the closest Ψ-operator, if any, we derive the Shift Together effect. If a single Ψ-operator is present, both Ψ-indexicals will shift; if multiple Ψ-operators are present (with scope over the clause in question), both Ψ-indexicals will shift as determined by the closest operator; otherwise, neither Ψ-indexical will shift.

Reference to particular classes of indexicals is a necessary component of these generalizations. Consider, for instance, an attitude complement containing both a first-person indexical and a second-person indexical. Whether we expect a limitation on the co-shifting behavior of these elements depends on the size of the complement structure allowed in the case in question. Suppose, for instance, that we are concerned with an attitude verb for which the structure in (238) is possible:

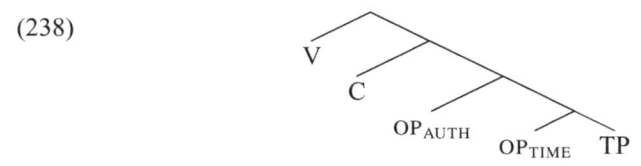

(238)

        V
     C
  OP$_{AUTH}$ OP$_{TIME}$ TP

Within the TP, in this structure, first persons (and temporal indexicals) will be shifted, but second persons will not be. This type of option, as discussed in chapter 3, is taken in Slave for complements of the verbs *hadi* 'say' and *yeniwę / hudeli* 'want/think'. In (239), first person shifts but second person does not.

(239) *Slave*
Simon [rásereyineht'u] hadi.
Simon [2SG.hit.1SG   ] 3SG.say
Simon said that you hit him. (Rice 1986, 53)

We also saw that certain Slave verbs, for instance, *édedi* 'tell/ask', require a larger structure, as in (240). In this structure, first and second person must both shift.

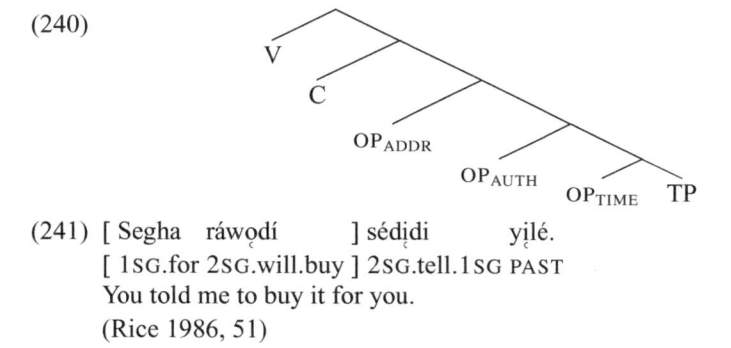

(240)

        V
     C
  OP$_{ADDR}$
      OP$_{AUTH}$ OP$_{TIME}$ TP

(241) [Segha ráwǫdí   ] sédįdi   yįlé.
[1SG.for 2SG.will.buy] 2SG.tell.1SG PAST
You told me to buy it for you.
(Rice 1986, 51)

Cases like (239) remind us that shift of first person without shift of second person does not run afoul of Local Determination or Shift Together. Conversely, the requirement that first and second persons both shift in cases like (241) follows not from these generalizations but from the subcategorization behavior of the verb *édedi* 'tell/ask', together with the hierarchy of shifty operators: this verb allows only complements that contain both OP$_{ADDR}$ and OP$_{AUTH}$. What *would* run afoul of Local Determination and Shift Together would be a minimal attitude complement in which, say, one second-person indexical but not another receives a shifted interpretation. Such cases are ruled out by the semantics of shifty operators. Once the addressee coordinate has been shifted, the previous value is overwritten and no longer available to second-person indexicals in the scope of the overwriting operator.

It should be noted that patterns like these are also fully captured on the approach to Slave in Anand and Nevins (2004) and Anand (2006). These approaches are exactly like the analyses just shown in that they involve shifty operators that manipulate certain coordinates of context but not others. (This should be no surprise, as Anand and Nevins 2004 and Anand 2006 are direct antecedents of the approach pursued here. For present purposes, the only relevant difference between the present approach and the earlier one is merely that shifty operators are not stacked on Anand and Nevins' and Anand's theories, and therefore there is no functional hierarchy of shifty operators.) These authors furthermore directly claim that Slave obeys Shift Together, based on (242), which involves two first-person pronouns (see Anand 2006, 99, Anand and Nevins 2004, (18)):

(242) [Sehlégé   segha   goníhkie rárulu   ] yudeli.
     [1SG.friend 1SG.for slippers 3SG.will.sew] 3SG.want.4SG
    a.   She$_i$ wants her$_i$ friend to sew slippers for her$_i$.
    b.   She$_i$ wants my friend to sew slippers for me.
    c.✗ She$_i$ wants my friend to sew slippers for her$_i$.
    d.✗ She$_i$ wants her$_i$ friend to sew slippers for me.
    (Rice 1986, 56)

Unfortunately, the explicit statements of the Shift Together constraint provided by these authors do not obviously match this analysis. I reprint the relevant formulations here:

(243) Shift Together constraint
All indexicals within a speech-context domain must pick up reference from the same context.
(Anand and Nevins 2004, 16)

(244) Shift Together constraint
All shiftable indexicals within a[n] attitude-context domain must pick up reference from the same context.
(Anand 2006, 100)

There is a natural interpretation available for both formulations which is falsified by (239). (This holds on the assumption that second person is a "shiftable indexical," in Anand's 2006 formulation; his theory does not provide for a characterization of this term.) One possibility—perhaps the most plausible one—is that Anand and Nevins see the embedded clause in (239) as interpreted with respect to a single context, which is partially shifted; both embedded indexicals draw their reference from this context and thus one shifts and the other does not. Another possibility is that the formulations of the constraint are to be understood as involving a contextual restriction to all indexicals *of the same class*, rather than all indexicals *tout court*.

Whatever the reason, the absence of explicit reference to indexical classes in the formulations reprinted in (243) and (244) has engendered significant confusion in the literature. Reports of "violations of Shift Together" involving separate classes of indexicals are made by Quer (2005), Korotkova (2016), and Hübl et al. (2019), among others. The data discussed by these authors show, as Slave (239) also does, that some classes of indexicals may shift without other classes of indexicals necessarily following suit. This shows that the cases in question do not feature a *total* series of shifty operators, shifting all coordinates of context; it does not in itself pose any empirical problem for the shifty operator theory.

Some of the insights that have come from an exploration of these cases have the potential to shed light on additional examples that have been recently put forward as putative Shift Together violations. Korotkova (2016), for instance, discusses the role of indexical elements in providing perspectival arguments for evidential expressions. In matrix clauses, evidentials reflect the evidence of the speaker, as in the following example from Bulgarian:

(245) *Bulgarian*
Context: The speaker sees pieces of a vase but did not see it break.
Sčupi-l-a   se.
break-IND.PAST-F REFL
It broke, I infer.
(Korotkova 2016, 214)

However, in various languages that permit embedded evidentials, the evidence holder—what Korotkova dubs the "origo"—may be not the speaker, but rather a participant in the embedding attitude event. Korotkova reports that this is an option for some Bulgarian speakers.[1] The interpretation of (246) exemplifies a shifted origo for the embedded evidential.

(246) Nataša popita   Stefan [dali   mechka e
Natasha ask.AOR.3SG Stefan [whether bear   be.3SG.PRES
mina-l-a   ottuk   ].
pass-IND.PAST-SG.F from.here]
Natasha asked Stefan whether, given what he hears/infers, a bear passed here.
(Korotkova 2016, 288)

Notably, Korotkova finds, Bulgarian atittude reports that embed multiple evidentials obey Shift Together: it is not possible to shift the origo for one evidential but not the other. Rather, a consistent choice of origo must be used throughout the embedded clause.

(247) Context: I'm exchanging news with Maria; we're discussing our cohort. I was mostly in touch with Jane and tell Maria that she lives in Japan. She was in touch with Lisa who is in Canada. Later on, Maria's mom joins us. Maria tells her: "Jane lives in Japan and Lisa lives in Canada."
Maria kaza na majka si che [Dzhein zhivee-l-a v Yaponia]
Maria said to mother her that [Jane live-IND.PAST-F in Japan]
i [Lisa zhivee-l-a v Kanada].
and [Lisa live-IND.PAST-F in Canada]
Impossible reading: Maria told her mother that, *as she was told*, Jane lives in Japan and—*as I was told*—Lisa lives in Canada.
(Korotkova 2016, 255)

Korotkova concludes that the behavior of embedded evidentials is well-suited for an indexical analysis; the origo is a contextual coordinate and may be shifted, yielding non-speaker-oriented evidential meanings. She notes, however, that there is no requirement that the evidential origo shift together with first-person pronouns. In Korean, shift of the evidential origo is obligatory, but shift of first-person pronouns is optional:

(248) *Korean*
Yenghi-nun [John-i na-lul po-te-la-ko]
Yenghi-TOP [John-NOM 1SG-ACC see-DIR-DECL-COMP]
malha-yess-ta.
say-PAST-DECL
a. Yenghi said that, as she perceived, John saw me.
b. Yenghi$_i$ said that, as she perceived, John saw her$_i$.
(Korotkova 2016, 258)

This fact reveals that the notion of an origo is not reducible to the notion of an author—and thus the working characterization of contexts we have made use of up to this point is incomplete. A context must separately specify an author and an origo. This is much like the way in which a context must separately specify an author and an addressee for the proper interpretation of examples like Slave (239). Accordingly, an operator that shifts origo without shifting author is readily definable:

(249) $[\![\text{OP}_{\text{ORIGO}}]\!]^{c,i,g} = \lambda p \in D_{<\kappa,\kappa t>} . p(i)(c^{origo(i)/origo})$

For unshifted contexts c, $origo(c)$ and $author(c)$ have the same value (which presumably reflects the fact, grounded in the pragmatics of assertion, that the evidence holder for a matrix utterance is the speaker herself). It is only by careful consideration of embedded contexts that Korotkova untangles these notions and thus makes a case for the inclusion of an origo coordinate in contextual tuples.

This case study potentially casts light on an additional phenomenon in Korean, which has been reported as an exception to Shift Together by Sundaresan (2018). In Korean, the verb meaning 'give' is subject to suppletive allomorphy. In matrix clauses, the allomorph *tal* is used where the speaker is the goal and the clause is imperative, as in (250a). When one or both conditions is not met, as in (250b) and (250c), the allomorph *cwu* is used, and *tal* is not possible.[2]

(250) a. (Ne) na-ekey satang-ul tal-la!
2SG.NOM 1SG-DAT candy-ACC give-IMP
Give me a candy!
b. Chingwu-ka na-ekey satang-ul cwu/*tal-ess-ta.
friend-NOM 1SG-DAT candy-ACC give-PAST-DECL
The friend gave me a candy.
c. Ne casin-eykey senmwul-ul cwu/*tal-la!
2SG ANAPH-DAT gift-ACC give-IMP
Give yourself a gift!
(Sundaresan 2018, 21)

Korean freely allows embedded imperatives (Pak, Portner, and Zanuttini 2008).[3] In embedded imperatives, *tal* may be used where the goal is an attitude holder, as shown in (251). (I use quotation here in the translation line only to clarify the intended meaning. Note that Sundaresan does not discuss the form of 'give' when the goal of an embedded imperative remains the overall speaker.)

(251) Swuci-ka Yuswu-eykey [Cimin$_1$-ika Cengmi-eykey [casin$_1$-eykey
Swuci-NOM Yuswu-DAT [Cimin-NOM Cengmi-DAT [self-DAT
senmwul-ul tal-la-ko] hay-ss-ta-ko] mal-hay-ss-ta.
gift-ACC give-IMP-C] v-PAST-DECL-C] say-PAST-DECL
Swuci told Yuswu that Cimin told Cengmi, "Give me a gift."

Such data are potentially analyzable in multiple ways. One analysis, given Korotkova's analysis, might invoke origo shift. On this analysis, *tal* would be used in imperatives when the origo (not necessarily the author) is the goal of 'give'. Korotkova argues that origo shift is obligatory in Korean. On this approach, one would expect the form *tal* to be impossible in embedded imperatives with the speaker as a goal, for instance, 'Yuswu told Cimin to give me a gift'. Another analysis would not invoke indexical shift at all and would treat the distribution of *tal* as involving an indexiphor (in the sense of chapter 5) sensitive to either *author*(*i*) or *origo*(*i*) values. On this approach, locality effects are predicted: e.g., (251) should lack a reading paraphrasable as 'Swuci told Yuswu that Cimin told Cengmi to give Swuci a gift'.

Sundaresan (2018) proposes a third option, which is that author shift is involved: *tal* requires a first-person goal, and the goal of the most embedded clause in (251) is a shifted first-person indexical. Based on this analysis, she reports that the example in (252) is a violation of Shift Together, as *tal* indicates first-person indexical shift but the indexical pronoun *nalul* 'me' is not shifted.[4]

(252) Context: My sister Cengmi, who is very fond of me, has a birthday coming up but doesn't know what to do to celebrate. Cimin, a mutual friend of ours, suggests to Cengmi that she have me visit her for her birthday, as a gift to herself on that day.
Cimin-ika   Cengmi-eykey   [casin-eykey   na-lul   tal-la-ko   ]
Cimin-NOM   Cengmi-DAT   [self-DAT   1SG-ACC   give-IMP-C]
mal-hay-ss-ta.
say-PAST-DECL
Cimin$_i$ told Cengmi$_j$ to give me to herself$_i$.

Use of this case as evidence against the shifty operator theory depends on ruling out the two alternative analyses just sketched, neither of which finds a Shift Together violation in this example. On a origo-indexical analysis, for instance, (252) is parallel to (248a), where an evidential is shifted but a personal pronoun is not. On an indexiphoric analysis, this case is parallel to Amharic data like (253); here one argument refers to *auth*(*i*) whereas the other refers to *auth*(*c*).

(253) *Amharic*
John [*pro*$_{subj}$ *pro*$_{obj}$ al-ittazzəzə-ññ   ] alə.
John [XPHOR   1SG   NEG.1S-obey.MKIMPERF-1SO] say.PERF.3SM
John$_i$ says he$_i$ will not obey me.
(Leslau 1995)

A general conclusion to be drawn here is that diagnosing a violation of Shift Together requires evidence of two sorts. First (as emphasized in chapter 5), it must be shown that the elements in question are indeed indexical. If they are instead indexiphoric, or subject to binding or other means of interpretation, no Shift Together effect is expected. Second, it must be shown that indexical elements make reference to the same coordinate of context. If they draw on separate coordinates of context, as for instance first- and second-person indexicals do, no Shift Together effect is expected. Rather, what is expected in this case is a hierarchical effect, given the hierarchy of shifty operators proposed in this book: one class of indexicals should be able to shift without the other shifting, though not vice versa. (For a caveat, see the discussion of lexical bundling in chapter 4.)

Both points are relevant for one final case I will mention here, related to Slovenian embedded imperatives. Stegovec and Kaufmann (2015) report that these clauses involve a violation of Shift Together: first- and second-person indexicals do not shift, but the "director" of the imperative—the individual who publicly commits to the preference that the imperative relates—does shift. In a matrix imperative, the director is the speaker. In the embedded imperative in (254), the director is Pero.

(254) *Slovenian*
Pero je rekel, da me ti poberi.
Pero is said.M that 1SG.ACC you pick.up.IMP
Pero said that you should pick me up.
(Stegovec 2019, 53)

One possible analysis of such data, like for the Korean data discussed above, involves a shifty indexical analysis involving a coordinate of context other than author or addressee. (This could in principle be a sui generis director coordinate—in which case we expect Shift Together effects among directors of imperatives in cases where multiple imperatives are embedded under a single verb, but no Shift Together effect with evidentials or pronouns. It could be an origo coordinate, as in Korotkova 2016. It could be a judge coordinate, as in McCready 2007 and Deal and O'Connor 2011.) In this case, we expect Shift Together effects in cases where the relevant coordinate of context is multiply invoked. But this is not the case in (254), which is therefore not a violation of Shift Together. Another style of analysis, pursued by Stegovec (2019), approaches such data as involving not indexicality but binding. Stegovec posits a PRO argument that saturates an argument position reserved for directors. PRO is itself then bound by attitude predicates or by illocutionary operators, yielding the attested pattern for matrix and embedded imperatives. This analysis posits no context shift of any type.

B Nez Perce Grammatical Background

Nez Perce has flexible word order within the clause and allows extensive use of null arguments, including for subjects, objects, and possessors. I gloss these arguments as *pro*; as a presentational convention, I linearize them in subject-verb-object order. In this appendix I briefly overview selected aspects of Nez Perce grammar that are relevant for the identification of null pronouns in the data presented in chapter 2. As we will see, identification of null arguments and recovery of their features is facilitated in Nez Perce by three grammatical systems: case, agreement, and clitics. I present these systems one by one, along with one or more examples drawn from chapter 2 in which the system in question can be used to identify the presence and/or person value of a null argument.

We begin with the case system. As discussed in Deal (2016a), the basic case pattern of Nez Perce varies between nominative-accusative (for first and second person) and tripartite ergative (for third person).[1] The pattern is exemplified for first person in (255) and third person in (256). As (256) shows, intransitive subjects, transitive subjects, and transitive objects are all marked distinctly in the third person. (Note that the examples in (255) are somewhat marked, as speakers prefer to use null pronouns rather than overt first-person pronouns. This situation has parallels in many other *pro*-drop languages.)

(255) a. 'Iin   waaqo' kuu-Ø-ye.
         1SG.NOM already go-P-REM.PAST
         I already went.
      b. 'Iin   'e-kiwyek-Ø-e   sik'eem-ne.
         1SG.NOM 3OBJ-feed-P-REM.PAST horse-ACC
         I fed the horse.
      c. Ciq'aamqal-m hi-ke'nip-Ø-e   'iin-e.
         dog-ERG   3SUBJ-bite-P-REM.PAST 1SG-ACC
         The dog bit me.

(256) a. 'Aayat waaqo' hi-kuu-Ø-ye.
woman.NOM already 3SUBJ-go-P-REM.PAST
The woman already went.
b. 'Aayato-nm pee-kiwyek-Ø-e sik'eem-ne.
woman-ERG 3/3-feed-P-REM.PAST horse-ACC
The woman fed the horse.
c. Ciq'aamqal-m pee-ke'np-Ø-e 'aayato-na.
dog-ERG 3/3-bite-P-REM.PAST woman-ACC
The dog bit the woman.

This pattern allows us to identify missing arguments in clauses that contain an accusative argument but no overt ergative, as well as in those that contain an ergative argument but no overt accusative. The two clauses of (257) exemplify these two possibilities.

(257) Context: Beth told me she met Harold. She doesn't know he is a teacher. When we are in class, I say to someone else:
Beth-nim hi-hi-n-e *pro* [*pro* 'e-wewkuny-Ø-e
Beth-ERG 3SUBJ-say-P-REM.PAST 1SG [1SG 3OBJ-meet-P-REM.PAST
sepehitemenew'etuu-ne].
teacher-ACC]
Beth told me she met the teacher.

We turn next to the agreement system. Nez Perce shows agreement in two loci: on verbs and on complementizers. These loci are divided in terms of which person categories they index directly. Verbs show overt person agreement affixes only for third person, whereas complementizers show overt person affixes only for first and second person. In addition, both systems index number (though the system of number inflection is richer on verbs than on complementizers). For verb agreement, the overt markers consist of the five prefixes listed in (258), along with the portmanteau suffixes listed in the rightmost column of (259). (Note that the use and combination of these affixes is subject to various additional restrictions not represented here. For instance, portmanteau markers of aspect/mood and subject plural do not co-occur with subject plural prefix *pe*; 3/3 portmanteau *pee* does not co-occur with other prefixes; and object plural marker *nees* cannot be controlled by plural second-person objects. These and other restrictions are discussed in Deal 2015b.)

(258) Verb agreement prefixes

> hi- third-person subject
> 'e- third-person object
> pee- third-person subject and third-person object
> pe- plural subject
> nees- plural object

(259) Portmanteau aspect/mood and agreement suffixes

	Basic form	Plural subject form
Imperfective	se/ce	siix/ciix
Habitual	teetu	tee'nix
Imperative	Ø/y/n	tx/nitx

Plural verb agreement occurs only for animate arguments (Deal 2016b). In the imperfective, habitual, and imperative, the plurality of an animate subject is marked as part of a portmanteau suffix, as in (259). The basic form of the aspect/mood suffix is used if the subject is singular and/or inanimate. In other aspect/mood categories, the plurality of an animate subject is marked by the plural subject prefix *pe*; this prefix is simply absent for singular and/or inanimate subjects. Full paradigms for verbal agreement are given in Deal 2015b.

Verb agreement plays a role in revealing the presence and properties of null arguments in two ways. First, the prefixes *'e* (3OBJ), *pee* (3/3), and *nees* (O.PL) may only index features from an (accusative) object and are therefore indicative of a transitive clause. This means that a null object argument must be present if none is overt. This pattern allows us to diagnose a null object argument for the main verb in (260). The agreement controlled by this argument unambiguously identifies it as third-person plural.

(260) Context: Elicited in Lapwai, ID.

> \# Kex kaa *pro* ciklii-toq-o' California-px, *pro*
> when.1 1SG return-back-PROSP California-to 1SG
> 'e-nees-Ø-nu' *pro* [*pro* we-ke'eyk-Ø-e
> 3OBJ-O.PL-say-PROSP 3PL.ACC [1SG fly-go-P-REM.PAST
> kinix kine-px].
> from.here here-to]
> When I return home to California, I will tell them that I flew from here*Idaho/California* to here*Idaho/California*.

Second, the prefixes *hi* (3SUBJ), *'e* (3OBJ), and *pee* (3/3) are obligatory in cases of third persons in the relevant argument position(s). A subject that does not appear with *hi* (3SUBJ) or *pee* (3/3) therefore cannot be third person. This allows us to determine local person status for the embedded subject in (260), as well as in (261). In the latter case, contrast the verb in the embedded clause (which has a shifted first-person indexical subject and no person prefix) with the verb in the 'but'-clause (which has a third-person subject and person prefix *hi-*).

(261) Context: my friend is calling me on his cellphone and describing his location. He is trying to make it to Lapwai, but he is lost.
Pro hi-hi-ce-Ø   [*pro* kine paay-ca-Ø   ],
3SG 3SUBJ-say-IMPERF-PRES [1SG here arrive-IMPERF-PRES]
met'u weet'u *pro* hi-paay-ca-Ø   kine.
but   not   3SG 3SUBJ-arrive-IMPERF-PRES here
He$_i$ says he$_i$ is arriving here, but he is not arriving here.

Likewise, an object in a clause without *'e* (3OBJ) or *pee* (3/3) on the verb cannot be third person.[2] In (262), ergative case on the embedded subject indicates that a null object is present in the embedded clause. The absence of third-person agreement with this object indicates that it is local person. (If the object were third person, the verb form would be *peeke'npe*.)

(262) Meeli   hi-i-caa-qa   [hi-ke'nip-Ø-e
      Mary.NOM 3SUBJ-say-IMPERF-REC.PAST [3SUBJ-bite-P-REM.PAST
      pro   Fido-nm].
      1SG.ACC Fido-ERG]
      Mary said that Fido bit her.

A final note on verb inflection concerns a suffix identified in Nez Perce grammars as the cislocative. On verbs of motion, cislocative marking indicates motion toward the speaker (Deal 2009a). This morpheme appears also to have acquired a secondary use as an agreement marker (or perhaps a very limited type of inverse marker), specifically in cases where the subject is second person and the object is first person. In the paradigms reported in Deal 2015b, the use of cislocative is categorical for this person combination (modulo morphological incompatibility with other adjacent suffixes). This fact is relevant for the interpretation of examples like (263), where both embedded arguments are local person. If the second person were the subject, the cislocative would be expected here. Its absence indicates that the first person is the subject. (The second-person clitic does not disambiguate; we return to the properties of second-person clitics below.)

(263) 'Iin-im lawtiwaa-nm hi-i-caa-qa *pro* [*pro*
1SG-GEN friend-ERG 3SUBJ-say-IMPERF-REC.PAST 1SG [1SG
'ee sok-saa-qa].
2SG.CL recognize-IMPERF-REC.PAST]
My friend told me I recognized you.

Complementizer agreement allows for partially similar argument-identification techniques to be deployed. As noted in chapter 2, Nez Perce does not use overt complementizers for attitude subordination. Accordingly, complementizer agreement is found primarily in relative and adverbial clauses, which are relatively underrepresented in the data of chapter 2. Unlike verbs, complementizers in Nez Perce show agreement according to a omnivorous pattern (in the sense of Nevins 2011). The same affix is used for second person, for instance, regardless of subject versus object status.

(264) Complementizer agreement suffixes

-(e)x	first person
-m	second person
-nm	first person inclusive
-pe	plural

The pattern of complementizer agreement shows various complexities in clauses containing plural arguments or more than one local person, as discussed in Deal 2015a, 2017. This complexity notwithstanding, the basic matter of inflection versus its absence can be used to show, for instance, that the subject of the 'when'-clause in (265) is second person; it controls *-m* inflection on the complementizer, and its clausemate arguments are clearly third person.

(265) Ke-m kaa *pro* 'ew-'nii-se-∅ laqaas-na
C-2 then 2SG 3OBJ-give-IMPERF-PRES mouse-ACC
cicyuk'iisin' k'aɨk'aɨ, kaa *pro* hi-wewluq-o'qa
cookie.NOM then 3SG 3SUBJ-want-MODAL
qahasnim wee'ikt kii taaqc.
milk.NOM same.day
When you give a mouse a cookie, he wants some milk that same day.

Complementizer agreement is clause-bounded (Deal 2015a, 2017). In (266), the relative clause shows no inflection on its complementizer *ke*. This supports the bracketing provided, wherein the first-person pronoun *'iin* is within the embedded clause, rather than an argument of the embedding attitude verb *hi* 'say'.

(266) Kii   hii-wes   'iniit   yox̂₁   ke   Jack
     this.NOM   3SUBJ-be.PRES   house.NOM   RP.NOM   C   Jack
     hi-hi-ce-Ø   ['iin   hani-Ø-ya t₁   ].
     3SUBJ-say-IMPERF-PRES [1SG.NOM   make-P-REM.PAST]
     This is the house that Jack says he built.

A third and final pattern that allows for the identification of null arguments concerns clitic pronouns. This system is particularly useful with respect to differentiation between first and second person. In the absence of a complementizer, first- and second-person arguments typically control identical agreement; pronouns of both persons may be null. Clauses containing a first- or second-person argument are therefore typically disambiguated by the use of full pronouns or by the presence of a clitic from the table in (267). Note that these clitics all reflect a second-person feature; there are no additional pronominal clitics beyond these three.

(267) Pronominal clitics
      'ee   second person singular
      'eetx   second person plural
      kiye   first person plural inclusive (first person + second person)

These clitics most commonly appear in immediate preverbal position and may double full second-person pronouns.

(268) 'Iim   'ee   wee-s   wepcuux.
      2SG.NOM 2SG.CLITIC be-PRES smart
      You (sg) are smart.
(269) *Pro* 'ime-ne   'ee   'iyoox̂oo-sa-Ø.
      1SG   2SG-ACC 2SG.CLITIC wait.for-IMPERF-PRES
      I'm waiting for you (sg).
(270) *Pro* 'imuu-ne 'eetx   tiwix-nu'.
      1SG   2PL-ACC 2PL.CLITIC follow-PROSP
      I will follow you (pl).

Unlike the full pronouns, the clitics may not be coordinated or host focus suffixes such as *-cim* 'only' or *-k'u* 'also'. They also differ from full pronouns in that they do not mark case distinctions. They may occur with subjects, as in (268), as well as objects, as in (269) and (270).

The presence of a second-person clitic allows us to identify as second person the subject of the embedded clause in (271) and the object of the embedded clause in (272):

(271) Lori   hi-neki-se-Ø   ['ee   wees   qetu   kuhet
     Lori.NOM 3SUBJ-think-IMPERF-PRES [2SG.CL be.PRES more tall
     'ip-nim-x   ].
     3SG-OBL-to]
     Lori$_i$ thinks that you$_j$ are taller than her$_i$.

(272) 'Iin-im   lawtiwaa-nm   hi-i-caa-qa   pro   [pro
     1SG-GEN   friend-ERG   3SUBJ-say-IMPERF-REC.PAST   1SG   [3SG
     'ee   hi-sok-saa-qa   ].
     2SG.CL 3SUBJ-recognize-IMPERF-REC.PAST]
     My friend$_i$ told me he$_i$ recognized you.

Conversely, the absence of a second-person clitic in numerous examples of chapter 2 gives rise to an unambiguously first-person parse. This is the case for instance in (273).

(273) Isii-ne$_i$ A.   hi-i-caa-qa   [cewcewin'es-ki
     who-ACC A.NOM 3SUBJ-say-IMPERF-REC.PAST [phone-with
     pro   'e-muu-ce-Ø   t$_i$]?
     1SG 3OBJ-call-IMPERF-PRES   ]
     Who did A$_i$ say I/she$_i$ was calling?

To ask 'Who did A say you (sg) were calling?', clitic 'ee would most naturally be present immediately before the embedded verb.

Further information on the grammar of Nez Perce can be found in the descriptions provided by Aoki (1970), Rude (1985), Crook (1999), and Deal (2010b), as well as in Aoki's (1994) extensive *Nez Perce Dictionary*.

Notes

Chapter 1

1. In this particular example this is no doubt due to the anaphoricity of *no* (on which see, for instance, Krifka 2013); without *no*, however, Berta's remark is simply a non sequitur in (2) (but not in (1)).

2. The following abbreviations are used in Nez Perce glosses: 3/3 3rd person subject + 3rd person object, 3SUBJ 3rd person subject, 3OBJ 3rd person object, ACC accusative, APPL applicative, C complementizer, CL clitic, CIS cislocative, ERG ergative, IMP imperative, IMPERF imperfective, IMPERF.PL imperfective + plural subject, HAB habitual, NEG negation, NOM nominative, OBL oblique, O.PL plural object, P perfect/perfective aspect (see Deal 2010b), PRES present tense, PROSP prospective aspect, REC.PAST recent past tense, REM.PAST remote past tense, RP relative pronoun, S.PL plural subject, μ functional head present in possessor raising (Deal 2013), 1SG (etc.) 1st person singular (etc.).

3. The status of the null subject here can be identified as first person rather than third person due to the lack of the subject agreement prefix *hi-* on the embedded verb. On details of glossing for Nez Perce examples, see appendix B.

4. I am aware of reports accompanied by at least some formal analysis for the following languages, listed here by language (sub)family or other typological group (though the reader is warned that I will not concur with analyses in terms of indexical shift for *all* these cases, as discussed in chapter 5 and appendix A): *Afro-Asiatic:* Amharic (Leslau 1995, Schlenker 1999, Anand 2006, Deal 2018b), Chaha (Schlenker 1999), Dhaasanac (Nishiguchi 2012, 2017), Tigrinya (Spadine 2019); *Athabaskan:* Navajo (Platero 1974, Schauber 1979, Speas 2000), Slave (Rice 1986, 1989, Anand and Nevins 2004); *Dravidian:* Malayalam (Anand 2006), Tamil (Sundaresan 2011, 2012, 2018), Telegu (Messick 2016; Sundaresan 2018); *Kartvelian:* Laz (Demirok and Öztürk 2015); Korean (Pak, Portner, and Zanuttini 2008, Park 2016) and Japanese (McCready 2007, Sudo 2012, Maier 2014a); *Kwa:* Engenni (Thomas 1978; Schlenker 1999); *Indo-Iranian:* Farsi (Anvari 2019), Kurmanji (Koev 2013, Akkuş 2018), Zazaki (Anand and Nevins 2004, Anand 2006, Akkuş 2018); *Other Indo-European:* Ancient Greek (Maier 2012), Bulgarian (Korotkova 2016), (nonstandard) English (Schlenker 2003 [though cf. Anand 2006, 92], Anderson 2015), Slovenian (Stegovec and Kaufmann 2015 [though cf. Stegovec 2019]); *Nakh-Dagestanian:* Tsez (Polinsky 2015); *Mongolic:* Kalmyk (Knyazev 2015);

Panoan: Matses (Munro et al. 2012); *Penutian:* Nez Perce (Deal 2014); *Turkic:* Mishar Tatar (Podobryaev 2014), Poshkart Chuvash (Knyazev 2019), Turkish (Gültekin Şener and Şener 2011, Özyıldız 2012, Akkuş 2018), Uyghur (Sudo 2012, Shklovsky and Sudo 2014, Major and Mayer 2019). In addition, the phenomenon is reported in a long list of sign languages (Zucchi 2004, Quer 2005, 2013, Herrmann and Steinbach 2012, Schlenker 2017a,b, inter alia), though on this last point cf. Davidson (2015) and Maier (2016, 2018), as well as the discussion in section 5.2. A number of additional languages have been discussed in the descriptive and typological literature in potentially similar terms, but require further attention before conclusive proposals can be made; these include *Trans-New Guinea* languages Gahuku (Deibler 1976), Golin (Loughnane 2005), Kobon (Davies 1981), Lower Grand Valley Dani (Bromley 1981), and Usan (Reesink 1993); *Nakh-Daghestanian* languages Icari Dargwa (Sumbatova and Mutalov 2003, 177–178) and Ingush (Nichols 2011); additional *Afroasiatic, Dravidian,* and *Kartvelian* languages Late Egyptian (Kammerzell and Peust 2002), Havyaka Kannada (Bhat 2004, 58), and Georgian (Thivierge 2019); as well as Aghem (Bantu; Hyman 1979), Manambu (Ndu; Aikhenvald 2008), and Wan (Mande; Nikitina 2012a). I will venture some hypotheses about languages from this last group throughout the discussion (and especially in chapter 5). Finally, I am aware of preliminary or unpublished reports of indexical shift in several additional languages—Buryat (Mongolic; Wurmbrand 2016), Cayuga (Iroquoian; Mike Barrie, pers. comm.); Magahi (Indo-Aryan; Mark Baker, pers. comm.); and Sakha (Turkic; Baker 2017)—for which, I hope, additional empirical discoveries will soon be forthcoming.

Chapter 2

1. Indeed these are two of the traditional tests distinguishing direct and indirect speech in English (Banfield 1973)—the other two relating to person and adverbial indexicals. For complementizers, note that while the presence of a complementizer is diagnostic (being restricted to the nonquotative case), the absence of a complementizer is not. For tense, note that while a simultaneous reading for past-under-past is diagnostic (again, restricted to the nonquotative case), the availability of present under past is not.

2. As I discuss in Deal (2019c), Nez Perce does allow some attitude complements with an overt complementizer, viz. the Ā complementizer *ke*. Tense in these complements allows simultaneous readings of past tense under past tense. I argue that this results from a *de re* reading of embedded tense, rather than from a sequence of tense rule. The behavior of these complements with respect to indexical shift is discussed at length in Deal (2019c).

3. On verbatim requirements on quotation, particularly outside of written language, see Clark and Gerrig (1990), Lillo-Martin (2012), and Davidson (2015).

4. On case patterns in Nez Perce, see Deal (2010a,b, 2019b).

5. For second person, Nez Perce has two series of pronouns: tonic pronouns *'iim* '2sg' and *'imé* '2pl' (along with their various case-marked variants), and noninflecting clitic pronouns *'ee* '2sg' and *'eetx* '2pl'. The clitic pronouns may double the tonic pronouns; see appendix B. I have not observed any difference between the two pronoun series with respect to indexical shift.

6. This example features object possessor raising: the direct object is 'me', rather than 'my flowers'. See Deal (2013) for in-depth discussion of this Nez Perce sentence type.

7. Kaplan's (1989) brief empirical discussion features a conditional; see his sections X and X(i).

8. This is not to say that there is any subject/object asymmetry to be found in the data in general. Recall that in (19) we see the reverse: a shifty indexical object and a *de re* subject.

9. There is a rich literature on this topic; see section 5.1 as well as Maier (forthcoming) and references there.

10. Nez Perce speakers often prefer shifty interpretations in cases where they are pragmatically possible. Under 'think', shift of second person is not possible (a point we return to in chapter 4), and thus the unshifty reading of (28) is uncontroversial. Under 'say', however, shift of second person is possible, and given the choice, speakers prefer shifty interpretations in most contexts. Note that, in spite of this preference, there is a clear distinction in consultant reactions to unshifty interpretation (30b) versus mixed interpretations (30c)/(30d), which are entirely unavailable. The same facts obtain in (31).

11. On the interaction of person shift and locative shift, see section 2.1.5 and especially section 3.1.3.

12. Consultants report that the only reading of (34)—flying from a location back to that same location—is one that is best described in a different way, e.g., as 'flying around'. In the same way, the English translation 'flying from here to here' is quite odd as a description of a flight that takes off from and returns to the speaker's location.

13. Note that there is only a single embedded clause here: the Nez Perce comparative allows only phrasal standards, not clausal ones (Deal and Hohaus 2019).

14. This point seems to have convinced Maier (2016) that at least some cases of purported indexical shift do not feature partial quotation.

15. For von Stechow, the particular mechanism of "disguise" relates to feature deletion under binding. See Anand (2006) for extensive discussion and critique of this view.

16. The phrase *qahasnim wee'ikt* literally means 'butter'.

17. In fact, *watiisx* serves as translation equivalents of both 'tomorrow' and 'yesterday'. The same type of symmetry is found for other temporal expressions in the language; similar patterns occur in Hindi (Rajesh Bhatt, pers. comm.).

18. See Anand (2006, section 2.6.1) for discussion of diacritics that would need to be added to von Stechow's (2003) binding-based view in order to account for patterns of Shift Together in Slave (Athabaskan).

19. This is a notational simplification of the proposal in Schlenker (1999, chapter 3); see Schlenker (2003).

20. On the syntax of prolepsis generally, see Davies (2005), Salzmann (2017a,b).

21. For arguments against a raising to object derivation of the (b) examples, see Deal (2017) (though the choice between prolepsis and raising derivations is largely orthogonal to the argument here).

22. On the morphosyntax of covert *res*-movement in Nez Perce, see Deal (2018a).

23. The ?? diacritic for (46a) indicates that this version was dispreferred to the unshifted version (46b), but not rejected as totally unacceptable. This preference, while not invariably absolute, is replicable: for instance, consultants demonstrated the same preference during elicitation sessions in 2016 and 2017. (In some elicitation sessions, as in (47), indexical shift was totally rejected with prolepsis.) Of my two consultants, one more strongly than the other disprefers indexical shift in proleptic complements. Notably, it is this same individual who more strongly prefers indexical shift in ordinary CP complementation, indicating a clear difference between these two complementation patterns in her grammar.

24. Additional partial support for this generalization comes from a class of embedding structures that in Deal (2019c) I have called "relative complements" (following Caponigro and Polinsky 2011): in these structures, there is a special syntax for the embedding CP, and person indexicals cannot shift. In Deal (2019c) I propose a semantic explanation for this behavior, based on the generalization that relative complements resist all dedicated *de se* phenomena (viz. shifty person indexicals and relative tense).

25. For further discussion of formal options for the modeling of contexts, see Schlenker (2018).

26. It might be asked whether this augmentation of the index is really so innocent, philosophically if not linguistically. I will say merely that I follow MacFarlane (2012, 135) in assuming that the presence of individual coordinates does not amount to an endorsement of relativism: "the presence of outlandish parameters of the index (taste, information state, etc.) does not itself make a semantic theory 'relativist' in any philosophically interesting sense. It does not prevent the theory from assigning truth values to sentences at contexts, or making absolute judgments of the accuracy of assertions."

27. Indeed, the received wisdom is that attitude verbs *always* do this; see, e.g., Schlenker (1999), Ogihara (1999), von Stechow (2003), Anand (2006), Grønn and von Stechow (2010), and Pearson (2015). In Deal (2019c) I argue, to the contrary, that this universal view is too strong: some attitude predicates indeed quantify merely over worlds.

28. I limit attention here and throughout this chapter to indirect discourse. Where what is embedded is a quote, multiple matters may be different (including, perhaps, the denotation of the verb).

29. Philippe Schlenker (pers. comm.) asks whether the different notational treatment of $w(i')$ and other i' coordinates (e.g., $author(i')$, $time(i')$) in (51) implies some deep difference between world-coordinates and other information in the index. It is not my intention to imply such a difference; rather, I treat the $w(i')$ coordinate in this way in (51) to highlight the connection with (50).

30. I will partially revise this view in chapter 3.

31. The formulation in (57) is a small touch-up of the proposal in Anand (2006, 72). See Klein (1980) for an antecedent. One detail left open in (56a) but not (56b) is the type of $[\![\alpha]\!]^{c,i,g}$; it is straightforward to provide a version of (56b) that allows other possibilities in this respect.

32. For simplicity, I set aside complications having to do with the *de re* reading of the indexical on its unshifted reading. (See Deal 2018a for relevant discussion.) I also ignore the *wh*-word and its associated predicate abstraction. I assume the trace is handled by

Heim and Kratzer's (1998) Traces and Pronouns rule and that *call* is handled in a very simple intensional way:

(i) $[\![call]\!]^{c,i,g} = \lambda x \in D_e . \lambda y \in D_e . y$ calls x at $t(i)$ in $w(i)$

33. These items are covert in Nez Perce, at least. It may be that they are overt in Laz (Demirok and Öztürk 2015), as touched on in chapter 4.

34. On an operators-as-C^0 view, the absence of shifty readings in prolepsis follows from competition for the C^0 position: if a clause-edge abstraction operator occupies this position, a shifty operator cannot. On a selectional view, the absence of a shifty reading in prolepsis structures like (46a) and (47c) is due to the fact that the shifty operator cannot select or be selected by the abstractor operator on the CP edge.

35. The representation of the binder index here follows Heim and Kratzer (1998): 2 is a trigger for Predicate Abstraction over this binding index.

36. Here two elements are understood to be in the same minimal attitude complement if they are contained within (a) the complement of an attitude verb and (b) all of the same clauses. In specifying this generalization only for the single-embedding case, I follow the strategy of Anand (2006). The multiclause case is discussed later in this section.

37. Similar remarks apply to Anand's (2006) original formulation of his constraint No Intervening Binder, reformulated in (77).

38. While this visualization depicts c_{utt} on par with syntactic elements, note that this is for conceptualization purposes only; the theory does not posit "context pronouns" or other syntactic representations of context. This distinguishes it from alternatives such as Schlenker (1999).

39. Note that, to derive a case where these values are not identical (and thus the indexicals do not shift together), ind_1 must not be the subject of $verb_1$. This holds in (76) as well; see discussion following example (85).

40. I propose this generalization as a replacement for the generalization that Anand (2006, 103) calls "No Intervening Binder." The shifty operator theory does not posit that indexicals (or shifty operators) have binders, making the name of this original constraint somewhat misleading. Local Determination also has broader empirical effects than Anand's No Intervening Binder constraint, if I understand Anand correctly: e.g., Local Determination but not No Intervening Binder rules out the reading schematized in (79), which is shown to be missing indeed in (83d).

41. I have little to say about this rather metaphysical question, beyond acknowledging Lewis's (1968) point that counterpart relations are not *always* transitive.

42. The reader will note that the predictions here follow from Shift Together, (72), as well as from the subsuming generalization Local Determination.

43. An alternative is to consider this OP a stand-in for the combination of OP_{AUTH} and OP_{ADDR}. This does not affect the reasoning here.

44. This is a respect in which person features, which are indexical, perhaps distinguish themselves from gender features, which are not:

(i) ? Sue is currently living as a woman, but is planning her gender transition. Whenever she transitions, he will change his name to Brian.

Judgments about this type of gender example are mixed; for discussion, see Sudo (2012).

Note also that a few cases of indexicals seemingly varying with quantifiers have been discussed by Nunberg (1993) and following work, most prominently Nunberg's example (ii):

(ii) *Condemned prisoner:* I am traditionally allowed to order whatever I like for my last meal.

Here the indexical seems to contribute something akin to the description *the condemned prisoner* (rather than *the speaker*). It seems to me that an e-type analysis is plausible here; see Elbourne (2008).

45. I address apparent counterexamples to this generalization (e.g., from Amharic [Semitic; Anand 2006] or Mutki Zazaki [Indo-Iranian; Akkuş 2018]) in chapter 5 and in appendix A. (I refer in the text to the variety of Zazaki documented by Anand 2006.)

46. The sentences required to test this generalization are quite complex, which explains why the set of languages in which it has been investigated is small. One apparent counterexample is found in Slave; see Anand (2006, section 2.7.1) and Bittner (2014) for discussion. Schlenker (2003, 68) discusses another, based on temporal expressions in English. See Anand (2006, 92) for an empirical argument that the temporal expressions in question are not in fact indexical, but rather anaphoric.

47. This position is defended by Shklovsky and Sudo (2014). Note however that recent work by Major and Mayer (2019) argues, based on prosodic behaviors, that the higher position is actually in the matrix clause—in which case, moved indexicals would be no longer clausemate with elements of their clause of origin. This would make these data more similar to the Farsi data on shift/movement interactions discussed by Anvari (2019).

48. The facts in Slave (a fellow Athabaskan language) are quite similar to those in Navajo; in particular, Rice (1986) demonstrates that verbs whose complements feature overt "complementizers" resist indexical shift. It may be that the putative complementizers are in fact markers of nominalization, though Rice (1989, chapter 42) presents challenges for this view.

49. Potential exceptions can be sorted into two types. The first involves two Turkic languages of Russia, Sakha and Balkar, as well as the Mongolic language Kalmyk. Baker (2017) and Knyazev (2015) report, respectively, that shift is possible in noun complement clauses in Sakha and Kalmyk. Sundaresan (2018) (citing unpublished work by Pavel Koval) reports that shift is possible in certain nominalized complements in Balkar. Given that very little information is available about these three languages, it is not yet clear to me that the relevant examples feature indexical shift as opposed to the phenomenon of indexiphoricity discussed in chapter 5. (The same goes for a species of rationale clause in Assamese [Indo-Aryan] and Telegu [Dravidian], analyzed by Sundaresan 2018 as indexical shift on the basis of unpublished work by Sushanta Rajkhowa and Rahul Balusu that had adopted a logophoric analysis.) The second type of potential exception involves shiftlike behavior in apparently matrix clauses in Tigrinya (Semitic; Spadine 2019) and Georgian (Thivierge 2019). Here it is not yet clear to me that the examples are not a species of Free Indirect Discourse, also discussed in chapter 5. Overall, however, it should be noted that, at least in the two Turkic languages and in Tigrinya, apparent shiftiness is still not possible across all syntactic complement

types—whatever the phenomenon responsible for the shifty reading, it is one that is sensitive to grammatical structure.

Chapter 3

1. On the semantics of *nízin* 'want/think', see Bogal-Allbritten (2016).

2. I follow here the descriptions by Platero (1974, 214) and especially Schauber (1979). In later work on Navajo, Speas (2000) reports a 'say'-only pattern. These findings remind us that talk of "languages" is loose talk; it is *grammars* we generalize over, and several grammars may be active in one speech community. It should be clear that this variation poses no problem for the overall pattern regarding attitude verbs, for both grammars of Navajo demonstrate expected possibilities.

3. An additional plausible example of this class is Amharic, where Anand (2006, 76) demonstrates shifting under 'say' and 'think' but does not discuss other verbs. Amharic is discussed in depth in chapter 5.

4. To assess factivity, Nez Perce speakers were asked to imagine that they had overheard a Nez Perce utterance that (in the crucial test cases) contained an attitude report embedded under negation, in a polar question, or in a conditional antecedent. They were then asked a follow-up question that probed for an entailment to the complement proposition, as exemplified in (i). (This task was prompted by the methodological discussion in Tonhauser et al. 2013.) Note that translations, given here in parentheses, were not provided in this task.

(i) ARD: "Suppose you overheard this:
C'alawi sepehiteemenew'eet hi-cuukwe-ce-Ø   ['iin
if   teacher.NOM   3SUBJ-know-IMPERF-PRES [1SG.NOM
k'oomay-ca-Ø   ], weet'u *pro* hi-cewcew-nuu-yu'-kum   *pro*.
be.sick-IMPERF-PRES] NEG   3SG 3SUBJ-call-APPL-PROSP-CIS 1SG
(If the teacher knows that I am sick, she won't call me.)
Would you think that person was ill?"
Consultant: "Well, I would think that person WAS ill. So he or she will not call her, if she knows."

With *cuukwe* 'know', consultants endorsed the complement proposition in five out of five total items. By contrast, with *neki* 'think', consultants declined to endorse the complement proposition in two of two downward entailing contexts and one out of one upward entailing context.

Nez Perce *cuukwe* also behaves like English knowledge predicates in the types of contexts discussed by Karttunen (1971), in which the factive inference appears not to be present. This is particularly clear in cases of inchoative knowledge reports, lexicalized in English with *find out* but expressed with *cuukwe* in Nez Perce:

(ii) Weetmet   kiy-u'!   C'alawi *pro* cuukwe-nu' ['ee   kuu-Ø-ye   ],
NEG.COMMAND go-PROSP if   1SG know-PROSP[2SG.CL go-P-REM.PAST],
konkí   *pro* q'eese'-nu'.
by.that 1SG be.upset-PROSP
Don't leave! If I find out you left, I'll be upset.

In exhorting the addressee not to leave, this discourse certainly does not presuppose that the contrary will occur.

5. An example is given in (i). The embedded structure here may either be a true embedded question (a CP) or else a free relative concealed question akin to 'the one she should call' (a DP). Further research is required to decide between these possibilities.

   (i) *Pro* hi-cuukwe-ce-∅   [ke 'isii-ne   *pro* pe-cewcew-nuu-yo'qa].
     3SG 3SUBJ-know-IMPERF-PRES [C who-ACC 3SG 3/3-call-APPL-MODAL]
     She knows who she should call.

6. Furthermore, various studies report behaviors for adverbials or other perspectival elements without ensuring that two crucial controls are in place. First, it must be shown that the elements in question are indeed indexical, rather than anaphoric or indexiphoric in the sense of chapter 5. Second, indexical elements related in a pretheoretic sense to the speaker or addressee must be carefully investigated to distinguish among what are potentially several distinct aspects of context, e.g., judge, origo, and author; see Korotkova (2016) and appendix A.

7. Speas demonstrates in particular that locative deictics glossed 'this here' and 'that there' do not shift, but person indexicals do.

8. See chapter 2 for Nez Perce and Anand (2006, 99) for Zazaki. The same presumably holds in Matses, given the generalizations set forth by Munro et al. (2012), but is not directly exemplified in their paper.

9. Nez Perce complements of emotive factives, introduced by the overt complementizer *ke* (mentioned in chapter 2, note 2) are a prima facie exception—though perhaps one that proves the rule: in Deal (2019c) I show that the behavior of person and locative indexicals in these complements crucially depends on the proposal to be given in this chapter regarding the relationship between person and locative shifting.

10. Some factors that can obscure these generalizations are discussed in connection with temporal indexicals in chapter 4 and in connection with nonindexical elements, Free Indirect Discourse, and sign language Role Shift in chapter 5.

11. Here and throughout I concentrate on optionality within particular grammars, rather than sociolinguistic or other variation within speech communities. Thus I do not consider the situation in Navajo described in note 2, for instance, to constitute optionality of the relevant sort.

12. A consequence is that the speaker/addressee of the context of utterance may not be referred to by first/second person in the complement clause; Munro et al. (2012) suggest that third person would have to be used for any individuals that do not participate in the reported attitude event. See their examples (19)–(20). Navajo exemplars of the same pattern are reported in Speas (2000, (2)); see also section 2.3. See also Anvari (2019) for discussion of connections between this type of pattern and the phenomenon of illeism.

13. *Nu* is in fact a portmanteau of first-person subject marking with some type of intention-related content; see Fleck (2003, 435–438). Note that the 'my wife' reading in (107b) is noted as impossible by Fleck; the interpretations in (107c) are not explicitly discussed, but are incompatible with the generalizations by Fleck and especially Munro et al. (2012). (For consistency, I present Matses material in the practical orthography used in Fleck's 2003 grammar of Matses.)

14. This context is inspired by a real-life example reported in the *Independent* online news, August 31, 2012, under the headline *'Missing' Icelandic tourist goes in search of herself*.

15. The same is reported for Mishar Tatar (Podobryaev 2014, 87–88), for which I defended an analysis without shifty indexicality in Deal (2018b). (I suspect, given the observations of Gültekin Şener and Şener 2011 and Özyıldız 2012, that the same general approach may apply to Turkish; *de se* restrictions for this language are noted in Gültekin Şener and Şener 2011.) On the multiple routes to *de se* interpretation, see Anand (2006).

16. Precise elicitation contexts for this sentence are not provided in Nishiguchi (2017) (though the relevant scenarios are well-known in the *de se* literature, owing to Kaplan 1989, section XVII). In personal communication, Sumiyo Nishiguchi confirms that in the elicitation scenarios, "Baali is looking at himself in a mirror. With [the] non–*de se* reading, he fails to recognize himself in the mirror, but the sentence is accepted."

17. This point will prove relevant to the discussion of nonstandard English temporal indexicals in chapter 4; Anderson (2015) observes that these do not require *de se* interpretations.

18. Nor, I might add, is indexical shift a necessary component of *de se* interpretation. See Anand (2006) and chapter 5 for discussion.

19. Beyond this, a treatment of *kine* as 'the vicinity of 1SG' (as per Harbour 2016) leads us incorrectly to expect Shift Together effects bidirectionally between person and locatives: the locative contains a first person indexical, and accordingly, shift of the author coordinate of context will shift both first person and locatives. See Deal (2019a) for discussion.

20. For the table in (G3), recall that neither Uyghur nor Dhaasanac allows shifty locative indexicals.

21. We return in section 4.2.1 to issues raised by the fact that a second-person shifted value is sometimes undefined, in particular with verbs of mental attitude.

22. Here I build on syntactic arguments that *v*P is always present, regardless of transitivity; see Legate (2003), Deal (2009b).

23. An anonymous reader asks whether this proposal is at odds with claims in the syntactic literature that there are covert left-peripheral elements that refer to the speaker and to the addressee, e.g., as arguments of a "Speech Act Phrase" or similar, especially given that many such claims involve a representation of the speaker that is structurally higher than the representation of the addressee (Speas and Tenny 2003, Sigurðsson 2004, Baker 2008, Haegeman and Hill 2013, Zu 2018, inter alia). It should be noted that this type of proposal is quite different from the proposal I have made: it involves referential elements that *refer* to the speaker and the addressee, rather than operators that simply adjust values for author and addressee coordinates of context. While I have yet to see convincing evidence for this sort of syntactic representation, I also do not see any inherent tension between these proposals and the proposal in the text. For much the same reasons, I do not see indexical shift as a source of evidence for syntactic proposals of the sort just mentioned, since merely making reference to the speaker and/or addressee

at the edge of the clause is not something that is likely to change the interpretation of first- or second-person pronouns.

24. Note that these are the possibilities for which Anand and Nevins (2004) propose the shifty operators OP$_\forall$ and OP$_{PERS}$. I discuss the choice between a syntactically articulated series of operators and this "single operator view" in chapter 4.

25. Crucial here is that the ellipsis mark conceals no shifty operators.

26. In the case of nominalizations, more properly it is the complement of the nominalizer that is clause–like but smaller than a full finite clause. See, e.g., Borsley and Kornfilt (2000) for discussion of the role of verbal and nominal projections inside nominalizations.

27. The word *systematic* is important here in view of the optionality of indexical shift in some languages. In Korean and Nez Perce, for instance, indexical shift is possible both with 'say' and 'think', but is not obligatory in either case. This means that these languages permit all of the following schematic structures:

(i) a. SAY [OP [TP   a′. THINK [OP [TP
    b. SAY   [TP   b′. THINK   [TP

Such cases suggest that the Speas/Sundaresan hierarchy of complement sizes should be taken to describe the *maximum* size for a particular complement type: the maximum size of a thought complement is always no greater than the maximum size of a speech complement.

28. A potential extension of this view might explore the behavior internal to the three classes of predicates discussed here, e.g., speech verbs. Given that the explanation I have posited is ultimately structural, one might in principle expect that variation internal to the class of speech verbs could divide that class into one subset that takes larger complements and allows (more) indexical shift versus another that takes smaller complements and takes no/less indexical shift. In this case, the dividing lines among classes of predicates would require further articulation.

29. For present purposes I set aside the possibility of an operator-free structure in Nez Perce and Zazaki, but not Uyghur, deriving optional indexical shift; see the discussion around (128).

30. This follows Deal (2014). Compare the similar move made by Bittner (2014) in Update with Eventuality Centering, where values for indexicals are functionally dependent on eventualities, including speech acts.

31. These denotations call for a straightforward extension of Monstrous Function Application beyond the formulation in chapter 2:

(i) If α is a branching node and $\{\beta, \gamma\}$ the set of its daughters, then for any context c, index i, and assignment g: if $[\![\gamma]\!]^{c,i,g} \in D_{<l,t>}$ and $[\![\beta]\!]^{c,i,g}$ is a function whose domain contains $\lambda i'.\lambda c'.\lambda e.[\![\gamma]\!]^{c',i',g}(e)$, then $[\![\alpha]\!]^{c,i,g} = [\![\beta]\!]^{c,i,g}(\lambda i'\lambda c'.\lambda e.[\![\gamma]\!]^{c',i',g}(e))$

32. A reader asks if we should then expect these shifters to occur outside intensional environments. While this is compatible with their semantics, it is not compatible with

the syntax for shifty operators I have defended throughout (which restricts the entire functional sequence of shifty operators to the edge of finite clauses).

33. Which counterpart? I take this to be a matter of the proper theory of modality *de re*, which is ultimately responsible for regulating how individuals belonging to one world are represented according to another.

Chapter 4

1. Also relevant to the relationship between embedded tenses and indexical shift are patterns of tense in relative clauses. While relativization is not reported to independently license indexical shift in any language, there are languages in which tenses in relative clauses are read relative to matrix tenses (e.g., Japanese); see Ogihara and Sharvit (2012) for recent discussion.

2. Though for some indication that the area of prima facie person marking is not fully devoid of this type of issue, see the discussion of indexiphoricity in chapter 5.

3. Seth Cable (pers. comm.) points out that facts like (153)/(154) are compatible with an indexical analysis of *watiisx/kii taaqc* on the assumption that an OP_{TIME} element (unlike other indexical shifters) may occur inside the scope of matrix adverbial quantifiers. (This analysis is consistent with the hierarchy proposed in this chapter, in that OP_{TIME} is the lowest shifty operator in the sequence. Thus matrix adverbial quantifiers could attach between OP_{TIME} and the next higher shifter up—were the sequence to be present in a matrix clause—yielding shift of temporal aspects of context only.) On this analysis, the difference between Nez Perce and English revealed in (153)/(154) would lie in the distribution of temporal shifters (which Nez Perce, but not English, allows in the relevant environments), rather than in the denotations of temporal adverbs. This analysis contrasts with the nonindexical analysis in that it predicts that temporal adverbials should show Shift Together effects in Nez Perce. But as we saw in chapter 2, this is not the case:

    (i) Halx̂pawit'aasx, Harold   hi-cuukwe-ce-ne   [*pro* wek-u'
         Saturday   Harold.NOM 3SUBJ-know-IMPERF-REM.PAST [1SG be-PROSP
         łepwey-pe watiisx   halx̂paawit-pa kaa kii taaqc lepiti-pe ka'aw-pa].
         Lapwai-LOC 1.day.away Sunday-LOC and same.day two-LOC day-LOC]
         On Saturday$_{t_1}$, Harold knew that I would be in Lapwai the next day$_{t_1+1}$, Sunday,
         and today$_{t*}$, Tuesday.   = (39)

4. For other cases where translation is affected in a way significant for semantic theory by pragmatic concerns in the language being translated into, see Deal (2015c).

5. Suggestive further evidence comes from Dhaasanac, where Nishiguchi (2017) shows that *gefere* 'yesterday' cannot vary with a temporal adverbial quantifier. The status of other temporal expressions in Dhaasanac remains to be clarified. It is, however, noteworthy that Dhaasanac allows shifting of temporal and person indexicals, but not locatives, in line with the articulation of the shifter hierarchy elaborated in this section.

6. Thanks to Min-Joo Kim and Sunwoo Jeong for this example.

7. Speaking of a single dialect here is a simplification, as experimental work by Anderson (2019) suggests several distinct subpopulations of speakers. One group of speakers disallows shifty *tomorrow* across the board; one permits it only in attitude reports; one permits it both in attitude reports and in a class of examples that are plausibly to be analyzed as Free Indirect Discourse. (Anderson argues against a Free Indirect Discourse analysis on the basis of the behavior of epithets and first-person pronouns. I do not find this case convincing; see Sharvit 2008 and Eckardt 2014 for some relevant data on first-person pronouns in Free Indirect Discourse. Moreover, Anderson argues against this analysis for a class of cases that are not "free" in the standard sense, but rather resemble standard attitude report embedding.)

8. While Nishiguchi (2017) reports that temporal indexical shift is possible in Dhaasanac, she does not report whether shifty temporals impose *de nunc* requirements. Thus it remains to be seen exactly how low C occurs in that language.

9. As information on the *de se* requirements of shifty indexicals is not available for Slave, no determination can be made regarding the location of C in this language.

10. Note that the glossing of the adverb *sacho̜* as 'tomorrow' follows Rice (1989). It is possible that this element is not in fact indexical, parallel to Nez Perce *watiisx* '1 day away'.

11. A potentially similar case is found in Laz, another language with obligatory indexical shift. Demirok and Öztürk (2015) show that Laz allows two types of finite complementizers, *ya/ma* and clitic *na=*, in complements of speech and thought verbs. Indexical shift is obligatory in *ya/ma* complements but forbidden in *na=* complements. (*Ya/ma* clauses need not be quotations; see Demirok and Öztürk 2015, section 3.2.)

(i) *Laz*
Arte-k [ma noseri vore] **ya** {iduşun-am-s / t'k'-u}.
Arte-ERG 1SG smart be.1SG C {think-IMPF-3SG / say-PST.3SG}
Arte$_i$ {thinks/says} that he$_i$ is /✗I am smart. (Demirok and Öztürk 2015, 51)

(ii) Arte-k [ma noseri **na=**vore] {iduşun-am-s / t'k'-u}.
Arte-ERG 1SG smart C=be.1SG {think-IMPF-3SG / say-PST.3SG}
Arte$_i$ {thinks/says} that I am /✗he$_i$ is smart. (Demirok and Öztürk 2015, 51)

This pattern suggests that the Laz lexicon contains both an unbundled C item, pronounced *na=*, and a bundled C + OP item, pronounced *ya/ma*. The bundling of C with shifty operators explains why the general purpose C head is missing in shifty complements. (On *na=* as a general purpose complementizer in Laz, see Lacroix 2012.) The expectation is that second persons will be forbidden when thought verbs take complements containing *ya/ma*, though Demirok and Öztürk do not discuss this.

12. For an independent case of potential lexical bundling of elements that are not structurally adjacent in a functional sequence, see Deal (2018c) (as well as discussion related to this point in Rizzi's 1997 discussion of English *that*-trace effects).

13. More precisely, this is the result of lexical bundling of series of *de se* operators.

14. See Charnavel (2019) for a similar proposal to treat local person pronouns as e-type (i.e., definite descriptions), extended to first person as well. If such an analysis were universally available for first and second persons, one might expect no *de se* requirements on shifted personal pronouns across the board.

15. This, however, would be difficult to diagnose, given that *de se* readings are available as a special case of *de re* readings. See Percus and Sauerland 2003a for a diagnostic that could be applicable.

16. This possibility was suggested in discussion by Pranav Anand, pers. comm.

17. I highlight this particular prediction because it is not *obviously* correct. For Slave, for instance, Rice (1989) provides examples wherein a first-person pronoun but not a word glossed 'tomorrow' shifts (e.g., Rice 1989, 1279, (37)). This suggests either that 'tomorrow' in Slave is not indexical, in line with the situation in Nez Perce (see (153)), or that Slave possesses a lexically bundled OP_ADV element of the type discussed for Korean (see (175)/(176)). The former predicts that temporal elements in Slave may not be "shiftable" at all in attitude complements (as this depends on the availability of binding, rather than actual indexical shift), but should show covariation under temporal quantification as in (153) and (154); the latter predicts that temporal and locative indexicals should be optionally shiftable in Slave, but that the two types of indexicals should have to shift together.

18. Note that the prediction for the interpretation of temporal indexicals in Nez Perce might be fulfilled vacuously, as the language plausibly does not have true temporal indexicals. Similar remarks may apply to Uyghur, though Sudo (2012) does not discuss temporal elements. A language with *de se* requirements on all indexicals is Zazaki; see Anand (2006, 80).

19. Proof: by the definition of function composition, $(\llbracket \text{OP}_1 \rrbracket \circ \llbracket \text{OP}_2 \rrbracket)(\llbracket \textit{XP} \rrbracket) = \llbracket \text{OP}_1 \rrbracket(\llbracket \text{OP}_2 \rrbracket(\llbracket \textit{XP} \rrbracket))$. Let XP = TP. If OP_2 is an index-based shifter, then $\llbracket \text{OP}_2 \rrbracket(\llbracket \textit{TP} \rrbracket) \in D_t$. If OP_1 is a event-based shifter, then it cannot compose with an argument of this type. Alternatively, let XP = CP. If OP_2 is an index-based shifter, its contribution is vacuous in this high position, and thus the bundled operator does not accomplish both types of shift.

20. This is the situation in Uyghur; see fn. 11 for a caveat.

21. Korean instantiates the "both" option for OP_ADV, as shown by Park (2016): all shifty indexicals require *de se* interpretation in Korean, revealing that C attaches quite high in that language (like in Zazaki).

Chapter 5

1. Note that unquotation of tenses does not automatically require unquotation of the entire word hosting the tense. Likewise, unquotation of pronouns does not automatically require unquotation of the entire word hosting agreement with the pronoun. Visibly marked unquotation of affixes is indeed routine in written registers, as in (i):

(i) a. Mueller's report contains evidence of "ten separate episodes of potentially obstructive conduct by the President, ranging 'from efforts to remove the Special Counsel and to reverse the effect of the Attorney General's recusal; to the attempted use of official power to limit the scope of the investigation': ... to 'encourage[ing] witnesses not to cooperate with the investigation.'" (*Washington Post*, August 8, 2019)

   b. "She said that she found people posting political points of view that oppose the US on my friend[s] list." (slate.com, August 27, 2019)

c. Despite a relatively poor average poll rating as Prime Minister, Thatcher has since ranked highly in retrospective opinion polling and, according to YouGov, she is "see[n] in overall positive terms" by the British public. (wikipedia.com)
d. In July 1977, during a live performance, the trio made a surprise announcement that "[they] want[ed] to return to being normal girls" and immediately end their careers. (wikipedia.com)

It seems to me that this possibility goes a ways toward addressing two objections to the quotation view by Eckardt (2014). First, Eckardt claims that a quotational view of FID forces quotation of material that is not otherwise quotable, e.g., single discourse particles, as in her example (ii). If, however, the verb stem is not quoted (as I display here), the quotation in this example contains more than just the particle.

(ii) *German*
[Sie] lieb[te] [ihn] ja.
She *ja* loved him.

Second, similarly, Eckardt objects that the quotation view requires quotation of only the abstract syntax of a question in cases such as (iii) (and its German counterpart). Again, this objection rests on the idea that the auxiliary, whose tense and person is adjusted, must be fully unquoted. Considering the example without this assumption (and keeping in mind that the lexical verb need not be unquoted either, in this case not even in part), the quotation here again contains more than just the abstract syntax of the question.

(iii) Peter looked at me. He was nervous. D[id] [he] please [me]?

2. The "Yes" in the second row for quotation is in reference to standard judgments about written examples—and note that FID lives exclusively in the written register. See Clark and Gerrig (1990), Lillo-Martin (2012), and Davidson (2015) on verbatim requirements, especially outside of spoken language.

3. This can be contrasted both with Lillo-Martin's (1995) treatment in terms of logophoricity and Schlenker's (2017a,b) recent proposal that Role Shift involves *both* indexical shift and iconicity requirements tantamount to quotation. See Lee et al. (1997), Davidson (2015), and Maier (2016, 2018) for critical discussion and arguments for a fully quotational analysis. An overview of the literature on Role Shift across sign languages can be found in Lillo-Martin (2012).

4. See however Charnavel (2019) for a class of exceptions to the requirement that first-person fake indexicals have first-person antecedents.

5. Kratzer (2009, 218) suggests that the availability of mixed readings is limited to cases where (roughly) the antecedent is local to the fake indexical. The English speakers I have consulted do not agree with the judgment she reports, however.

6. Properly, Sudo's proposal is slightly more complex: an index is a triple of a number, a type, and a person feature.

7. This example provides further evidence against restricting embedded -*N* to cases where the embedded subject is a logophoric pronoun. Culy (1994, 114) shows that logophoric pronouns in Donno Sɔ (as in many languages) must have third-person

antecedents. Heath (2016, 303) refers to the logophor *ǹjèmɛ́* as a "third person logophoric pronoun," suggesting that the same restriction holds in the variety he documents. In the most embedded clause of (207), the null subject has a second-person pronoun as its antecedent, meaning therefore that this element is presumably a null second-person pronoun rather than a null logophoric pronoun. I have glossed the example accordingly.

8. This is a reformatting of Coppock and Wechsler's proposal, aimed at clarifying its relation to its various antecedents. These include, for instance, Anand and Nevins (2004), who propose this type of analysis for controlled PRO and for logophors, and Ninan (2010), who considers this analysis for Amharic "first person." Ninan ultimately rejects this analysis of Amharic as it does not extend to Zazaki. My analysis of Amharic in this section is similar to the approach Ninan rejects (in view of the multiple empirical differences between the Amharic facts and their Zazaki counterparts).

9. Note that this is a different (and, I believe, improved) use for the term 'indexiphoric' than the one found in Deal 2018b. In that work, 'indexiphor' is a term used for a logophor (a special type of bound pronoun) that agrees like an indexical. I believe the present account handles agreement with indexiphors in a more explanatory way. Note that one important empirical difference between the current treatment of indexiphors versus the Deal 2018b approach is that, on the present approach, the [AUTH-I] feature may in principle be borne by a first- or second-person pronoun, which will accordingly be *both* indexical and indexiphoric; for instance, a first-person indexiphor is required to refer to both *author*(i) and *author*(c) (and thus is appropriate only in contexts in which the values for these are the same). By contrast, no element may be both indexical and indexiphoric in the sense of Deal 2018b. The reader is advised, however, that in the text I largely abstract away from possibility of indexiphoric indexicals for the sake of simplicity, and contrast elements that are merely indexical with elements that are merely indexiphoric.

10. If attitude verbs always express centered quantification, we expect the requirement of locality for indexiphors to be absolute. If, however, some attitude predicates may involve uncentered quantification (Deal 2019c), exceptions to this locality are expected. In cases where indexiphors are not locally construed, we expect all other dedicated *de se* devices to also be missing or behave specially. This is not expected in cases in which indexicals are long-distance shifted, such as (218).

11. This analysis follows a suggestion by Mark Baker (pers. comm.).

12. Golin (New Guinea; Loughnane 2005) is a possible case of a language where the syncretism holds for pronouns but not for verbal inflection. This language is like Kathmandu Newari and Donno Sɔ in allowing only *author*(i) elements to control embedded "first-person" agreement; as for these other cases, I assume this agreement is in fact agreement with an [AUTH-I] feature. It differs from Kathmandu Newari and Donno Sɔ in that embedded "first-person" pronouns may refer to either *author*(i) or *author*(c) (and mixed readings within a single clause are possible). I conclude that the pronouns reflect not an indexical first person feature, but rather a syncretism in the subfeature [AUTH].

13. Anand lists only readings (b) and (c), which are most relevant to his discussion; readings (a) and (d) are predicted by all approaches to Amharic of which I am aware.

14. A more general statement of the constraint, intended to apply equally well to cases such as the Turkish one discussed by Akkuş (2018), is given in Deal (2018b).

15. Akkuş (2018) argues that the Turkish and Mutki Zazaki data cannot feature indexiphoricity because they do not show the locality property reviewed earlier in connection with (216) and (217). However, this diagnosis is confounded by the possibility that the languages in question contain OP_{auth} shifty operators. On languages with both indexiphoricity and indexical shift, see the discussion of Amharic examples (229)–(231).

16. Sundaresan (2018) argues that the *De Re* Blocking effect is violated in Tamil. However, her example, reprinted in (i), features not a simple indexical as a potential *de re* competitor for an indexiphor (here *taan*, glossed 'anaphor'), but rather the expression 'me with my three sisters'; evidence for the syntactic position of this expression (at LF) is based purely on the scope-taking behavior of the numeral 'three' with respect to a sentential adverb.

(i) *Tamil*
Sri [taan enn-oo:ɖæ muu:ɳŭ akkaa-vooɖæ ennæ orŭ daram
Sri.NOM [ANAPH.NOM me-GEN three sister-with me-ACC one time
parr.tt-iru-kkir-een-nnŭ] so-nn-aan.
see.ASP-COP-PRES-1SG-C] say-PAST-3M.SG
Sri$_i$ said that he$_i$ has seen me with my three sisters once.
Possible scopal reading: three > once

Predictions for *De Re* Blocking in this case depend on the syntax of the comitative and the means of scope-taking. On the former count, we see in (227) that an expression that contains a first person pronoun, e.g., as a possessor, is not necessarily a *de re* competitor for an indexiphor. (This is presumably because the indexical does not c-command out of the containing phrase.) The same may apply to the comitative construction of interest for Sundaresan. On the second count, the argument depends on ruling out a means of scope-taking for the numeral that is not based on (covert) movement, e.g., choice functions (Reinhart 1997, Winter 1997, Kratzer 1998b, Matthewson 1999, Dawson 2019, inter alia). If 'me with my three sisters' is interpreted in its surface position, it does not c-command the indexiphoric subject and is not expected to serve as a *de re* competitor.

17. A potential additional language with a syncretism in [AUTH] but not [ADDR] is Golin (New Guinea; Loughnane 2005). In this language, the same form is used for *author(i)* and *author(c)* pronouns (see note 12). Nikitina (2012b) claims this asymmetry does not extend to *addr*-based elements: *addr(c)* elements in speech reports are realized as second-person pronouns, whereas *addr(i)* elements are realized as third-person pronouns. Note, however, that Nikitina cites Loughnane (2005) for this pattern, and I have been unable to locate any discussion of reported addressees in that work.

18. Judgment diacritics including "(?)" are taken from Akkuş's paper.

Appendix A

1. Note that this is contrary to earlier findings by Sauerland and Schenner (2007).

2. Sundaresan (2018) also reports a third condition for the use of *tal*, which I set aside here for the sake of simplicity: the goal must be "construed as an eventual recipient of the theme," meaning that *tal* is not possible in the negated version of (250a).

3. Pak, Portner, and Zanuttini (2008) explicitly propose that some Korean indexicals are shiftable whereas others are not; in particular, they propose that the only shiftable person features in Korean are those associated with embedded imperatives. This is contrary to the findings of Park (2016), who shows that ordinary person indexicals are shiftable in Korean. Pak et al.'s proposal might be taken to suggest that Korean embedded imperatives give rise to violations of Shift Together, but they provide no examples that demonstrate potential violations.

4. A question facing this account involves the morphology of the embedded goal argument, namely its realization with the pronoun *casin*. Park (2016) shows that the Korean logophor *caki* cannot be co-referential with a shifted first-person indexical. She attributes this fact to third-person features on *caki*. If the same effect holds for *casin*, used in (251) and (252), this challenges an account in terms of first-person indexical shift: *casin* would need to bear first-person features, contrary to its behavior in other cases.

Appendix B

1. The language also allows notionally transitive clauses in which both arguments are nominative. As discussed at length in Rude (1985, 1986), Deal (2010a), and especially Deal (2010b, 188–423), this clause type arises when either the object is a weak indefinite or the subject binds the possessor of the object. In such clauses, the case of visible arguments does not provide an unambiguous clue to the presence of a clausemate null argument.

2. This generalization is subject to a caveat (though not one that is relevant to the examples of chapter 2): if the subject is third person and the object is third person plural, then the verb inflection is *hi-nees-*. In this form, the person of the object is not reflected. See Deal (2015b).

References

Abusch, Dorit. 1997. Sequence of tense and temporal de re. *Linguistics and Philosophy* 20 (1): 1–50.

Adesola, Oluseye. 2005. Pronouns and null operators: A-bar dependencies and relations in Yoruba. PhD diss., Rutgers University.

Adesola, Oluseye. 2006. A-bar dependencies in the Yoruba reference-tracking system. *Lingua* 116: 2068–2106.

Aikhenvald, Alexandra. 2008. Semi-direct speech: Manambu and beyond. *Language Sciences* 30: 383–422.

Akkuş, Faruk. 2018. Un-shifting indexicals. Manuscript, University of Pennsylvania.

Anand, Pranav. 2006. De *de se*. PhD diss., MIT.

Anand, Pranav, and Valentine Hacquard. 2008. Epistemics with attitude. In *SALT XVIII*, eds. T. Friedman and S. Ito, 37–54. Ithaca, NY: CLC Publications.

Anand, Pranav, and Andrew Nevins. 2004. Shifty operators in changing contexts. In *Proceedings of SALT XIV*, ed. Robert B. Young, 20–37. Ithaca, NY: CLC Publications.

Anderson, Carolyn. 2015. *Tomorrow* isn't just another day: shifty temporal indexicals in English. Manuscript, University of Massachusetts, Amherst.

Anderson, Carolyn. 2019. Tomorrow isn't always a day away. In *Proceedings of Sinn und Bedeutung 23*, ed. M. Teresa Espinal et al., Vol. 1, 37–56. Barcelona: Universitat Autònoma de Barcelona, Bellaterra (Cerdanyola del Vallès).

Anvari, Amir. 2019. Meaning in context. PhD diss., École Normale Supérieure.

Aoki, Haruo. 1970. *Nez Perce grammar*. Berkeley: University of California Press.

Aoki, Haruo. 1994. *Nez Perce dictionary*. Berkeley: University of California Press.

Baker, Mark C. 2008. *The syntax of agreement and concord*. Cambridge: Cambridge University Press.

Baker, Mark C. 2017. Comments on "Shifty asymmetries: universals and variation in shifty indexicality." Rutgers Semantics/Pragmatics Workshop, Rutgers University Center for Cognitive Science.

Banfield, Ann. 1973. Narrative style and the grammar of direct and indirect discourse. *Foundations of Language* 10 (1): 1–39.

Bassi, Itai, and Nicholas Longenbaugh. 2018. Features on bound pronouns: an argument against syntactic agreement approaches. In *Proceedings of NELS 48*, eds. Sherry Hucklebridge and Max Nelson, Vol. 1, 59–72. Amherst, MA: GLSA Publications.

Beck, Sigrid, Sveta Krasikova, Daniel Fleischer, Remus Gergel, Stefan Hofstetter, Christiane Savelsberg, John Vanderelst, and Elisabeth Villalta. 2009. Crosslinguistic variation in comparison constructions. *Linguistic Variation Yearbook* 9: 1–66.

Bhat, DNS. 2004. *Pronouns*. Oxford: Oxford University Press.

Bittner, Maria. 2014. Perspectival discourse referents for indexicals. In *Proceedings of SULA 7*, ed. H. Greene, 1–22. Amherst, MA: GLSA Publications.

Bobaljik, Jonathan David, and Höskuldur Thráinsson. 1998. Two heads aren't always better than one. *Syntax* 1 (1): 37–71.

Bochnak, Ryan, Vera Hohaus, and Anne Mucha. 2019. Variation in tense and aspect, and the temporal interpretation of complement clauses. *Journal of Semantics* 36 (3): 407–452.

Bogal-Allbritten, Elizabeth. 2016. Building meaning in Navajo. PhD diss., University of Massachusetts, Amherst.

Borer, Hagit. 1984. *Parametric syntax*. Dordrecht: Foris Publications.

Borsley, Robert D., and Jaklin Kornfilt. 2000. Mixed extended projections. In *The nature and function of syntactic categories*, ed. Robert D. Borsley, 101–131. San Diego: Academic Press.

Bresnan, Joan. 1972. Theory of complementation in English syntax. PhD diss., MIT.

Bromley, H. Myron. 1981. *A grammar of Lower Grand Valley Dani*. Canberra: Pacific Linguistics.

Cable, Seth. 2005. Binding local person pronouns without semantically empty features. Manuscript, MIT.

Caponigro, Ivano, and Maria Polinsky. 2011. Relative embeddings: a Circassian puzzle for the syntax/semantics interface. *Natural Language and Linguistic Theory* 29 (1): 71–122. doi:10.1007/s11049-011-9121-9.

Cappelen, Herman, and Ernie Lepore. 1997. Varieties of quotation. *Mind* 106: 429–450.

Cappelen, Herman, and Ernie Lepore. 2017. Quotation. In *The Stanford encyclopedia of philosophy (fall 2017 edition)*, ed. Edward N. Zalta. https://plato.stanford.edu/archives/fall2017/entries/quotation/.

Cecchetto, Carlo, Carlo Geraci, and Sandro Zucchi. 2009. Another way to mark syntactic dependencies: the case for right-peripheral specifiers in sign languages. *Language* 85 (2): 278–320.

Charlow, Simon, and Yael Sharvit. 2014. Bound *de re* pronouns and the LFs of attitude reports. *Semantics and Pragmatics* 7 (3): 1–43. doi:10.3765/sp.7.3.

Charnavel, Isabelle. 2019. Supersloppy readings: indexicals as bound descriptions. *Journal of Semantics* 36 (3): 453–530.

Chierchia, Gennaro. 1998. Reference to kinds across languages. *Natural Language Semantics* 6 (4): 339–405.

Chomsky, Noam. 1995. *The minimalist program*. Cambridge, MA: MIT Press.

References

Cinque, Guglielmo. 1999. *Adverbs and functional heads: a cross-linguistic perspective*. New York: Oxford University Press.

Clark, Herbert C. 1996. *Using language*. Cambridge: Cambridge University Press.

Clark, Herbert C., and Richard J. Gerrig. 1990. Quotations as demonstrations. *Language* 66 (4): 764–805.

Coppock, Elizabeth, and Stephen Wechsler. 2018. The proper treatment of egophoricity in Kathmandu Newari. In *Expressing the self: cultural diversity and cognitive universals*, eds. Kasia M Jaszczolt and Minyao Huang, 40–57. Oxford: Oxford University Press.

Cristofaro, Sonia. 2003. *Subordination*. Oxford: Oxford University Press.

Crook, Harold David. 1999. The phonology and morphology of Nez Perce stress. PhD diss., University of California, Los Angeles.

Culy, Christopher. 1994. A note on logophoricity in Dogon. *Journal of African Languages and Linguistics* 15: 113–125.

Cumming, Samuel. 2003. Two accounts of indexicals in mixed quotation. *Belgian Journal of Linguistics* 17 (1): 77–88.

Curnow, Timothy. 2002. Three types of verbal logophoricity in African languages. *Studies in African Linguistics* 31: 1–25.

Cysouw, Michael. 2003. *The paradigmatic structure of person marking*. Oxford: Oxford University Press.

Davidson, Kathryn. 2015. Quotation, demonstration and iconicity. *Linguistics and Philosophy* 38 (6): 477–520.

Davies, John. 1981. *Kobon*. Amsterdam: North-Holland Publishing.

Davies, William D. 2005. Madurese prolepsis and its implications for a typology of raising. *Language* 81 (3): 645–665. doi:10.1353/lan.2005.0121.

Dawson, Virginia. 2019. Paths to exceptional wide scope: choice functions in Tiwa. Manuscript, University of California, Berkeley.

Deal, Amy Rose. 2009a. Events in space. In *Proceedings of SALT XVIII*, eds. T. Friedman and S. Ito, 230–247. Ithaca, NY: CLC Publications.

Deal, Amy Rose. 2009b. The origin and content of expletives: evidence from "selection." *Syntax* 12 (4): 285–323.

Deal, Amy Rose. 2010a. Ergative case and the transitive subject: a view from Nez Perce. *Natural Language and Linguistic Theory* 28 (1): 73–120. doi:10.1007/s11049-009-9081-5.

Deal, Amy Rose. 2010b. Topics in the Nez Perce verb. PhD diss., University of Massachusetts, Amherst.

Deal, Amy Rose. 2013. Possessor raising. *Linguistic Inquiry* 44 (3): 391–432. doi:10.1162/LING_a_00133.

Deal, Amy Rose. 2014. Nez Perce embedded indexicals. In *Proceedings of SULA 7: Semantics of under-represented languages in the Americas*, ed. H. Greene, 23–40. Amherst, MA: GLSA Publications.

Deal, Amy Rose. 2015a. Interaction and satisfaction in ϕ-agreement. In *Proceedings of NELS 45*, eds. Thuy Bui and Deniz Özyıldız, 179–192. Amherst, MA: GLSA Publications.

Deal, Amy Rose. 2015b. A note on Nez Perce verb agreement, with sample paradigms. In *Proceedings of the International Conference on Salish and Neighbouring Languages 50*, ed. Natalie Weber et al., 389–413. Vancouver: UBC Working Papers in Linguistics.

Deal, Amy Rose. 2015c. Reasoning about equivalence in semantic fieldwork. In *Methodologies in semantic fieldwork*, eds. R. Bochnak and L. Matthewson, 157–174. Oxford: Oxford University Press.

Deal, Amy Rose. 2016a. Person-based split ergativity in Nez Perce is syntactic. *Journal of Linguistics* 52 (3): 533–564. doi:10.1017/S0022226715000031.

Deal, Amy Rose. 2016b. Plural exponence in the Nez Perce DP: a DM analysis. *Morphology* 26 (3): 313–339. doi:10.1007/s11525-015-9277-9.

Deal, Amy Rose. 2017. Covert hyperraising to object. In *Proceedings of NELS 47*, eds. Andrew Lamont and Katerina Tetzloff, 257–270. Amherst, MA: GLSA Publications.

Deal, Amy Rose. 2018a. Compositional paths to *de re*. In *Proceedings of SALT 28*, ed. Sireemas Maspong et al., 622–648. Ithaca, NY: CLC Publications.

Deal, Amy Rose. 2018b. Indexiphors: notes on embedded indexicals, shifty agreement, and logophoricity. In *The leader of the pack: a festschrift in honor of Peggy Speas*, ed. Rodica Ivan, 59–86. Amherst, MA: GLSA Publications.

Deal, Amy Rose. 2018c. Locality in allomorphy and presyntactic bundling: a case of tense and aspect. *Snippets* 34: 8–9.

Deal, Amy Rose. 2019a. Person features and shiftiness. Paper presented at the Alphabet of Universal Grammar, British Academy, London.

Deal, Amy Rose. 2019b. Raising to ergative: remarks on applicatives of unaccusatives. *Linguistic Inquiry* 50 (2): 388–415. doi:10.1162/ling_a_00310.

Deal, Amy Rose. 2019c. Uncentered attitude reports. Manuscript, University of California, Berkeley.

Deal, Amy Rose, and Vera Hohaus. 2019. Vague predicates, crisp judgments. In *Proceedings of Sinn und Bedeutung 23*, ed. M. Teresa Espinal et al., 347–364. Barcelona: Universitat Autònoma de Barcelona, Bellaterra (Cerdanyola del Vallès).

Deal, Amy Rose, and M. C. O'Connor. 2011. The perspectival basis of fluid-S case-marking in Northern Pomo. In *Proceedings of SULA 5*, ed. Suzi Lima, 173–188. Amherst, MA: GLSA Publications.

De Brabanter, Philippe. 2010. The semantics and pragmatics of hybrid quotations. *Language and Linguistics Compass* 4 (2): 107–120.

Deibler, Ellis. 1976. *Semantic relationships of Gahuku verbs*. Dallas, TX: SIL International.

Demirok, Ömer, and Balkız Öztürk. 2015. The logophoric complementizer in Laz. *Dilbilim Araştırmaları Dergisi (Journal of Linguistics Research)* 26 (2): 45–69.

Eckardt, Regine. 2014. *The semantics of free indirect discourse: how texts allow us to mind-read and eavesdrop*. Leiden: Brill.

Elbourne, Paul. 2008. Ellipsis sites as definite descriptions. *Linguistic Inquiry* 39 (2): 191–220.

Engberg-Pedersen, Elisabeth. 1995. Point of view expressed through shifters. In *Language, gesture and space*, eds. K. Emmorey and J. S. Reilly, 133–154. Hillsdale, NJ: Lawrence Erlbaum Associates.

Evans, Nicholas. 2006. View with a view: towards a typology of multiple perspective constructions. In *BLS 31: General session and parasession on prosodic variation and change*, eds. Rebecca Cover and Yuni Kim, 93–120. Berkeley, CA: Berkeley Linguistics Society.

Fleck, David. 2006. Complement clause types and complementation strategies in Matses. In *Complementation: a cross-linguistic typology*, eds. R. M. W. Dixon and Alexandra Aikhenvald, 224–244. Oxford: Oxford University Press.

Fleck, David W. 2003. A grammar of Matses. PhD diss., Rice University.

Grashchenkov, Pavel, and Vita Markman. 2008. Non-core arguments in verbal and nominal predication: high and low applicatives and possessor raising. In *Proceedings of the 27th West Coast Conference on Formal Linguistics*, eds. Natasha Abner and Jason Bishop, 185–193. Somerville, MA: Cascadilla.

Grønn, Atle, and Arnim von Stechow. 2010. Complement tense in contrast: the SOT parameter in Russian and English. In *Russian in contrast*, eds. Atle Grønn and Irena Marijanovic, 109–153. Oslo: University of Oslo.

Gültekin Şener, Nilfüfer, and Serkan Şener. 2011. Null subjects and indexicality in Turkish and Uyghur. In *Proceedings of the 7th Workshop on Altaic Formal Linguistics*, ed. Andrew Simpson, 269–283. Cambridge, MA: MITWPL.

Hacquard, Valentine. 2006. Aspects of modality. PhD diss., MIT.

Haegeman, Liliane, and Virginia Hill. 2013. The syntacticization of discourse. In *Syntax and its limits*, eds. Raffaella Folli, Christina Sevdali, and Robert Truswell, 370–390. Oxford: Oxford University Press.

Harbour, Daniel. 2016. *Impossible persons*. Cambridge, MA: MIT Press.

Hargreaves, David. 2018. "Am I blue?": privileged access constraints in Kathmandu Newar. In *Egophoricity*, eds. Simeon Floyd, Elisabeth Norcliffe, and Lila San Roque, 79–107. Amsterdam: John Benjamins.

Harley, Heidi. 2013. The 'bundling' hypothesis and the disparate functions of little *v*. Handout from the Little v Workshop, Leiden University.

Heath, Jeffrey. 2016. A grammar of Donno So or Kamma So (Dogon language family, Mali). Manuscript, University of Michigan. http://hdl.handle.net/2027.42/123062.

Heim, Irene. 1994. Comments on Abusch's theory of tense. In *Ellipsis, tense and questions*, ed. Hans Kamp, 143–170. Amsterdam: University of Amsterdam.

Heim, Irene. 2008. Features on bound pronouns. In *Phi theory*, eds. Daniel Harbour, David Adger, and Susana Béjar, 35–56. Oxford: Oxford University Press.

Heim, Irene, and Angelika Kratzer. 1998. *Semantics in generative grammar*. Malden, MA: Blackwell.

Herrmann, Annika, and Markus Steinbach. 2012. Quotation in sign languages—a visible context shift. In *Quotatives: Cross-linguistic and cross-disciplinary perspectives*, eds. Isabelle Buchstaller and Ingrid van Alphen, 203–228. Amsterdam: John Benjamins.

Heycock, Caroline. 2006. Embedded root phenomena. In *The Blackwell companion to syntax*, eds. Martin Everaert and Henk van Riemsdijk, 174–209. Malden, MA: Blackwell. doi:https://doi.org/10.1002/9781118358733.wbsyncom068.

Hübl, Annika. 2013. Role shift, indexicals and beyond—new evidence from German Sign Language. In *Proceedings from the 13th meeting of the Texas Linguistics Society*, ed. Leah C. Greer, 1–11. Austin, TX: Texas Linguistics Society.

Hübl, Annika, Emar Maier, and Markus Steinbach. 2019. To shift or not to shift: quotation and attraction in DGS. *Sign Language & Linguistics* 22 (2): 248–286.

Hunter, Julie, and Nicholas Asher. 2005. A presuppositional account of indexicals. In *Proceedings of the fifteenth Amsterdam colloquium*, eds. Paul Dekker and Michael Franke, 119–124. Amsterdam: Institute for Logic, Language and Computation.

Hyman, Larry M., ed. 1979. *Aghem grammatical structure*. Los Angeles: Department of Linguistics, University of Southern California.

Jacobson, Pauline. 2012. Direct compositionality and 'uninterpretability': the case of (sometimes) 'uninterpretable' features on pronouns. *Journal of Semantics* 29: 305–343.

Kammerzell, Frank, and Carsten Peust. 2002. Reported speech in Egyptian: forms, types and history. In *Reported discourse: a meeting ground for different linguistic domains*, eds. Tom Güldemann and Manfred von Roncador, 289–322. Amsterdam: John Benjamins.

Kaplan, David. 1989. Demonstratives: An essay on the semantics, logic, metaphysics, and epistemology of demonstratives and other indexicals. In *Themes from Kaplan*, eds. Joseph Almog, John Perry, and Howard Wettstein, 481–564. Oxford: Oxford University Press.

Karttunen, Lauri. 1971. Implicative verbs. *Language* 47 (2): 340–358.

Kasimir, Elke. 2008. Prosodic correlates of subclausal quotation marks. *ZAS Papers in Linguistics* 49: 67–77.

Klein, Ewan. 1980. A semantics for positive and comparative adjectives. *Linguistics and Philosophy* 4: 1–45.

Knyazev, Mikhail. 2015. Verbal complementizers in Kalmyk: V, C, or both. In *Proceedings of the 9th Workshop on Altaic Formal Linguistics*, eds. Andrew Joseph and Esra Predolac, 145–158. Cambridge, MA: MITWPL.

Knyazev, Mikhail. 2019. Two say-complementizers in Poshkart Chuvash. Manuscript, Saint Petersburg State University.

Koev, Todor. 2013. Apposition and the structure of discourse. PhD diss., Rutgers University.

Koopman, Hilda, and Dominique Sportiche. 1989. Pronouns, logical variables, and logophoricity in Abe. *Linguistic Inquiry* 20 (4): 555–588.

Korotkova, Natalia. 2016. Heterogeneity and uniformity in the evidential domain. PhD diss., University of California, Los Angeles.

Kratzer, Angelika. 1989. An investigation of the lumps of thought. *Linguistics and Philosophy* 12 (5): 607–653.

Kratzer, Angelika. 1998a. More structural analogies between pronouns and tenses. In *Proceedings of SALT VIII*, eds. Devon Strolovitch and Aaron Lawson, 92–110. Ithaca, NY: CLC Publications.

Kratzer, Angelika. 1998b. Scope or pseudoscope? Are there wide-scope indefinites? In *Events and grammar*, ed. Susan Rothstein, 163–196. Dordrecht: Kluwer.

Kratzer, Angelika. 2006. Decomposing attitude verbs. Talk given at The Hebrew University of Jerusalem.

Kratzer, Angelika. 2009. Making a pronoun: fake indexicals as windows into the properties of pronouns. *Linguistic Inquiry* 40 (2): 187–237.

Krifka, Manfred. 2013. Response particles as propositional anaphors. In *Proceedings of SALT 23*, ed. Todd Snider, 1–18. Ithaca, NY: CLC Publications.

Kusumoto, Kiyomi. 2005. On the quantification over times in natural language. *Natural Language Semantics* 13 (4): 317–357.

Lacroix, René. 2012. The multi-purpose subordinator *na* in Laz. In *Clause linkage in cross-linguistic perspective*, eds. Volker Gast and Holger Diessel, 77–104. Berlin: De Gruyter.

Landau, Idan. 2016. Agreement at PF: an argument from partial control. *Syntax* 19 (1): 79–109.

Lasersohn, Peter. 2005. Context dependence, disagreement, and predicates of personal taste. *Linguistics and Philosophy* 28 (6): 643–686.

Lee, Robert G., Carol Neidle, Dawn MacLaughlin, Benjamin Bahan, and Judy Kegl. 1997. Role shift in ASL: a syntactic look at direct speech. In *Syntactic structure and discourse function: an examination of two constructions in American Sign Language*, eds. Carol Neidle, Dawn MacLaughlin, and Robert G. Lee, 24–45. Boston: American Sign Language Linguistic Research Project. ftp://louis-xiv.bu.edu/pub/asl/rpt4/ASLLRPr4.pdf.

Legate, Julie Anne. 2003. Some interface properties of the phase. *Linguistic Inquiry* 34 (3): 506–516.

Leslau, Wolf. 1995. *A reference grammar of Amharic*. Wiesbaden: Harrassowitz.

Lewis, David. 1980. Index, context, and content. In *Philosophy and grammar*, eds. Stig Kanger and Sven Öhman, 79–100. New York: Springer.

Lewis, David K. 1968. Counterpart theory and quantified modal logic. *Journal of Philosophy* 65: 113–126.

Liddell, Scott K., and Melanie Metzger. 1998. Gesture in sign language discourse. *Journal of Pragmatics* 30: 657–697.

Lillo-Martin, Diane. 1995. The point of view predicate in American Sign Language. In *Language, gesture and space*, eds. K. Emmorey and J. S. Reilly, 155–170. Hillsdale, NJ: Lawrence Erlbaum Associates.

Lillo-Martin, Diane. 2012. Utterance reports and constructed action. In *Sign language – an international handbook*, eds. Roland Pfau, Markus Steinbach, and Bencie Woll, 365–387. Berlin: Walter de Gruyter.

Loughnane, Robyn. 2005. Reported speech constructions in Golin. In *Materials on Golin: grammar, texts and dictionary*, ed. N. Evans et al, 129–150. Melbourne: University of Melbourne.

MacFarlane, John. 2012. Relativism. In *The Routledge companion to the philosophy of language*, eds. Delia Graff Fara and Gillian Russell, 132–142. New York: Routledge.

Maier, Emar. 2007. Quotation marks as monsters, or the other way around? In *Proceedings of the 16th Amsterdam colloquium*, eds. Maria Aloni and Floris Roelofsen, 145–150. Amsterdam: ILLC/Department of Philosophy.

Maier, Emar. 2012. Switches between direct and indirect speech in Ancient Greek. *Journal of Greek Linguistics* 12: 118–139.

Maier, Emar. 2014a. Japanese reported speech: towards an account of perspective shift as mixed quotation. In *Formal approaches to semantics and pragmatics*, ed. E. McCready, 135–154. New York: Springer.

Maier, Emar. 2014b. Language shifts in free indirect discourse. *Journal of Literary Semantics* 43 (2): 143–167.

Maier, Emar. 2015. Quotation and unquotation in free indirect discourse. *Mind and Language* 30 (3): 345–373.

Maier, Emar. 2016. A plea against monsters. *Grazer Philosophische Studien* 93 (3): 363–395.

Maier, Emar. 2017. The pragmatics of attraction: explaining unquotation in direct and free indirect discourse. In *The semantics and pragmatics of quotation*, eds. Paul Saka and Michael Johnson, 259–280. New York: Springer.

Maier, Emar. 2018. Quotation, demonstration, and attraction in sign language role shift. *Theoretical Linguistics* 44 (3/4): 165–176.

Maier, Emar. Forthcoming. Mixed quotation. In *The companion to semantics*, eds. Cécile Meier, Thomas Ede Zimmerman, Hotze Rullmann, and Lisa Matthewson. Hoboken, NJ: Wiley Blackwell.

Major, Travis, and Connor Mayer. 2019. What indexical shift sounds like: Uyghur intonation and interpreting speech reports. In *Proceedings of NELS 49*, eds. Maggie Baird and Jonathan Pesetsky, 255–264. Amherst, MA: GLSA Publications.

Matthewson, Lisa. 1999. On the interpretation of wide-scope indefinites. *Natural Language Semantics* 7 (1): 79–134.

Matthewson, Lisa. 2013. Strategies of quantification in St'át'imcets and the rest of the world. In *Strategies of quantification*, eds. Kook-Hee Gil, Stephen Harlow, and George Tsoulas, 15–38. Oxford: Oxford University Press.

McCready, E. 2007. Context shifting in questions and elsewhere. In *Proceedings of Sinn und Bedeutung 11*, ed. E. Puig-Waldmüller, 433–447. Barcelona: Universitat Pompeu Fabra.

Messick, Troy. 2016. Pronouns and agreement in Telugu embedded contexts. In *Proceedings of the 33rd West Coast Conference on Formal Linguistics*, ed. Kyeong-min Kim et al., 309–319. Somerville, MA: Cascadilla Proceedings Project.

Moulton, Keir. 2009. Natural selection and the syntax of clausal complementation. PhD diss., University of Massachusetts, Amherst.

Moulton, Keir. 2015. CPs: copies and compositionality. *Linguistic Inquiry* 46 (2): 305–342.

Munro, Robert, Rainer Ludwig, Uli Sauerland, and David Fleck. 2012. Matses reported speech: perspective persistence and evidential narratives. *International Journal of American Linguistics* 78 (1): 41–75.

Nevins, Andrew. 2011. Multiple agree with clitics: person complementarity vs. omnivorous number. *Natural Language and Linguistic Theory* 29: 939–971.

Nichols, Johanna. 2011. *Ingush grammar*. Berkeley, CA: University of California Press.

Nikitina, Tatiana. 2012a. Logophoric discourse and first person reporting in Wan (West Africa). *Anthropological Linguistics* 54 (3): 280–301.

Nikitina, Tatiana. 2012b. Personal deixis and reported discourse: towards a typology of person alignment. *Linguistic Typology* 16: 233–263.

Ninan, Dilip. 2010. De se attitudes: ascription and communication. *Philosophy Compass* 5 (7): 551–567.

Ninan, Dilip. 2012. Counterfactual attitudes and multi-centered worlds. *Semantics and Pragmatics* 5 (5): 1–57. doi:10.3765/sp.5.5.

Nishiguchi, Sumiyo. 2012. Shifty operators in Dhaasanac. *Snippets* 26: 14–15.

Nishiguchi, Sumiyo. 2017. Indexical shifting in Dhaasanac and Somali. In *Proceedings of TripleA 3*, eds. Vera Hohaus and Wanda Rothe, 47–55. Tübingen: Universitätsbibliothek Tübingen.

Nunberg, Geoffrey. 1993. Indexicality and deixis. *Linguistics and Philosophy* 16 (1): 1–43.

Ogihara, Toshiyuki. 1989. Temporal reference in English and Japanese. PhD diss., University of Texas at Austin.

Ogihara, Toshiyuki. 1996. *Tense, attitudes, and scope*. Dordrecht: Kluwer Academic.

Ogihara, Toshiyuki. 1999. Double access sentences generalized. In *Proceedings from SALT IX*, eds. T. Matthews and D. Strolovitch, 224–236. Ithaca, NY: CLC Publications.

Ogihara, Toshiyuki, and Yael Sharvit. 2012. Embedded tenses. In *The Oxford handbook of tense and aspect*, ed. Robert I. Binnick, 638–668. Oxford: Oxford University Press.

Oshima, David Y. 2006. Perspectives in reported discourse. PhD diss., Stanford University.

Ouhalla, Jamal. 1991. *Functional categories and parametric variation*. New York: Routledge.

Özyıldız, Deniz. 2012. When I is not me: a preliminary case study of shifted indexicals in Turkish. Manuscript, École Normale Supérieure.

Pak, Miok, Paul Portner, and Rafaella Zanuttini. 2008. Agreement in promissive, imperative and exhortative clauses. *Korean Linguistics* 14: 157–175.

Park, Yangsook. 2016. Indexical shift and the long-distance reflexive *caki* in Korean. Manuscript, University of Massachusetts, Amherst.

Partee, Barbara. 1989. Binding implicit variables in quantified contexts. In *Chicago Linguistics Society 25*, ed. C. Wiltshire et al., 342–365. Chicago: Chicago Linguistics Society.

Pearson, Hazel. 2015. The interpretation of the logophoric pronoun in Ewe. *Natural Language Semantics* 23: 77–118. doi:10.1007/s11050-015-9112-1.

Percus, Orin. 2000. Constraints on some other variables in syntax. *Natural Language Semantics* 8 (3): 173–229.

Percus, Orin, and Uli Sauerland. 2003a. On the LFs of attitude reports. In *Proceedings from Sinn und Bedeutung 7*, ed. M. Weisgerber, 228–242. Konstanz: University of Konstanz.

Percus, Orin, and Uli Sauerland. 2003b. Pronoun movement in dream reports. In *Proceedings of NELS 33*, eds. Makoto Kadowaki and Shigeto Kawahara, 265–283. Amherst, MA: GLSA Publications.

Platero, Paul. 1974. The Navajo relative clause. *International Journal of American Linguistics* 40 (3): 202–246.

Podobryaev, Alexander. 2014. Persons, imposters and monsters. PhD diss., MIT.

Podobryaev, Alexander. 2017. Three routes to person indexicality. *Natural Language Semantics* 25: 329–354.

Polinsky, Maria. 2015. Embedded finite complements, indexical shift, and binding in Tsez. *Languages of the Caucasus* 1 (1): 1–37.

Pylkkänen, Liina. 2008. *Introducing arguments*. Cambridge, MA: MIT Press.

Quer, Josep. 2005. Context shift and indexical variables in Sign Language. In *Proceedings of SALT XV*, eds. Effi Georgala and Jonathan Howell, 152–168. Ithaca, NY: CLC Publications.

Quer, Josep. 2011. Reporting and quoting in signed discourse. In *Understanding quotation*, ed. E. Brendel et al., 277–302. Berlin: Mouton de Gruyter.

Quer, Josep. 2013. Attitude ascriptions in sign languages and role shift. In *Proceedings from the 13th meeting of the Texas Linguistics Society*, ed. Leah C. Greer, 12–38. Austin, TX: Texas Linguistics Society.

Ramchand, Gillian. 2018. *Situations and syntactic structures*. Cambridge, MA: MIT Press.

Ramchand, Gillian, and Peter Svenonius. 2014. Deriving the functional hierarchy. *Language Sciences* 46 (B): 152–174.

Reboul, Anne, Denis Delfitto, and Gaetano Fiorin. 2016. The semantic properties of free indirect discourse. *Annual Review of Linguistics* 2: 255–271.

Recanati, François. 2001. Open quotation. *Mind* 110: 637–687.

Reesink, Ger. 1993. "Inner speech" in Papuan languages. *Language and Linguistics in Melanesia* 24: 217–225.

Reinhart, Tanya. 1997. Quantifier scope: how labor is divided between QR and choice functions. *Linguistics and Philosophy* 20 (4): 335–397.

Reuland, Eric. 2010. Minimal versus not so minimal pronouns: feature transmission, feature deletion, and the role of economy in the language system. In *The linguistics enterprise: from knowledge of language to knowledge in linguistics*, ed. Martin Everaert et al., 257–282. Amsterdam: John Benjamins.

Rice, Keren. 1986. Some remarks on direct and indirect speech in Slave (Northern Athapaskan). In *Direct and indirect speech*, ed. F. Coulmas, 47–76. Berlin: Mouton de Gruyter.

Rice, Keren. 1989. *A grammar of Slave*. Berlin: Mouton.

Rizzi, Luigi. 1997. The fine structure of the left periphery. In *Elements of grammar*, ed. Liliane Haegeman, 281–337. Dordrecht: Kluwer Academic.

Rizzi, Luigi. 2005. On the grammatical basis of language development: a case study. In *The Oxford handbook of comparative syntax*, eds. Guglielmo Cinque and Richard S. Kayne, 70–109. Oxford: Oxford University Press.

Roberts, Craige. 2015. Indexicality: de se semantics and pragmatics. Manuscript, OSU.

Rochette, Anne. 1988. Semantic and syntactic aspects of Romance sentential complementation. PhD diss., MIT.

Rude, Noel. 1985. Studies in Nez Perce grammar and discourse. PhD diss., University of Oregon.

Rude, Noel. 1986. Topicality, transitivity, and the direct object in Nez Perce. *International Journal of American Linguistics* 52 (2): 124–153.

Rullmann, Hotze. 2004. First and second person pronouns as bound variables. *Linguistic Inquiry* 35 (1): 159–168.

Salzmann, Martin. 2017a. Prolepsis. In *The Wiley Blackwell companion to syntax*, eds. Martin Everaert and Henk van Riemsdijk. Malden, MA: Wiley-Blackwell.

Salzmann, Martin. 2017b. *Reconstruction and resumption in indirect A'-dependencies*. Berlin: Mouton de Gruyter.

Sams, Jessie. 2010. Quoting the unspoken: an analysis of quotations in spoken discourse. *Journal of Pragmatics* 42: 3147–3160.

Sauerland, Uli. 2013. Presuppositions and the alternative tier. In *Proceedings of SALT 23*, ed. Todd Snider, 156–173. Ithaca, NY: CLC Publications.

Sauerland, Uli, and Mathias Schenner. 2007. Embedded evidentials in Bulgarian. In *Proceedings of Sinn und Bedeutung 11*, ed. E. Puig-Waldmüller et al., 525–539. Barcelona: Universitat Pompeu Fabra.

Schauber, Ellen. 1979. *The syntax and semantics of questions in Navajo*. New York: Garland.

Schlenker, Philippe. 1999. Propositional attitudes and indexicality: a cross-categorial approach. PhD diss., MIT.

Schlenker, Philippe. 2003. A plea for monsters. *Linguistics and Philosophy* 26: 29–120.

Schlenker, Philippe. 2004. Context of thought and context of utterance: a note on free indirect discourse and the historical present. *Mind and Language* 19 (3): 279–304.

Schlenker, Philippe. 2011. Indexicality and *de se* reports. In *Semantics: an international handbook of contemporary research*, eds. K. von Heusinger, C. Maienborn, and P. Portner, 1561–1603. Berlin: de Gruyter.

Schlenker, Philippe. 2017a. Super monsters I: attitude and action role shift in sign language. *Semantics and Pragmatics* 10 (9).

Schlenker, Philippe. 2017b. Super monsters II: role shift, iconicity and quotation in sign language. *Semantics and Pragmatics* 10 (12).

Schlenker, Philippe. 2018. Indexicals. In *Introduction to formal philosophy*, eds. Sven Ove Hansson and Vincent F. Hendricks, 297–321. New York: Springer.

Scontras, Greg, Judith Degen, and Noah Goodman. 2017. Subjectivity predicts adjective ordering preferences. *Open Mind* 1 (1): 53–66.

Shan, Chung-chieh. 2010. The character of quotation. *Linguistics and Philosophy* 33 (5): 417–443.

Sharvit, Yael. 2008. The puzzle of free indirect discourse. *Linguistics and Philosophy* 31: 353–395.

Sharvit, Yael. 2018. Sequence of tense: syntax, semantics, pragmatics. In *Pronouns in embedded contexts at the syntax-semantics interface*, eds. Pritty Patel-Grosz, Patrick Grosz, and Sarah Zobel, 215–247. New York: Springer.

Shklovsky, Kirill, and Yasutada Sudo. 2014. The syntax of monsters. *Linguistic Inquiry* 45 (3): 381–402.

Sigurðsson, Halldór Ármann. 2004. The syntax of person, tense, and speech features. *Rivista di Linguistica–Italian Journal of Linguistics* 16 (1): 219–251.

Spadine, Carolyn. 2019. The syntax of attitude holders: evidence from Tigrinya. Manuscript, MIT.

Speas, Margaret. 2000. Person and point of view in Navajo. In *Papers in honor of Ken Hale*, eds. Andrew Carnie, Eloise Jelinek, and MaryAnn Willie, 259–273. Cambridge, MA: MITWPL.

Speas, Margaret. 2004. Evidentiality, logophoricity and the syntactic representation of pragmatic features. *Lingua* 114: 255–276.

Speas, Margaret, and Carol Tenny. 2003. Configurational properties of point of view roles. In *Asymmetry in grammar*, ed. Anna Maria di Sciullo, 315–344. Amsterdam: John Benjamins.

Stalnaker, Robert. 1978. Assertion. In *Pragmatics*, ed. Peter Cole. Vol. 9 of *Syntax and semantics*, 315–332. New York: Academic Press.

Stegovec, Adrian. 2019. Perspectival control and obviation in directive clauses. *Natural Language Semantics* 27: 47–94.

Stegovec, Adrian, and Magdalena Kaufmann. 2015. Slovenian imperatives: you can't always embed what you want! In *Proceedings of Sinn und Bedeutung 19*, eds. Eva Csipak and Hedde Zeijlstra, 621–638. Göttingen: LinG.

Stephenson, Tamina. 2007. Towards a theory of subjective meaning. PhD diss., MIT.

Stirling, Lesley. 1993. *Switch-reference and discourse representation*. Cambridge: Cambridge University Press.

Sudo, Yasutada. 2012. On the semantics of phi features on pronouns. PhD diss., MIT.

Sumbatova, Nina R., and Rasul O. Mutalov. 2003. *A grammar of Icari Dargwa*. Munich: Lincom Europa.

Sundaresan, Sandhya. 2011. A plea for syntax and a return to first principles: monstrous agreement in Tamil. In *Proceedings of SALT 21*, eds. Neil Ashton, Anca Chereches, and David Lutz, 674–693. Ithaca, NY: CLC Publications.

Sundaresan, Sandhya. 2012. Context and (co)reference in the syntax and its interfaces. PhD diss., University of Tromsø.

Sundaresan, Sandhya. 2018. An alternative model of indexical shift: variation and selection without context-overwriting. Manuscript, University of Leipzig.

Thivierge, Sigwan. 2019. High shifty operators in Georgian indexical shift. Poster presented at MACSIM.

Thomas, Elaine. 1978. *A grammatical description of the Engenni language*. Dallas, TX: Summer Institute of Linguistics.

Tida, Syuntaroo. 2006. A grammar of the Dom language, a Papuan language of Papua New Guinea. PhD diss., University of Kyoto.

Tonhauser, Judith, David Beaver, Craige Roberts, and Mandy Simons. 2013. Toward a taxonomy of projective content. *Language* 89 (1): 66–109.

von Stechow, Arnim. 1995. On the proper treatment of tense. In *Proceedings of SALT V*, eds. Mandy Simons and Teresa Galloway, 362–386. Ithaca, NY: Cornell University.

von Stechow, Arnim. 2003. Feature deletion under semantic binding: tense, person and mood under verbal quantifiers. In *Proceedings of NELS 33*, eds. Makoto Kadowaki and Shigeto Kawahara, 379–404. Amherst, MA: GLSA Publications.

von Stechow, Arnim, and Thomas Ede Zimmermann. 2005. A problem for a compositional treatment of *de re* attitudes. In *Reference and quantification: the Partee effect*, eds. Greg Carlson and Francis Jeffrey Pelletier, 207–228. Stanford: CSLI Publications.

Winter, Yoad. 1997. Choice functions and the scopal semantics of indefinites. *Linguistics and Philosophy* 20 (4): 399–467.

Wurmbrand, Susi. 2016. Restructuring as the regulator of clause size. Handout from Shrinking Trees, Leipzig.

Wurmbrand, Susi. 2017. Feature sharing, or, how I value my son. In *The pesky set: Papers for David Pesetsky*, eds. Claire Halpert, Hadas Kotek, and Coppe van Urk, 173–182. Cambridge, MA: MITWPL.

Zamparelli, Roberto. 1995. Layers in the determiner phrase. PhD diss., University of Rochester.

Zu, Vera. 2018. Discourse participants and the structural representation of the context. PhD diss., New York University.

Zucchi, Alessandro. 2004. Monsters in the visual mode? Manuscript, Università degli Studi di Milano.

Index

Abbreviations, 141n2
Addressee (parameter of index or context), 29, 38, 43, 65, 73, 83–86, 111, 119–120, 123, 129, 148nn6,12, 156n17. *See also* Indexiphor; Second person
 defective value for, 73, 84, 85, 87, 149n23
 function on events, 74
Adioukrou, 120
Adverbial quantifiers, 15–16, 20, 35–36, 121
Aghem, 120
Agreement, 110, 133, 134–138
Akkuş, Faruk, 117, 119, 156nn14–15
Akɔɔse, 120
American Sign Language (ASL), 97, 103
Amharic, 60, 113–114, 115–116, 117–118, 119, 120, 131, 147n3, 155n8
A' movement. *See wh-*movement
Anand, Pranav, 8, 18, 27, 29, 31, 34, 38, 49, 52, 54, 59, 65, 72, 78, 85, 89, 91, 98, 114–116, 117, 127, 143nn13,18, 144nn27,31, 145n40, 146nn45–46, 147n3, 148n8, 149nn15,18
Anderson, Carolyn, 82–83, 149n17, 152n7
Assertion, 130
Assignment, variable, 28, 35, 37, 44, 106
Attitude verbs
 covert, 45
 event semantics for, 72–73
 meaning, 29, 72–73, 85
Attraction, pragmatic, 102

Author (parameter of index or context), 2, 28–29, 33, 37, 38, 39, 48, 65, 73, 85, 94, 104, 106, 107, 109–111, 113–114, 119, 120, 123, 129–130, 131, 148n6, 149nn19,23, 155nn9,12. *See also* First person; Indexiphor

Babungo, 120
Balkar, 146n49
Binding, 15–16, 19–23, 36–37, 43, 47, 63, 69, 78, 79, 80, 82, 98, 104, 106, 114, 116, 131, 132, 145n35
 of context pronouns 21–23
Bittner, Maria, 8, 23, 49, 65, 150n30
Bulgarian, 128–129
Bundling, 5, 83–87, 89, 94–95, 123, 132, 152nn11–13

Case pattern, 133–134, 142n4
Catalan Sign Language, 103–104
C-command, 114, 115, 116
Centering, 29, 72, 74, 92, 155n10
Character, Kaplanian, 30
Cislocative, 136
Clitics, 133, 136, 138–139, 142n5
Cognition, verbs of, 50–51, 68–70, 78, 81–82, 83–87, 90, 91, 93, 147n4
Comparative construction, 143n13
Complementation strategy, 23–27, 34
Complementizer
 bundling with shifty operators, 83, 86–87, 95, 152n11
 meaning of, 73, 92
 overt vs. covert, 9–10, 137, 142n2

Complementizer (cont.)
  syntactic domain (CP domain), 34, 47
  syntactic position, 74–76, 77, 83, 123
Complement size, 66–69, 91, 93, 97, 126
Concept generators, 92
Content, 72–73
Context, 35, 37, 44, 65, 110, 114, 120, 125, 129–130
  improper, 32, 65
  modeling of, 28–29, 32, 144n25
  modification of, 31
  pronouns, 21–23, 145n38
Counterpart relation, 42, 74, 92, 145n41, 151n33

Dani, 116
Danish Sign Language, 103, 104
Definite descriptions, 14, 63, 91–92
De re, 10–11, 13, 16, 24–27, 92, 97, 98, 100, 102, 103, 114–116, 121, 144n32, 151n33
De re blocking effect, 114–117, 119, 120, 156n16
De se, 29, 31, 33, 59–64, 70–76, 77, 81, 83, 91–92, 94–95, 97, 109, 110, 111, 114, 118, 120, 144n24, 149nn15–18, 155n10
Dhaasanac, 49, 50, 51, 53, 60, 61, 62, 63, 69, 71, 76, 83, 149n20, 151n4
Director, imperative, 132
Direct reference theory of indexicals, 1, 4, 7, 28, 107
Disagreement, coherence of, 1–3
Discourse anchoring, 23
Dom, 116
Donno Sɔ, 107–112, 113, 154–155n7
Dream reports, 114

Eckardt, Regine, 99, 154n1
Egophoricity, 98, 107, 109
Egyptian, Late, 113, 114
Embedded root phenomena, 93
Engenni, 120
English, 1–2, 54, 55, 58, 64, 69, 77, 78–79, 80, 82–83, 99, 104–105, 120, 146n46, 151n3

E-type pronouns, 146n44, 152n14. *See also* Definite descriptions
Evans, Nicholas, 116–117
Event semantics, 72, 74, 97
Evidentials, 109, 110, 128–129, 132

Factivity, 51, 147n4, 148n9
Fake indexicals, 98, 104–107
Farsi, 45, 49, 146n47
Feature deletion under binding, 106, 143n15
Features, nominal, 109–110, 113, 145–146n44
Feature transmission under binding, 106
Finiteness, 48, 67, 69, 93, 97
First person, 2–3, 9, 15–16, 17–18, 22–23, 28, 30, 31, 33, 37, 38, 39, 41, 43, 45, 47, 52, 53, 54, 55, 56, 57, 58, 59–60, 63, 75, 76, 81–82, 83, 84, 85, 87, 102, 104, 106, 107, 108, 109, 110, 111, 113, 118, 119, 120, 125, 126, 129, 131, 133, 134, 136, 137, 138–139, 148n13, 149n19, 152n14, 155nn8,12
Focus, 98, 105, 106–107, 121
Free Indirect Discourse, 97, 99–102, 146n49, 148n10, 152n7
French Sign Language. *See* LSF
Functional heads, 33, 66, 76
Functional sequence, 66–68, 76, 77, 78, 82, 86, 87, 89, 90, 93, 95, 97, 123, 127, 132, 152n12
Function composition, 85, 86, 95

Gahuku, 117
Georgian, 45, 60, 100, 146n49
German, 104
German Sign Language, 103
Golin, 117, 155n12, 156n17

Hacquard, Valentine, 72, 90
Hebrew, 10
Hindi, 10, 143n17

Iconicity, 102, 103, 154n3
Illeism, 148n12
Imperative, 130, 132, 157n3

Implicational hierarchy
  of *de se* requirements (G3), 63, 71–76, 83, 91–92, 94–95, 124
  of indexical classes (G2), 54, 58, 64, 67–68, 89–90, 93–94, 118, 124
  of verbs (G1), 51, 68–70, 77, 93, 124
Impoverishment, structural, 66-68, 76, 93
Index (binding index on pronouns), 106, 154n6
Index (circumstance of evaluation), 28–29, 35–36, 72, 95, 109–110, 114, 116, 120, 144nn26,29
Indexiphor, 98, 107–121, 131
  locality, 111–113, 118, 120, 131, 155n10, 156n15
  mixed readings with clausemate indexicals, 111, 117–118, 119
  previous use of term, 155n9
Intensional function application, 29, 116
Interrogative flip, 109

Jacobson, Pauline, 106–107
Japanese, 10, 48, 50, 60, 76, 151n1
Judge (coordinate of context), 95, 132, 148n6

κ (type), 31
Kalmyk, 146n49
Kaplan, David, 1, 7, 14–15, 28, 30, 31, 35, 107, 110
Kathmandu Newari, 107, 109–112, 113
Kiowa, 10
Knowledge, verbs of, 50–51, 68–70, 83, 93, 147n4
Kobon, 47, 55
Korean, 45, 46, 48, 50, 60, 61, 63, 69, 71, 80–82, 87–89, 90–91, 94, 112, 129, 130–131, 150n27, 157nn3–4
Korotkova, Natalia, 95, 128–130, 148n6
Kurmanji, 49, 117

l (type), 74
Laz, 45, 46, 50, 53, 55, 145n33, 152n11
Lewis, David, 28, 32, 145n41
Local Determination, 39–44, 45–46, 125–126. *See also* Shift Together

replacement for No Intervening Binder, 145n40
Locative
  adverbials, 98
  function on events, 74
  indexicals, 12, 14, 15–16, 19, 22–23, 28, 37, 52, 53, 54, 56, 57, 58, 61, 63, 65, 66, 67, 70, 71, 78, 82, 85, 87–88, 94, 125, 149n20
  parameter of index or context, 29, 65, 73, 123
Logophors, 69, 92, 98, 107–108, 114, 116, 120, 146n49, 154nn3,7, 155nn8–9, 157n4
LSF (French Sign Language), 97, 103

Maier, Emar, 7, 17, 97, 101, 102, 104, 143nn9,14
Manambu, 47
Mandarin, 10
Matrix clause, 34–36, 107, 109, 110, 146nn47,49
Matses, 47, 50, 52, 55, 58, 64, 67, 101, 148n8
Mishar Tatar, 10, 113, 114, 120, 149n15
Mixed quotation. *See* Quotation, partial
Monsters begat by elegance, 31
Monstrous function application, 31, 32, 150n31
Movement, 46-47, 67. *See also* wh-movement
Mundang, 120
Multiple embedding, 40–44, 45, 47–48, 98, 111–112, 118, 121

Navajo, 47–48, 50, 51, 53, 55, 69, 100, 112, 146n48, 147n2, 148nn11–12
Negative polarity, 10–11, 97, 101, 103
Nevins, Andrew, 18, 27, 30–31, 38, 127–128, 137
Nez Perce, 2–3, 7–44, 46, 51, 52, 53, 56–58, 59, 60, 61, 62, 63, 65, 67, 69, 70–71, 73–74, 76, 78–79, 84–85, 87, 89, 91, 94, 100, 150nn27,29, 151n3
Ngwo, 120
No Intervening Binder, 145n40
Nominalization, 48, 69, 146n48, 150n26

Obolo, 120
OP$_\forall$, 31, 38, 89, 150n27
OP$_{ADDR}$, 38–39, 65, 66, 67, 68, 70, 74, 75, 76, 77, 82, 84, 85, 86, 87, 90, 93, 105, 123, 126
OP$_{ADV}$, 87–88, 94–95, 153nn17,21
OP$_{AUTH}$, 38–39, 65, 66, 67, 68, 70, 72, 75, 76, 77, 80, 82, 84, 85, 86, 87, 89, 93, 123, 126
OP$_{LOC}$, 65, 66, 67, 68, 70, 73, 74, 75, 76, 77, 80, 82, 86, 87, 88, 90, 93, 94, 123, 124
OP$_{ORIGO}$, 129
OP$_{PERS}$, 31, 37, 38, 39, 43, 85, 86, 88, 89, 95, 150n24
OP$_{TIME}$, 78, 79, 80, 81, 82, 83, 84, 87, 88, 93, 94, 123, 126, 151n3
Optionality, 54–58, 80, 95, 148n11
Origo coordinate of context, 95, 128–130, 131, 132, 148n6
Oshima, David, 38, 52, 54
Overwriting, 36–44, 47–48, 111, 127

Park, Yangsook, 80, 87, 157nn3–4
Partial indexical shift, 56, 65
Pearson, Hazel, 92
Perspective, 29, 72, 128. *See also* De se
Principle B, 115, 118
PRO, 114, 132, 155n8
Prolepsis, 23–27, 34, 143nn20–21, 145n34

Quer, Josep, 103–104, 128
Question embedding, 51, 148n5
Quotation, 3, 7, 9–14, 33, 80, 97, 117, 121, 144n28, 153–154n1
  opacity of, 11–13, 103, 121
  partial, 16–19, 98–99, 102, 103, 121
  verbatim requirement, 14, 100–101, 102, 142n3, 154n2

Relativism, 144n26
Role Shift, 97, 103–104, 148n10, 154n3
Russian, 10

Sakha, 146n49
Salience, 23, 27

Schlenker, Philippe, 7, 8, 21, 49, 59, 99, 100, 103
Second person, 12, 15–16, 17–18, 31, 37, 38, 43, 52, 53, 54, 55, 56, 58, 60–61, 63, 71, 75, 76, 78, 83–87, 91–92, 94, 106, 107, 109, 117–118, 119–120, 125, 126, 131, 134, 136, 137, 138–139, 148n12, 155n9
Selection, 68, 77, 81, 83, 85, 91, 126, 145n34
Sequence of tense, 9–10, 142n2
Sharvit, Yael, 99, 101
Shift Together, 17–23, 37–44, 45, 80, 105, 111, 117–118, 125–132, 143n18, 145n42, 149n19, 151n3, 157n3. *See also* Local Determination
  putative violations, 128, 130–132
Shklovsky, Kirill, 46–47, 86, 104, 146n47
Sign Languages, 97, 103–104, 141–142n4, 148n10, 154n3
Slave, 45, 50, 51, 53–54, 55–56, 58, 64, 65, 68, 69, 84, 85, 126–127, 128, 129, 143n18, 146nn46,48, 153n17
Slovenian, 132
Somali, 50
Speech Act Phrase, 149n23
Speaker. *See* Author
Speas, Peggy, 69, 147n2, 150n27
Speech, verbs of, 49–52, 53, 56, 68–70, 81, 83, 90, 91, 93, 150n28
Subcategorization. *See* Selection
Subject, 34, 110, 115, 117, 118, 137, 143n8, 145n39
Sudo, Yasutada, 34, 46, 47, 50, 61, 62, 78, 86, 91, 104, 106
Sundaresan, Sandhya, 52, 69, 108, 130, 131, 146n49, 150n27, 156nn16,2
Syncretism, 114, 120, 155n12, 156n17

Tamil, 113, 114
Temporal adverb, 3, 20–21, 78, 98, 104, 146n46, 151n3, 152n8
Temporal indexical, 37, 78, 81–82, 87–88, 94, 125, 126, 148n10
Tense, 78, 99–100, 102, 142n2, 151n1. *See also* Sequence of Tense

Third person, 100, 133, 134–135, 136, 137, 157nn4,2
Thought, verbs of. *See* Cognition, verbs of
Tigrinya, 146n49
Time (parameter of index or context), 29, 73, 123
Translation, 20, 78–79, 98, 151n4
Tsez, 10, 45, 46, 48, 53, 100
Turkish, 113, 114, 117, 118, 119, 120, 156nn14–15

Unquotation, 102, 104, 153–154n1
Usan, 117
Uyghur, 45, 46–47, 48, 50–51, 53, 54, 55, 56, 58, 60, 61, 62, 63, 64, 65, 67, 69, 70–71, 74, 75, 76, 77, 86, 87, 91, 94, 149n20

von Stechow, Arnim, 7, 20, 29, 106, 143n15

Wan, 120
wh-movement, 10–12, 33, 97, 99, 101, 103, 104, 117

Yoruba, 114–115, 116

Zazaki, 45, 46, 49–50, 51, 52, 53, 54, 55, 56, 58, 59, 60, 61–62, 63, 67, 69, 70, 71, 73, 75, 76, 91, 101, 148n8, 155n8
Mutki dialect, 113, 114, 117, 118

Linguistic Inquiry Monographs
Samuel Jay Keyser, general editor

1. *Word Formation in Generative Grammar*, Mark Aronoff
2. *Syntax: A Study of Phrase Structure*, Ray Jackendoff
3. *Recent Transformational Studies in European Languages*, S. Jay Keyser, editor
4. *Studies in Abstract Phonology*, Edmund Gussmann
5. *An Encyclopedia of AUX: A Study of Cross-Linguistic Equivalence*, Susan Steele
6. *Some Concepts and Consequences of the Theory of Government and Binding*, Noam Chomsky
7. *The Syntax of Words*, Elisabeth O. Selkirk
8. *Syllable Structure and Stress in Spanish: A Nonlinear Analysis*, James W. Harris
9. *CV Phonology: A Generative Theory of the Syllable*, George N. Clements and Samuel Jay Keyser
10. *On the Nature of Grammatical Relations*, Alec P. Marantz
11. *A Grammar of Anaphora*, Joseph Aoun
12. *Logical Form: Its Structure and Derivation*, Robert May
13. *Barriers*, Noam Chomsky
14. *On the Definition of Word*, Anna-Maria Di Sciullo and Edwin Williams
15. *Japanese Tone Structure*, Janet Pierrehumbert and Mary E. Beckman
16. *Relativized Minimality*, Luigi Rizzi
17. *Types of Ā-Dependencies*, Guglielmo Cinque
18. *Argument Structure*, Jane Grimshaw
19. *Locality: A Theory and Some of Its Empirical Consequences*, Maria Rita Manzini
20. *Indefinites*, Molly Diesing
21. *Syntax of Scope*, Joseph Aoun and Yen-hui Audrey Li
22. *Morphology by Itself: Stems and Inflectional Classes*, Mark Aronoff
23. *Thematic Structure in Syntax*, Edwin Williams
24. *Indices and Identity*, Robert Fiengo and Robert May
25. *The Antisymmetry of Syntax*, Richard S. Kayne
26. *Unaccusativity: At the Syntax–Lexical Semantics Interface*, Beth Levin and Malka Rappaport Hovav
27. *Lexico-Logical Form: A Radically Minimalist Theory*, Michael Brody
28. *The Architecture of the Language Faculty*, Ray Jackendoff
29. *Local Economy*, Chris Collins
30. *Surface Structure and Interpretation*, Mark Steedman
31. *Elementary Operations and Optimal Derivations*, Hisatsugu Kitahara

32. *The Syntax of Nonfinite Complementation: An Economy Approach*, Željko Bošković
33. *Prosody, Focus, and Word Order*, Maria Luisa Zubizarreta
34. *The Dependencies of Objects*, Esther Torrego
35. *Economy and Semantic Interpretation*, Danny Fox
36. *What Counts: Focus and Quantification*, Elena Herburger
37. *Phrasal Movement and Its Kin*, David Pesetsky
38. *Dynamic Antisymmetry*, Andrea Moro
39. *Prolegomenon to a Theory of Argument Structure*, Ken Hale and Samuel Jay Keyser
40. *Essays on the Representational and Derivational Nature of Grammar: The Diversity of* Wh-*Constructions*, Joseph Aoun and Yen-hui Audrey Li
41. *Japanese Morphophonemics: Markedness and Word Structure*, Junko Ito and Armin Mester
42. *Restriction and Saturation*, Sandra Chung and William A. Ladusaw
43. *Linearization of Chains and Sideward Movement*, Jairo Nunes
44. *The Syntax of (In)dependence*, Ken Safir
45. *Interface Strategies: Optimal and Costly Computations*, Tanya Reinhart
46. *Asymmetry in Morphology*, Anna Maria Di Sciullo
47. *Relators and Linkers: The Syntax of Predication, Predicate Inversion, and Copulas*, Marcel den Dikken
48. *On the Syntactic Composition of Manner and Motion*, Maria Luisa Zubizarreta and Eunjeong Oh
49. *Introducing Arguments*, Liina Pylkkänen
50. *Where Does Binding Theory Apply?*, David Lebeaux
51. *Locality in Minimalist Syntax*, Thomas S. Stroik
52. *Distributed Reduplication*, John Frampton
53. *The Locative Syntax of Experiencers*, Idan Landau
54. *Why Agree? Why Move?: Unifying Agreement-Based and Discourse-Configurational Languages*, Shigeru Miyagawa
55. *Locality in Vowel Harmony*, Andrew Nevins
56. *Uttering Trees*, Norvin Richards
57. *The Syntax of Adjectives*, Guglielmo Cinque
58. *Arguments as Relations*, John Bowers
59. *Agreement and Head Movement*, Ian Roberts
60. *Localism versus Globalism in Morphology and Phonology*, David Embick
61. *Provocative Syntax*, Phil Branigan
62. *Anaphora and Language Design*, Eric J. Reuland

63. *Indefinite Objects: Scrambling, Choice Functions, and Differential Marking*, Luis López
64. *A Syntax of Substance*, David Adger
65. *Subjunctive Conditionals*, Michela Ippolito
66. *Russian Case Morphology and the Syntactic Categories*, David Pesetsky
67. *Classical NEG Raising: An Essay on the Syntax of Negation*, Chris Collins and Paul M. Postal
68. *Agreement and Its Failures*, Omer Preminger
69. *Voice and v: Lessons from Acehnese*, Julie Anne Legate
70. *(Re)labeling*, Carlo Cecchetto and Caterina Donati
71. *A Two-Tiered Theory of Control*, Idan Landau
72. *Concepts, Syntax, and Their Interface: Tanya Reinhart's Theta System*, Martin Everaert, Marijana Marelj, and Eric Reuland, editors
73. *Contiguity Theory*, Norvin Richards
74. *Impossible Persons*, Daniel Harbour
75. *Agreement Beyond Phi*, Shigeru Miyagawa
76. *The Final-Over-Final Condition: A Syntactic Universal*, Michelle Sheehan, Theresa Biberauer, Ian Roberts, and Anders Holmberg
77. *Situations and Syntactic Structures: Rethinking Auxiliaries and Order in English*, Gillian Ramchand
78. *Features of Person: From the Inventory of Persons to their Morphological Realization*, Peter Ackema and Ad Neeleman
79. *Cardinals: The Syntax and Semantics of Cardinal-Containing Expressions*, Tania Ionin and Ora Matushansky
80. *Composing Questions*, Hadas Kotek
81. *Probes and Their Horizons*, Stefan Keine
82. *A Theory of Indexical Shift: Meaning, Grammar, and Crosslinguistic Variation*, Amy Rose Deal